# Death of a Taxpayer

## 8th Edition

Suzanne I.R. Hanson, B.A., LL.B
Sandra A. Bussey, C.A.

www.cch.ca
A WoltersKluwer Company

CCH CANADIAN LIMITED
90 Sheppard Avenue East, Suite 300
Toronto, ON M2N 6X1
Telephone: (416) 224-2248  Toll Free: 1-800-268-4522
Fax: (416) 224-2243  Toll Free: 1-800-461-4131
www.cch.ca

Published by CCH Canadian Limited

The CCH design is a registered trademark of CCH Incorporated.

**Library and Archives Canada Cataloguing in Publication**

Hanson, Suzanne

    Death of a taxpayer/Suzanne Hanson, Sandra Bussey. — 8th ed.

Includes bibliographical references and index.

ISBN 1-55367-516-9

1. Decedents' estates — Taxation — Canada.
2. Trusts and trustees — Taxation — Canada.
I. Bussey, Sandra.  II.  Title.

KE5976.H36  2005      343.7105'3      C2005-904306-7
KF6584.H36  2005

## © 2005, CCH Canadian Limited

Typeset by CCH Canadian Limited.
Printed in Canada.

# Acknowledgement

The authors wish to acknowledge with gratitude the participation of Edward C. Northwood and Carol A. Fitzsimmons[1], partners with the firm of Hodgson, Russ LLP, Attorneys at Law, Toronto, Ontario[2] and Buffalo, New York in the preparation of Appendix 2, "United States Estate Tax".

The authors are also grateful for the assistance of Mary Louise Dickson, Q.C. and Llana Nakonechny of Dickson, MacGregor, Appell, Toronto, Ontario, in reviewing and updating the materials in Chapter 6, "Some Income Tax Aspects of the Ontario Family Law Act", and Sheila Matson of KPMG in reviewing the materials in Appendix 1, "Canadian Taxation and the Non-Resident".

In accordance with Internal Revenue Service Circular 230, we advise that any discussion of a federal tax issue in this communication is not intended or written to be used, and it cannot be used, by any recipient, for the purpose of avoiding penalties that may be imposed on the recipient under United States federal tax laws.

---

[1] enorthwo@hodsonruss.com, cfizsim@hodgsonruss.com

[2] Practice registered to U.S. law.

# Preface

The only two certainties in life are death and taxes — and the taxman will persist even after death to collect what is owing. Just as an individual is subject to income tax while alive, so too do the federal and provincial income tax laws continue to impose tax upon and beyond death. Death also creates one or more taxpayers in the person of the deceased's estate and any testamentary trusts which may arise as a consequence of the taxpayer's death, and will often impact the tax position of the deceased's beneficiaries.

Compliance with income tax legislation as it affects both deceased persons and their estates can be riddled with complexity. Accrual basis reporting for income in the year of death, deemed dispositions of capital property subject to available tax-deferred rollovers, and multiple returns for the year of death are only a few of the numerous departures from the standard reporting of personal income. Although there is a variety of opportunities under the *Income Tax Act* for tax minimization, both for the deceased taxpayer and for the estate, there are serious traps for the unwary. Planning for the estate during one's lifetime, with particular attention to the will as a primary planning tool, is the essential base for tax minimization on death. Planning should be an on-going process, well organized in the beginning and monitored throughout.

Changing laws and evolving family circumstances can upset even the most meticulous estate plans. One notable example was the introduction of the *Family Law Act* in Ontario which can have the effect of completely unwinding plans and overriding the provisions of the deceased's will unless appropriate steps are taken within the parameters of that Act to ensure that the wishes of the deceased prevail.

Opportunities for post mortem planning are available to the deceased's executor and personal representatives as the estate is administered and distributed and the tax obligations of the deceased are satisfied. An aware and responsible executor or trustee may be able to realize significant tax savings for the deceased and estate merely by taking advantage of the planning opportunities available under the *Income Tax Act.* However, an executor or trustee can also be at personal risk for the outstanding tax liability of the deceased and the estate should the estate be distributed without the appropriate tax clearance certificates being obtained from the Canada Revenue Agency.

*Death of a Taxpayer* provides not only a comprehensive review of the relevant income tax aspects of death, but also summarizes various non-tax considerations including will planning and some implications of the Ontario *Family Law Act* relating to death and the estate planning process. Also considered are Canadian income tax issues which could affect the non-resident, as well as United States Estate Tax issues as they may apply on the death of a Canadian resident.

Suzanne I. R. Hanson, B.A., LL.B.
Sandra A. Bussey, C.A.
*June 2005*

# Table of Contents

# I

# Introduction

## ¶100

## Tax Planning at Death

The *Income Tax Act* (R.S.C. 1985, c. 1 (5th Supp.)) (the "Act") contains numerous provisions which could apply to the income and property of a deceased taxpayer. Consequently, knowledge of the imposition of income tax as it affects the deceased, the estate and the beneficiaries of the deceased's estate is important both in formulating an estate plan and administering an estate after death. The Act provides specific rules which may facilitate income splitting and allow a deferral of the recognition of income and capital gains or losses on death. Accordingly, the incidence of tax on death will depend on the sources of the deceased taxpayer's income, the nature of the assets held at death and the relationship of the estate beneficiaries to the deceased.

## ¶102

## Intestacy

If a person dies without leaving a will, or the will is determined to be invalid, or ineffective (either in whole or in part), the person is said to have died "intestate". The intestacy rules may apply either to the distribution of the entire estate or may apply to only that portion of the estate which is not otherwise dealt with under the will.

A court of competent jurisdiction — for example, in Ontario the Ontario Court (General Division) — will determine whether a person died intestate, and if so, will appoint an administrator by granting a certificate of appointment of estate trustee without a will. This is conclusive evidence of the intestacy of the deceased and of the right of the administrator or estate trustee to deal with the property of the deceased. Generally, the courts look to the spouse, children, grandchildren, parents and brothers or sisters of the deceased to grant such certificate of appointment. However, the grant of the certificate of appointment is in the sole discretion of the court, and the court may appoint a trust company, for example, where the next of kin of the deceased are unable or unwilling to accept the appointment.

The administrator or estate trustee, once appointed, is responsible for the collection, management, supervision and realization of the assets of the deceased, payment of the deceased's debts and tax liabilities, and ultimately distributing assets to those persons entitled to inherit in accordance with the relevant provincial legislation.

## ¶104   Scheme of Distribution

Provincial laws providing for intestate succession govern the distribution of the estate of an intestate. In Ontario, an estate of a person who died intestate on or after March 31, 1978, would be subject to Part II of the *Succession Law Reform Act* (R.S.O. 1990, c. S.26, as amended) (the "SLRA") which provides as follows:

(1) If the deceased left a surviving spouse and no children ("issue"), the surviving spouse would take the entire estate absolutely (section 44).*

(2) If the deceased left a surviving spouse and issue, but the estate is valued at an amount equal to $200,000 or less, then the surviving spouse would take the entire estate absolutely (subsection 45(1)).

(3) If the deceased left a surviving spouse and issue, and the estate is valued at an amount greater than $200,000, then:

(a) if there is one child,

---

* Unless otherwise provided, the following references are to the SLRA.

(i) the surviving spouse would take a preferential share of $200,000, plus one-half of the excess over $200,000 (subsection 46(1)), and

(ii) the child would take the remaining one-half of the excess over $200,000 (subsection 46(1));

(b) if there is more than one child,

(i) the surviving spouse would take a preferential share of $200,000, plus one-third of the excess over $200,000 (subsection 46(2)), and

(ii) the remaining two-thirds of the excess over $200,000 would be divided equally among the issue *per stirpes*.[3]

(4) If the deceased did not leave a surviving spouse, then the entire estate would be divided equally among the issue of the deceased *per stirpes* (subsection 47(1)).

(5) If the deceased did not leave a surviving spouse or issue, then the parents of the deceased would share equally *per capita*, or all would go to the surviving parent (subsection 47(3)).

(6) If the deceased did not leave a surviving spouse, issue or parents, then the deceased's brothers and sisters would share equally *per capita*.

Note: If the brother or sister of the deceased is deceased, representation by children of the deceased's brother or sister is allowed, but only to the extent of nieces and nephews of the deceased and not to the extent of grandnieces and grandnephews, as this is not *per stirpes* representation (subsections 47(4), (5)).

(7) If the deceased did not leave a surviving spouse, issue, parents, brothers or sisters, then the nieces and nephews of the deceased take *per capita* (subsection 47(5)).

(8) If the deceased did not leave a surviving spouse, issue, parents, brothers, sisters, nieces or nephews, then all other next of kin take *per capita* on the basis of equal degrees of consanguinity (subsection 47(6)).

---

[3] *Per stirpes* means all issue flowing from the body, i.e., children of the deceased and grandchildren of the deceased share by representation. Hence, where a child of the deceased parent (the intestate) has predeceased the intestate and that child has left surviving children, the excess referred to in (a)(ii) and (b)(ii) above (the distributive share) would pass as though the child had not predeceased the intestate.

¶104

To determine equal degrees of consanguinity one must count up from the deceased to the nearest common ancestor and then down to the relative being considered (subsection 47(8)).

*Table of Consanguinity*

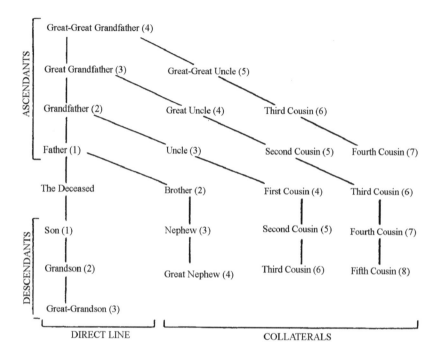

(9) Where there are no surviving next of kin, the property becomes property of the Crown and *The Escheats Act* applies (subsection 47(7)).

# ¶106

# Will Planning

## ¶108   Why Have a Will?

It is essential to have a valid will if property is to pass on death in a manner other than in accordance with the intestacy provisions of provincial statutes. However, as discussed below, certain property, including property held in joint tenancy and property subject to a valid beneficiary designation, pass by operation of law outside the will.

The administration of an estate is usually more expeditious if there is a will because:

(a) the executor may act immediately after the death;

(b) there is generally a shorter waiting period for a certificate of appointment of estate trustee with a will than for a certificate of appointment of estate trustee without a will;

(c) provincial statutes may prescribe a waiting period of up to one year from the death of the intestate before the beneficiaries cease to be liable for the debts of the deceased; and

(d) because the beneficiaries are named ascertainable under the will, it may be easier to locate beneficiaries of the deceased's estate.

It may be more cost effective to have a will in certain circumstances, for example:

(a) the will may provide that a beneficiary survive the deceased for a certain period of time, for example thirty days, and thereby avoid duplicate estate settlement costs which would be levied if the beneficiary were to die within days or weeks of the deceased;

(b) the will may authorize the executor to make particular investments which are not authorized by statutes such as the *Trustee Act*;

(c) the will may provide for advantageous distribution of assets in accordance with the provisions of the *Income Tax Act*; and

(d) the cost of administering the estate where there is a will may be lower.

## ¶110 Form of Will

A will may be defined to include:

- a testament;

- a codicil;

- an appointment by will or by writing in the nature of a will in exercise of a power; and

- any other testamentary disposition (SLRA subsection 1(1)).

## Testament

A testament is a document executed in accordance with relevant provincial legislation by a competent testator who intended that the disposition of the testator's property take effect upon death.

## Codicil

A codicil is an amendment to a will and requires a reference to a written instrument then existing and readily ascertainable. The doctrine of incorporation by reference requires that the will and the codicil be read together to carry out the testator's intention.

## Holograph

Subject to provincial legislation, a testator may make a valid will wholly in the testator's own handwriting and signature, without formality and without the presence, attestation or signature of one or more witnesses.

## Multiple Wills

Depending on the nature and location of the testator's assets, multiple wills might be executed. It is essential that the wills be drafted so as to contemplate the execution of one or more other wills and to ensure that such wills do not inadvertently revoke one another. Multiple wills might be used to segregate assets which would not otherwise require a probated will in order to be transferred or dealt with, for example, shares in a private corporation or personal property. Multiple wills may also be appropriate to deal with assets in a foreign jurisdiction so as to expedite the administration of such assets.

¶110

# ¶112   Requirements for Validity

*Formalities*

Provincial legislation prescribes the formalities which must be adhered to in order that a document be recognized as a valid will. The Ontario *Succession Law Reform Act* provides:

> Section 3.   A will is valid only when it is in writing.

> Section 4.   (1) Subject to sections 5 (Privileged Wills) and 6 (Holograph Wills), a will is not valid unless,

> (a) at its end it is signed by the testator or by some other person in his or her presence and by his or her direction;

> (b) the testator makes or acknowledges the signature in the presence of two or more attesting witnesses present at the same time; and

> (c) two or more of the attesting witnesses subscribe the will in the presence of the testator.

> Section 7.   (1) Insofar as the position of the signature is concerned, a will, whether holograph or not, is valid if the signature of the testator made either by him or her or the person signing for him or her is placed at, after, following, under or beside or opposite to the end of the will so that it is apparent on the face of the will that the testator intended to give effect by the signature to the writing signed as his or her will.

> (2) A will is not rendered invalid by the circumstances that,

> (a) the signature does not follow or is not immediately after the end of the will;

> (b) a blank space intervenes between the concluding words of the will and the signature;

> (c) the signature,

> (i) is placed among the words of a testimonium clause or of a clause of attestation,

> (ii) follows or is after or under a clause of attestation either with or without a blank space intervening, or

> (iii) follows or is after, under or beside the name of a subscribing witness;

(d) the signature is on a side, page or other portion of the paper or papers containing the will on which no clause, paragraph or disposing part of the will is written above the signature; or

(e) there appears to be sufficient space on or at the bottom of the preceding side, page or other portion of the same paper on which the will is written to contain the signature.

(3) The generality of subsection (1) is not restricted by the enumeration of circumstances set out in subsection (2), but a signature in conformity with section 4, 5 or 6 or this section does not give effect to,

(a) a disposition or a direction that is underneath the signature or that follows the signature; or

(b) a disposition or direction inserted after the signature was made.

## Capacity

Provincial legislation governs the capacity of infants to make a valid will. The Ontario *Succession Law Reform Act* provides as follows:

Section 8.   (1) A will made by a person who is under the age of eighteen years is not valid unless at the time of making the will the person,

(a) is or has been married;

(b) is contemplating marriage and the will states that it is made in contemplation of marriage to a named person except that such a will is not valid unless and until the marriage to the named person takes place;

(c) is a member of a component of the Canadian Forces,

(i) that is referred to in the *National Defence Act* (Canada) as a regular force, or

(ii) while placed on active service under the *National Defence Act* (Canada); or

(d) is a sailor and at sea or in the course of a voyage.

(2) A certificate purporting to be signed by or on behalf of an officer having custody of the records certifying that he or she has custody of the records of the force in which a person was serving at the time the will was made, setting out that the person was at that time a member of a regular force or was on active service within clause (1)(c), is proof, in the absence of evidence to the contrary, of that fact.

(3) A person who has made a will under subsection (1) may, while under the age of eighteen years, revoke the will.

The common law governs the mental capacity required of a testator to make a valid will. A person must be of sound mind, memory and understanding. At the time of making the will or giving instructions to the lawyer, the testator must have been able to understand that it was a will being made, that the testator could comprehend and recollect the extent of the property that the testator had an interest in, that the testator had relatives or other persons who might be expected to benefit by this will, and the extent of what is given to each beneficiary, to the exclusion of others.

When the will is executed, case law has held that it is only necessary that the testator understand that it is a will that is being executed and that the testator had previously given instructions which have been reflected in this document.

## ¶114 Naming Executors

Executors who are named in and accept their nomination under the will are responsible for the administration and distribution of the estate. Their duties include arranging the burial, locating the last will and codicils, if any, of the deceased, collecting any estate assets, ascertaining the beneficiaries, filing tax returns for the deceased and the estate, making payment of debts and legacies of the deceased, setting aside any trust funds established under the will and distributing the residue to the persons entitled. Since executors have full legal authority to deal with all the assets of the estate, the testator should have the utmost faith in the executor's honesty and ability to make prudent investments, manage funds, maintain accounts and manage similar responsibilities. While the testator may appoint any number of executors, it simplifies administration if there are no more than three executors. In order to avoid a stalemate, it is generally preferable to provide for all decisions by majority. Otherwise, decisions must be unanimous. If the estate is not highly complex, the testator may consider appointing a beneficiary, family member, friend or possibly a professional advisor who is younger than the testator as executor. In the event that an executor predeceases the testator, the court will appoint a replacement unless the will provides for the appointment of a second or substitute executor/trustee. Where the executor has commenced the administration of the testator's estate and has proven (or probated) the will but dies before the estate administration has been completed, the executor of the deceased executor would become the executor of the original testator provided that the latter executor proves (or probates) the will of the former executor.

An institutional trustee might be appointed where the estate is complex or continuing for an extended period of time, for example, where an infant is not to take under the will until attaining a specified age or where the will establishes a trust for the lifetime of the beneficiary. Appointing an institutional trustee may be more expensive, less flexible and less compassionate. However, one is generally assured of professional expertise and continuity in the administration of the estate.

## ¶116   Certificate of Appointment of Estate Trustee With a Will

A court of competent jurisdiction, in Ontario the Ontario Court (General Division), issues a document, the certificate of appointment of estate trustee with a will, which certifies that the will attached has been approved and registered in the court. The persons named in the will as executors derive their authority from the will. The grant of the certificate is evidence that the will is valid.

## ¶118   Powers of Attorney

Where a person, the donor or principal, gives authority to another person, the donee or attorney, to act on behalf of the donor in conducting the donor's financial affairs, a power of attorney has been created. The relationship created by this appointment is governed by the common law of agency and by provincial statutes (in Ontario, *The Substitute Decisions Act* S.O. 1992, c. 30, as amended).

Powers of attorney may be general in nature in that they may be intended for general purposes at some unknown future time and they contain broad powers. Conversely, powers of attorney may be limited to specific acts at specific dates. In some jurisdictions, including Ontario, separate powers of attorney may be executed and separate attorneys named to deal with either financial or personal care matters.

The donor may revoke the power of attorney at any time provided that the donor has the mental capacity at the time of the revocation and the donor gives notice in writing of the revocation to the donee.

However, a power of attorney is valid only while the donor is alive. After death, the affairs of the deceased are governed by the will or the laws of intestacy.

# ¶120

## Will Planning and the Ontario Family Law Act

In Ontario, the *Family Law Act* (R.S.O. 1990, c. F.3, as amended) (the "FLA") applies where a person dies after March 1, 1986 without contracting out of the FLA, and leaves a surviving spouse whose net family property value is less than that of the deceased spouse.

Under section 6 of the FLA, the surviving spouse is required to elect to take under the will of the deceased spouse (or under the intestacy provisions of the Ontario *Succession Law Reform Act* if there is no will), or to receive the statutory entitlement of section 5 of the FLA. Unless the election is filed within six months after the deceased's death, the spouse is deemed to give up his or her rights under the FLA for property equalization, subject to any relief the court may grant for delays in filing.

Section 5 of the FLA provides that where the net family property of the deceased spouse exceeds the net family property of the surviving spouse, the surviving spouse is entitled to one-half of the difference between the two values less specific amounts such as life insurance and lump-sum pension benefits received by the surviving spouse as a result of the death of the deceased spouse.

Section 4 of the FLA defines net family property as the *value* of all property except excluded property, as listed in subsection 4(2) of the FLA, that a spouse owns on the relevant valuation date, in this case, the day prior to the date of death, after deducting,

(1) the spouse's debts and other liabilities; and

(2) the value of the property, other than a matrimonial home, that the spouse owned on the date of marriage, after deducting the spouse's debts and other liabilities, calculated as of the date of marriage.

Note: *Value* is a term which has not been defined by the FLA. Accordingly, where there is any ambiguity, its meaning may have to be determined by negotiation or ultimately by the courts.

If, by will or by statutory intestacy provisions, the surviving spouse inherits the deceased spouse's entire estate, generally the FLA would have no effect. If something less than the entire estate is to pass by will or intestacy, for example, where the surviving spouse is the beneficiary of a lifetime spousal trust, the spouse might consider whether filing an election under the FLA would be appropriate.

If the surviving spouse is incapacitated, the FLA election may be made by his or her attorney acting on their behalf. In fact, the attorney may have no choice but to make the election if the spouse's entitlement under the will is less than their FLA equalization entitlement, in that the attorney has an obligation to protect the financial security of the incapacitated spouse.

## ¶122

## Property Passing Outside the Will

Certain property interests held by a testator may pass, by operation of law, outside of the testator's will. The following are examples of property interests which may pass to beneficiaries without being provided for in the will.

## ¶124    Insurance Proceeds

The *Insurance Act* (R.S.O. 1990, c. I.8) divides insurance policies into two categories by date. Policies issued prior to July 1, 1962 require that beneficiaries be designated by one of three classes:

1. where a person gave valuable consideration, other than marriage, to the insured and was described as a beneficiary for value in the insurance policy, such beneficiary has priority over all other beneficiaries for value or assignees for value, provided that such beneficiary gives written notice of the interest to the insurance company's head office;

2. where a named beneficiary is a relative of the insured as defined in the *Insurance Act*, the proceeds of the insurance policy do not form part of the estate of the deceased and generally are not subject to the claims of the deceased's creditors;

3. all other beneficiaries are ordinary beneficiaries and can claim no priority over the interests of the beneficiaries for value, or assignees for value, or a preferred beneficiary (section 172).

Policies issued after July 1, 1962 provide that the designation of a beneficiary under an insurance policy is revocable unless the insured expressly makes the designation irrevocable (sections 190, 191). Where the beneficiary designation is revocable, the insured may change the beneficiary without the consent of or notice to the beneficiary. Where the beneficiary designation is irrevocable, the consent of the beneficiary is required prior to any change of beneficiary being implemented. In both situations, the proceeds are not part of the estate of the deceased unless the named beneficiary is the estate, and provided the beneficiary under a revocable policy is within the definition of immediate relative as provided in the *Insurance Act.*

## ¶126  Joint Tenancy

Generally, where property is registered in the name of the deceased and another person as joint tenants, the property automatically vests in the surviving joint tenant or tenants on the death of one of the joint tenants. An exception to this general rule occurs where the real property is a matrimonial home owned by one spouse and a person other than the spouse as joint tenants. Under such circumstances in Ontario, the FLA provides that the joint tenancy is deemed to be severed on the death of the spouse. As such, the interest of the deceased spouse would devolve in accordance with the will or the rules of intestacy if there is no will, subject to any claim under the FLA.

Where property is registered in the name of the deceased and another person as tenants in common, the surviving tenant is not entitled to claim the undivided interest of the deceased in the property. The undivided interest in the property of the deceased must be dealt with in the manner prescribed by the deceased's will, or by the intestacy provisions of the relevant provincial statute where there is no will, again subject to any FLA claim.

## ¶128  Joint Bank Accounts

Where the bank account is a joint account, the surviving joint owner will generally be permitted to deal with the account on presentation of evidence of the death of the deceased joint owner.

Where the bank account is not a joint account, the *Bank Act* requires delivery of certain documents to authorize the bank to release deposits, property held by the bank as security or safekeeping, or rights with respect to a safety deposit box.

## ¶130   Shareholders' Agreements

Where the deceased held shares which were subject to a shareholders' agreement, the agreement must be reviewed by the executor or other personal representative of the deceased to determine the rights and obligations of the deceased, the surviving shareholders and the corporation. Frequently, shareholders' agreements have provisions which, on the death of one of the shareholders, provide a right of first refusal to surviving shareholders, or an obligation by the surviving shareholders or the corporation to purchase the shares of the deceased. There may also be provisions for the transfer of shares held by the deceased shareholder to the shareholder's spouse and/or children.

(See ¶306 "Shareholdings and Death" for further consideration of this issue.)

## ¶132   Pension Benefits

Pension plans may provide a number of different options in the event of the death of a member. If at the time of death the member had not already retired and commenced receiving pension benefits, the plan may provide for the payment of a lump-sum death benefit to the designated beneficiary. If the member were already receiving pension benefits, the plan may provide for the payment of survivorship benefits to a surviving spouse or dependants which are usually a reduced percentage of the amount received by the deceased member.

In view of the variety of options available, the executor or personal representative may wish to review the pension plan document as registered under the pension benefits act of the relevant province.

Under the *Canada Pension Plan/Quebec Pension Plan*, a death benefit is payable to the estate of a contributor who has made contributions for the minimum qualifying period. The executor or personal representative of the deceased, or any eligible recipient of the death benefit, may apply for the benefit. In addition, a surviving spouse and dependent children may be entitled to survivors' benefits provided the deceased contributor has made contributions for the minimum qualifying period.

## ¶140

## Estate Administration

## ¶142 Introduction

Estate administration includes arranging for the payment of the deceased's funeral and testamentary expenses, debts and taxes, and for the distribution of the residue of the estate to the persons legally entitled, all as soon as reasonably possible. The time required to complete the administration of an estate usually depends upon the size and nature of its assets, whether the estate is subject to contest, and the cooperation received from third parties in supplying information or documentation required in the course of the estate administration. Although an executor or administrator is generally allowed one year from the testator's death to settle the affairs of the estate, the administration of some estates may be substantially completed and the estate ready for distribution (or a substantial partial distribution) within six months of death. However, it may not be possible to obtain the information necessary to file tax returns within that period. Further, it is unlikely that clearance certificates, which release the personal representative from personal liability for taxes owing by the deceased or the estate, will be received from the Canada Revenue Agency within one year of death.

## ¶144 Mechanics of Estate Administration

The administration of an estate involves two types of work: solicitor's work and executor's work. Although it may appear that the two types of work are inter-related, they are in fact separate and distinct.

*Solicitor's Work*

Solicitor's work includes advising the executor as to the executor's rights, duties and responsibilities in connection with the administration of the deceased's estate; preparing and filing applications for letters probate, letters of administration or, in Ontario, for a certificate of appointment of estate trustee with or without a will, with supporting material (when required); obtaining letters probate, letters of administration or, in Ontario, a certificate of appointment of estate trustee, and making sufficient notarial copies for the purpose of estate administration; preparing and filing returns or applications required to obtain consents for the transfer of property (e.g., U.S. Estate Tax Consents); preparing all transmission declarations, and other documents required for the transfer of the deceased's assets into the executor's name on behalf of the estate or to establish the executor's authority to sell or otherwise deal with those assets; arranging to advertise for creditors (where appropriate); preparing forms of indemnity and release to be signed by the beneficiaries (where appropriate); and general legal advice and recommendations during the course of estate administration.

*Executor's Work*

The executor who was appointed by the testator under the will, or the administrator or estate trustee who was appointed by the court, bears the ultimate responsibility for the administration of the deceased's estate. The executor's or administrator's work involves: arranging the funeral; ascertaining, locating and notifying the deceased's relatives and beneficiaries; preparing an inventory of the deceased's assets and liabilities and arranging valuations where necessary; disposing of the deceased's perishable assets and securing and protecting all other assets; reviewing the deceased's insurance coverage and obtaining increased or additional coverage on assets held in the estate where necessary; making provision for the immediate needs of the dependants; collecting income generated by the deceased's assets; opening and maintaining an estate bank account; making investment decisions (where required) pending distribution of the estate; notifying various government and private institutions of the deceased's death; arranging for the sale of estate assets (where required) to generate funds required to pay debts, taxes and legacies; maintaining estate accounts for approval by beneficiaries or examination by the Court (where appropriate); preparing and filing the deceased's terminal tax return and all tax returns for prior years due but not yet filed as at the date of death; preparing and filing the estate income tax return; obtaining clearance certificates from the Canada Revenue Agency; settling claims of creditors and paying all legitimate claims; arranging for the payment or distribution of all bequests, legacies and residue in accordance with the terms of the deceased's will; and reporting from time to time to the deceased's beneficiaries.

## ¶146   Income Tax Returns

One of the most complex tasks of estate administration relates to tax matters, including the determination of the number and types of income tax returns and tax elections to be filed. Substantial tax savings may be achieved through the appropriate choice of tax returns and elections.

## ¶148 Potential Liabilities of Executor

*Debts*

The deceased's creditors are entitled to payment before distribution is made to the deceased's beneficiaries. An executor who distributes estate funds without advertising for creditors is personally liable to any creditors who are subsequently ascertained to the extent of the lesser of:

(a) the debts owed to such creditors; and

(b) the value of the estate.

Consequently, many executors advertise for creditors in a newspaper having general circulation in a municipality in which the deceased resided or carried on business. The cost of such advertisements will vary depending on the size and circulation of the newspaper in which the advertisement is placed.

An executor or personal representative who is certain that the deceased has few or no liabilities at the time of death may decide that the estate should not be put to the expense of advertising for creditors. In such case, it is recommended that the executor request each residuary beneficiary to indemnify the executor against any claims which may arise to the extent of such beneficiary's proportionate share of the estate.

*Income Tax Liabilities*

An executor or personal representative who distributes estate funds without obtaining a final clearance certificate from the Canada Revenue Agency is personally liable to the Canada Revenue Agency for any unpaid taxes, interest and penalties to the extent of the lesser of:

(a) such tax liabilities; and

(b) the value of the estate.

Consequently, executors and personal representatives generally should not distribute the entire estate until a clearance certificate is received, holding back whatever amount is considered appropriate under the circumstances to cover any outstanding tax liability. The executor or personal representative should request the residuary beneficiaries to indemnify the executor against any income tax liability which may arise to the extent of such beneficiary's proportionate share of the estate.

## Purchase of Estate Assets

It is a well-established principle of estate law that an executor or trustee must not purchase estate assets unless there is specific authorization in the will or the purchase receives court approval. If an executor or trustee purchases estate assets without such authorization or approval, the purchase may be set aside or the executor or trustee may be required to account to the beneficiaries for any profit made by reason of the purchase.

## Distribution

If the deceased's will or any codicil to the will was executed after March 31, 1978, the terms "child", "children" and "issue" include children and issue born out of wedlock unless the will provides otherwise. In particular, wills generally provide that only persons who may trace their legitimacy through marriage or adoption are entitled to inherit under the will. However, many wills now provide an exception to this general provision to allow a person born outside marriage if, in the unanimous opinion of the executors and trustees, that person was always acknowledged and treated as the legitimate child of their parent. If the will is silent, the executor or personal representative should not distribute estate funds without making reasonable enquiries and undertaking searches at the office of the Registrar General for the province to determine the identity of all proper beneficiaries.

Unless the will otherwise provides, an executor or personal representative should not deliver a bequest or pay a legacy to a minor (as defined in the relevant provincial legislation) since a minor cannot give a valid receipt. Furthermore, the executor is not justified in delivering a bequest or paying a legacy to the minor's parents or other relatives unless the will or a court order authorizes such delivery or payment.

# ¶150  Solicitor's Fees

Historically, the fees allowed to a solicitor for the performance of the solicitor's work outlined above was calculated by a tariff which related the solicitor's fee to the value of the estate. That tariff has been revoked and the solicitor's fee should be calculated so as to reflect time and effort required and spent, any special skill or service required and provided, the amount involved or value of the subject matter, and the results obtained in any special circumstances relating to the matter.

Although it is difficult to determine in advance the precise fee to be charged by the solicitor, after review of the deceased's will and the nature and extent of the assets, and after ascertaining the number of beneficiaries, the solicitor should be able to provide a reasonable estimate of the fee for solicitor's work. If an executor is not satisfied with the solicitor's account when finally rendered, the executor may ask the court to review the account and reduce it if it is found to be excessive.

## ¶152   Executor's Compensation

An executor or personal representative is entitled to a fair and reasonable allowance for their care, pains and trouble, and time expended for the performance of their work. As a rule, where the estate provides for an immediate distribution, an executor is allowed a fee equal to 5% of the value of the estate. Based on the court guidelines, where the will provides for a continuing trust, an executor is generally entitled to:

- $2^1/_2$% of the value of all assets and income received;

- $2^1/_2$% of all assets and income disbursed or distributed; and

- $2/_5$ of 1% per year of the average fair market value of the capital of the trust as a care and management fee.

In addition, where the nature of the assets requires special services, a court may permit an increased or special fee.

Where there is more than one executor of an estate, the amount of the compensation is divided among the executors in whatever proportion they may agree.

In many instances, executors who have little experience or expertise in estate administration may request a solicitor to perform a part of or all of the estate administration. In such case, the solicitor may expect to receive a portion of the executor's compensation in addition to the solicitor's fee referred to above. The allocation of executor's work and executor's compensation between the executor and solicitor should be determined at an early stage of the estate administration.

## ¶154   General Comments

The comments in this section are intended only as a general outline of the steps, rights and liabilities involved in estate administration. They are not an exhaustive statement of the law and procedure relating to estate administration. In addition, the requirements and obligations may vary from province to province.

# 2

# Computation of Income and Taxes Payable

## ¶200

### Filing of Returns

It is the responsibility of the personal representative of the deceased, in his or her capacity as executor, administrator or trustee, to file the requisite terminal period income tax returns. The taxation year for the terminal period extends from January 1 of the year of death up to the date of death.[4] When the death of the taxpayer occurs during a year and before November 1, the terminal period income tax return must be filed by April 30 following the year of death, or June 15 following the year of death if the deceased or deceased's spouse[5] or common-law partner was carrying on a business in the year of death, effective for 1995 and subsequent taxation years (paragraph 150(1)(d)). The later filing deadline of June 15 does not apply if the expenditures of the business are primarily the cost or capital cost of tax shelter investments. When the death of the taxpayer occurs during a

---

[4] See *Katz Estate v. The Queen*, 76 DTC 6377 (F.C.T.D.).

[5] Effective in 1993, subsection 252(4) provided that words referring to a spouse of a taxpayer include the person of the opposite sex who cohabits at that time with the taxpayer in a conjugal relationship and

- has cohabited with the taxpayer throughout a 12-month period, or
- would be a parent of a child of whom the taxpayer would be a parent.

Subsection 252(4) was repealed effective for 2001 and later years as a result of the definition of common-law partner being added in subsection 248(1). The definition of common-law partner is similar to the extended definition of spouse contained in subsection 252(4) but has been extended to cover same-sex partners.

year and after October 31, the terminal period income tax return must be filed by the later of the day on or before which the return would otherwise be required to be filed and six months following the date of death (paragraph 150(1)(*b*)). Therefore, if the taxpayer died on March 15, 2005, and the deceased or the deceased's spouse or common-law partner was not carrying on a business in 2005, the terminal period return would have to be filed by April 30, 2006. However, if the taxpayer died on November 15, 2005, the terminal period return would be due on May 15, 2006 or June 15, 2006 if the deceased or the deceased's spouse or common-law partner were carrying on a business in 2005.

With respect to the payment of any taxes due on the terminal period income tax return, the balance-due day will depend on the date of the taxpayer's death. When the death of the taxpayer occurs during a year and before November 1, any unpaid taxes are due by April 30 following the year of death (subsection 156.1(4) and subsection 248(1)). This balance-due day applies even if the terminal period income tax return is not due until June 15 following the year of death because the deceased or deceased's spouse or common-law partner was carrying on a business in the year of death. When the death of the taxpayer occurs after October, any unpaid taxes are due by six months after the date of death (subsection 156.1(4) and subsection 248(1)). Interest at the prescribed rate[6] would, however, be charged on any tax which is unpaid by the balance-due day (subsection 161(1)).

Tax in respect of resource property, land inventory, amounts included in income as rights or things, and deemed dispositions of capital property may be paid in instalments as discussed in greater detail at ¶286 (subsection 159(5)).

Where the deceased's will creates a tainted spouse trust to which subsection 70(7) applies, the terminal return may be filed up to 18 months following death (paragraph 70(7)(*a*)). This extension applies whether or not such a trust is successfully untainted under paragraph 70(7)(*b*). However, even though the actual time for filing a return is extended, tax owing is payable by the later of April 30 of the year following the year of death or six months following the date of death. Otherwise, interest at the prescribed rate will be calculated on any unpaid amounts. (See ¶504, Untainting a Spouse Trust, for a discussion of these provisions.)

The time for filing is also extended for a separate return filed for rights or things (see ¶216).

---

[6] Compounded quarterly for time period before 1987 and compounded daily thereafter (subsection 248(11)).

¶200

Where a taxpayer dies before the filing deadline of his/her tax return for the year prior to the year of death, that return is due the later of the day on which the return would otherwise be required to be filed and the day that is six months after the date of death (paragraph 150(1)(*b*)). For example, if a taxpayer died on March 15, 2005 and the deceased or the deceased's spouse or common-law partner was not carrying on a business, the taxpayer's 2004 tax return would be due on September 15, 2005 and unpaid taxes would be due on that day as well.

In addition to the filing of the terminal period income tax return and the elective separate returns (see ¶206), the personal representative will also be required to determine if the deceased was required to file any of the foreign reporting forms required by sections 233.2 to 233.4 and 233.6. Form T1141 (section 233.2 — transfers or loans to non-resident trusts), T1135 (section 233.3 — foreign income verification statement) and T1142 (section 233.6 — distributions from and indebtedness to a non-resident trust) are due on the filing due date of the deceased's terminal income tax return. Forms T1134-A (section 233.4 — foreign affiliates that are not controlled foreign affiliates) and T1134-B (section 233.4 — controlled foreign affiliates) for the year in which the deceased died are due within 15 months from the date of death.

## ¶202

## Liability of Personal Representative

Since it is the responsibility of the personal representative to discharge all outstanding liability for income tax, where a taxpayer has not filed returns for any years prior to the year of death, those returns must also be prepared by the trustee or executor and filed. Should the representative fail to do this, and distribute the assets of the estate without obtaining an income tax clearance certificate from the Canada Revenue Agency, the representative is strictly liable for any tax, interest or penalty which remains payable (subsection 159(3)). Accordingly, before any distribution is made to the beneficiaries of the estate, the representative should obtain a clearance certificate from the Canada Revenue Agency (subsection 159(2)). Otherwise, the representative will be personally liable to the extent of the lesser of the value of the property distributed or the tax, interest and penalties which are owing.

## ¶204

## Clearance Certificates

A clearance certificate certifies that all income tax, *Canada Pension Plan* contributions, employment insurance premiums, interest and penalties payable by the taxpayer have either been paid or have been secured to the satisfaction of the Minister. Subsection 159(2) requires a personal representative to obtain a clearance certificate prior to distributing any property under the representative's control.

Canada Revenue Agency's Information Circular 82-6R3 considers the property of an estate to be distributed on the date when the personal representative gives up control over the property and transfers it to the person entitled to receive it. Distribution is not considered to be the date when the person has acquired the right to receive the property.

Where a personal representative intends to distribute property of an estate to a beneficiary in satisfaction of an income interest in the estate (subsection 106(3)) to a non-resident beneficiary (subsection 107(5)) or to a beneficiary of a spouse trust (or of a reversionary trust in certain circumstances) in satisfaction of his or her capital interest (subsections 107(4) and (4.1)), the fair market value of such property must be ascertained as at the distribution date.

Prior to winding up the estate and distributing its assets, the personal representative should establish a scheme of distribution as of a date chosen by the representative. That date would be one which is prior to the date on which the request in the certificate is in fact made. A final T3 estate income tax return for that part of the taxation year ending on the chosen date must be prepared and filed, and the tax payable on that return is calculated as if the distribution had occurred on the chosen date. Provided all returns have been filed and all income tax, interest and penalties have been paid, the Canada Revenue Agency will issue a certificate, Form TX 21, for final distribution of all property in the estate. Upon issuance of that form, the Canada Revenue Agency considers the date chosen by the personal representative as being the actual date of distribution for tax purposes. From that time, the personal representative is considered to hold the property on behalf of the beneficiaries of the estate, and the beneficiaries would pay tax on any income earned after the chosen date.

The Canada Revenue Agency has indicated in Information Circular 82-6R3 that since a clearance certificate cannot be issued until all returns have been filed and assessed and all amounts payable have been paid or secured, the request for a certificate should not be made until all the required income tax returns have been assessed. To request a clearance certificate, Form TX 19 must be completed and forwarded to the relevant tax services office.

Generally, a distribution of capital to a non-resident beneficiary of an estate will not result in a capital gain to the beneficiary. However, before an exectutor makes a distribution of property (including a distribution of cash) to a non-resident beneficiary of the estate in respect of the beneficiary's capital interest, consideration should be given to the requirements for a certificate of compliance under section 116. "Taxable Canadian property", as defined in subsection 248(1), includes a capital interest in a trust, other than a unit trust, resident in Canada. A beneficiary of an estate is considered to have a disposition of all or a part of his/her capital interest where a payment is received after 1999 from the estate that can reasonably be considered to have been made because of their capital interest (see definition of "disposition" in subsection 248(1)). As a result, the requirements of section 116 must be compiled with. It should be noted that the trust would be considered the purchaser for purposes of subsection 116(5) and as such, the trust would be liable to pay, on behalf of the non-resident beneficiary, the amount determined under that subsection.

Under the provisions of section 116, the request for a certificate of compliance can be made pursuant to subsection 116(1), prior to the distribution or pursuant to subsection 116(3), not later than 10 days after the distribution. As the provisions of subsection 107(1) only apply for purposes of calculating the adjusted cost base of a capital interest where that capital interest has been disposed of, different amounts may need to be remitted depending on whether the request for a certificate of compliance is made pursuant to subsection 116(1) or subsection 116(3). (Reference should be made to Information Circular 72-17R4 and technical interpretations 2001-0093155 dated October 5, 2001 and 2002-0131015 dated February 24, 2003.)

## ¶206
### Elections to File Separate Returns

There are several choices for filing provided in the Act which cover a variety of sources of income a taxpayer might have at the time of death. As a result, more than one income tax return may be filed for the year of death on behalf of the deceased.

The first is the ordinary return covering the deceased's income for the period from January 1 of the year of death to the date of death (subsection 70(1)).

The second is a separate return where the taxpayer operated a business as a proprietorship, or was a member of a partnership, and an election was made to use an off-calendar fiscal year end (subsection 150(4)). The subsection 150(4) election is applicable where death occurred after the close of the fiscal year, but before the end of the calendar year in which the next fiscal year closed and, in the case of a partnership, the death of the partner caused that second fiscal period of the partnership to end. The return filed pursuant to subsection 150(4) will report the above-noted stub period income in a separate return as if the taxpayer were another person whose only income for the year was that income. If there were no deemed or actual fiscal year end of the partnership as a result of the death of the partner, the partnership income of the stub period which accrued to the partner to the date of death would be a right or thing (Interpretation Bulletin IT-278R2). In this case, a separate return may be filed (pursuant to subsection 70(2)), including only the income from the business which arose after the close of the fiscal year to the date of death (see below).

For 1996 and subsequent years, a legal representative can report on a subsection 150(4) return the balance of the individual's reserve in respect of December 31, 1995 income (subsection 34.2(8)). See the discussion at ¶220 with respect to the calculation of the income reported on a subsection 150(4) return for 1996 and subsequent years where the taxpayer has elected under subsection 249.1(4) to retain an off-calendar fiscal year end, and the treatment of an individual's reserve in respect of December 31, 1995 income in the year of death.

The third is a separate return where the taxpayer was an income beneficiary of a testamentary trust with a taxation year other than a calendar year (paragraph 104(23)(*d*)). A return may be filed including only the income from the trust which arose after the end of the taxation year of the trust, up to the date of death of the taxpayer.

Returns filed under subsections 70(1), 150(4) and paragraph 104(23)(*d*) are generally due by the later of April 30 of the year following death, or six months following the date of death, with interest at the prescribed rate payable on any tax which remains unpaid after the due date. However, for 1995 and subsequent taxation years, the due date for such returns may be extended for a deceased person if the deceased or deceased's spouse or common-law partner carried on a business in the year of death. See ¶200 for a discussion of the extended filing deadline.

Finally, an election may be made to file a separate return for the value of rights or things owed to the taxpayer at the time of death (subsection 70(2)). (This is discussed in greater detail at ¶210.) This return must be filed by the later of one year from the date of death or 90 days after the mailing of any notice of assessment in respect of the tax return of the taxpayer for the year of death. For example, if a taxpayer died on May 1, 2005 and the notice of assessment for the terminal period return was mailed prior to January 31, 2006, the personal representative would have until April 30, 2006 to file a separate return for rights or things. However, if the personal representative

¶206

had not filed the terminal period return until April 30, 2006, and the notice of assessment of that return was not mailed until June 15, 2006, the separate rights or things return would not have to be filed until September 13, 2006. It should be noted that any tax payable on the rights or things return is due on the same day as any taxes due on the terminal period return. Therefore, in the above example where the separate rights or things return would be due on September 13, 2006, any taxes payable on that return would be due on April 30, 2006 (see Technical Interpretation 2001-0096585).

## ¶208

### Periodic Payments[7]

The difference between periodic payments and rights or things generally creates a good deal of confusion. In fact, the Canada Revenue Agency has taken the position that, in cases where an income item cannot be categorized as a periodic payment or as a right or thing with any degree of certainty, the item may be reported so as to place the taxpayer in the most favourable position (Interpretation Bulletins IT-210R2, IT-212R3). In many cases, it would be advantageous to classify a doubtful item as a right or thing.

Periodic payments include those amounts which were accruing but not yet due as at the date of death. Such items are deemed to accrue in equal daily amounts in the period for which that amount is payable. As a result, even though an amount is not actually received as at the date of death, this deeming provision in subsection 70(1) requires any amount deemed to accrue to the date of death to be included in income on the terminal period return. Some examples of items considered to be periodic payments are rents, interest, royalties, annuities and remuneration from an office or employment. If a deceased taxpayer has incurred expenses with respect to those periodic payments, those expenses may be deducted on an accrual basis even though they may not have been paid as at the date of death. Because it is the value of accrued amounts which is included in income, the face amount of the accrual might be decreased if it is established that some accrued amounts might not be collectable. As with the calculation of income, expenses are accrued on a daily basis up to death (Interpretation Bulletin IT-210R2, paragraph 5). If by accruing expenses a loss is realized on the terminal period return, that loss may be deducted from all other income (Interpretation Bulletin IT-210R2, paragraph 5).

As a result of this method of computing income, periodic payments are separated into those which are taxed in the hands of the individual prior to death and those which are taxed in the estate, being those amounts accruing

---

[7] Subsection 70(1).

after death. For example, if a taxpayer died with funds in a bank account, interest on that account, accrued from the last interest date to the date of death, would be included in the terminal period return. Any interest accruing after that time would be taxed in the estate when actually received from the bank.

Where a taxpayer claims an investment tax credit in the year of death or a preceding taxation year, and the amount has neither been included in income nor deducted from the cost of property to which the credit relates, paragraph 70(1)(*b*) will cause the amount to be included in income in the year of death.

## ¶210
## Rights or Things

As noted above, rights or things may be reported on a separate return. Generally, rights or things include items of income which have been earned and are receivable as at the date of death but which have not been collected as at that time. In the absence of the provisions of the Act that include rights or things in the income of the deceased taxpayer, these amounts would not be subject to tax since, subject to specific exceptions, individual taxpayers are considered to receive income on a cash rather than accrual basis. That is, since income is not taxed until it is received, as at the time of death, being the end of the deceased's taxation year, amounts which are rights or things would not be received by the taxpayer.

## ¶212   What Constitutes Rights or Things

Rights or things include items other than capital property, an interest in a life insurance policy (other than an annuity contract of a taxpayer which was deductible from income under paragraph (60)(*l*) or acquired in circumstances to which subsection 146(21) applies), eligible capital property, land inventory of a business and a Canadian or foreign resource property which would have been included in the computation of the deceased's income when those amounts were actually realized or disposed of (subsection 70(3.1), Interpretation Bulletin IT-212R3, paragraph 2).[8] The amount to be included in the taxpayer's income is the amount or value of the right or thing at the date of death.

---

[8] The notice of Ways and Means Motion tabled on October 30, 2003, proposes that for taxation years that began after 2002, a right or thing will not include property in respect of which proposed new subsection 94.2(3) applies (and proposed new subsection 94.2(20) does not apply) to the individual for the individual's taxation year in which the individual dies.

Rights or things include: matured uncashed bond coupons, farm crops, herds on hand less basic herd, accounts receivable for taxpayers such as farmers or fishermen reporting on a cash basis, unpaid salary and wages or commissions (including employment insurance benefits), *Canada Pension Plan* and Old Age Security benefits, vacation pay not taken and vested rights in employee compensation plans. However, unpaid salary would be considered to be a right or thing only if it related to pay periods ending prior to the date of death. Declared and unpaid dividends are rights or things if the ex-dividend date (or date of record if no ex-dividend date) is prior to the date of death. These dividends are subject to the normal gross-up and credit mechanisms.

According to Interpretation Bulletin IT-212R3, work in progress of a professional practising as a sole proprietor is also a right or thing where the taxpayer has elected under section 34 to exclude the value of work in progress in computing income. This election was repealed for the 1983 and subsequent taxation years for professionals other than accountants, dentists, lawyers, medical doctors, veterinarians and chiropractors.

Pursuant to Interpretation Bulletin IT-337R4, paragraph 18, where a retired employee dies before receiving all of a retiring allowance entitlement, any payments made to a dependant, relation, or the deceased's estate will be included in the recipient's income under subparagraph 56(1)(a)(ii). Alternatively, the value of any retiring allowance entitlement at the time of death may be included in the deceased's income as a right or thing.

Where the deceased taxpayer was a member of a partnership, see ¶704 for a discussion of the treatment of the "stub period" as a right or thing.

In summary, whether an amount is considered a right or thing for tax purposes turns on whether the amount is receivable by the taxpayer at the time of death. If the taxpayer has no absolute right to receive the item of income at that time, the income would be taxed to the estate (or possibly the beneficiary) when received.

Excluded as rights or things are 1971 receivables under ITAR 23 which are included in the taxpayer's income on death pursuant to ITAR 23(3)(c), income-averaging annuity contracts, lump-sum payments out of a pension fund or plan unless the employee could have required payment out of the plan during the employee's lifetime, matured or unmatured RRSPs, RRIFs and an amount in the deceased taxpayer's NISA Fund No. 2.

## ¶214   Computation of Rights or Things

The Act provides that it is the value of rights or things which must be included in income, not their face amount. This would be relevant, for example, in the case of a receivable where collectibility is doubtful. The amount to be included in income would be the amount which could be collected. In some circumstances this amount would be nil.

In many instances, the value of rights or things may be determined only after the deduction of expenses relating to those items, calculated to the date of death. Only those expenses which have become payable or which have been incurred specifically in respect of those rights or things are deductible. In addition, the amount claimed as a deduction must be such that it would have been an allowable deduction to the taxpayer had death not occurred. Where the income from a right or thing is less than the expenses relating to that item, the excess may be deducted from other income (Interpretation Bulletin IT-212R3, paragraphs 4 and 5).

## ¶216   Separate Filing

In order for the personal representative of the deceased to be able to file a separate return reporting only income from rights or things, an election must be filed with the Canada Revenue Agency by the later of one year after the taxpayer's death, or 90 days after the notice of assessment of the terminal return is mailed. This election may be revoked only if the personal representative signs and files a notice of revocation with the Minister within the relevant filing time for a rights or things return (subsection 70(4)). Because this return is considered to be that of another person, full personal tax credits may be claimed on this return. If it is advantageous, the personal representative may choose to claim other tax credits in respect of medical expenses, charitable donations, disability, tuition fees, education amount and pension income provided that these amounts have not been claimed on any other of the terminal return filings (subsection 70(2), section 118.93). See ¶206 for a detailed discussion of filing deadlines and due dates of any taxes payable on a subsection 70(2) return.

## ¶218   Transfer to Beneficiary

The tax liability for rights or things may be transferred to a beneficiary provided the right or thing is distributed to the beneficiary within the later of one year from the date of death, or within 90 days from the date of the notice of assessment in respect of the year of death (subsection 70(3), Interpretation Bulletin IT-212R3, paragraph 25). Pursuant to subsection 69(1.1), the beneficiary is deemed to acquire the rights or things at a cost equal to such part of the cost to the deceased that was not deducted in computing income for any taxation year, plus any expenses incurred by the beneficiary to acquire the rights or things. At such time as the beneficiary disposes of those items, the amount received on realization or disposition of the rights or things included in income at that time will be the difference between the proceeds of disposition and the beneficiary's cost as established above (paragraph 70(3)(*b*)).

It is possible for only some rights or things to be transferred to a beneficiary or beneficiaries. Any rights or things not transferred to a beneficiary must be reported either in the terminal period return or in a separate return (Interpretation Bulletin IT-212R3, paragraph 20). If a separate return is filed pursuant to subsection 70(2), the total value of all rights or things minus the value of those transferred to a beneficiary or beneficiaries must be included on that return.

## ¶220

## Income from a Business

Business income may also be reported on a separate return, as if the taxpayer were another person, if the fiscal period of a business of which the taxpayer is a proprietor or partner is not on a calendar year basis and death occurs after the close of the fiscal period (subsection 150(4)). In the case of a partner's death, a separate return is filed under subsection 150(4) only if the death causes the fiscal period of the partnership to end. If there is no deemed or actual fiscal year end, the deceased's partnership profits for the stub period immediately prior to death are considered a right or thing (Interpretation Bulletin IT-278R2, paragraph 2). The advantage of the latter characterization is the extended time for filing a rights or things return (see ¶210).

The ability to report business income on a separate return for 1996 and subsequent years is limited to circumstances where the proprietor or the members of the partnership have elected to use an off-calendar fiscal year end, or where an individual has a reserve in respect of December 31, 1995 income.

Effective for 1995 and subsequent years, the provisions of section 34.1 apply to the computation of an individual's income from a business where the taxpayer has made an election under subsection 249.1(4) to use an off-calendar fiscal year end. The election is available for individuals carrying on business as a proprietorship or as a member of a partnership where all of the members are individuals. Under the provisions of subsection 34.1(3), any additional business income included in the preceding year, pursuant to subsection 34.1(1) or 34.1(2), is to be deducted in computing the individual's business income for the taxation year. Subsection 34.1(8) provides that subsections 34.1(1) and 34.1(2) do not apply to include any additional business income in the individual's business income for a taxation year where the individual dies in the year. However, pursuant to subsection 34.1(9) where

(a) an individual carries on a business in a taxation year,

(b) the individual dies in the year and after the end of the fiscal period of the business that ends in the year,

(c) another fiscal period of the business ends because of the individual's death (referred to as the short period), and

(d) the individual's legal representative elects that subsection 34.1(9) apply in computing the individual's income for the year or files a separate return of income under subsection 150(4) in respect of the individual's business,

then in computing the individual's income for the year reported on the terminal period income tax return from the business (other than for the short period), there will be an addition to the income similar to that computed under subsections 34.1(1) and 34.1(2). To the extent that there is an income inclusion under subsection 34.1(9), in computing the income reported under subsection 150(4) in respect of the stub period, a deduction of an equal amount will be claimed. The rules in subsection 34.1(9) are applicable for 1996 and subsequent years except that for 1996 and 1997, a legal representative who filed a subsection 150(4) return in respect of the stub period income had the option of not adding an amount under subsection 34.1(9), and not deducting it from income on the subsection 150(4) return.

For 1996 and subsequent years, the balance of an individual's reserve in respect of December 31, 1995 income can be included on a subsection 150(4) return. In the year of death, an individual who carries on a business, either as a proprietor or as a partner, will be required to include in income reported on the terminal period income tax return any reserve claimed in the year immediately preceding death in respect of December 31, 1995 income, pursuant to subsection 34.2(5). No reserve in respect of December 31, 1995 income is allowed under subsection 34.2(4) where the individual dies in the calendar year in which the taxation year of the business ends (subsection 34.2(6)). However, where an amount is included under subsection 34.2(5) in the deceased's business income for the year of death, subsection 34.2(8) allows the legal representative to claim the reserve that would have otherwise been available under subsection 34.2(4) if the individual had not died. If the legal representative elects to have the provisions of subsection 34.2(8) apply, the reserve claimed must be included in a subsection 150(4) return.

The personal representative may claim on that subsection 150(4) return the usual personal tax credits in full and other tax credits in respect of medical expenses, charitable donations, disability, tuition fees, education amounts and pension income to the extent that these amounts have not been previously claimed in other terminal return filings (section 118.93, subsection 150(4)).

Generally this election for splitting income in the year of death will result in tax savings. However, it may be advantageous to include the income from both periods in the same return where, for example, the net allowable capital losses in the year of the taxpayer's death, in excess of the total capital gains exemption claimed, cannot be applied in full against other income in the year of death and the year immediately preceding the year of death. Therefore, by including the stub period income in the terminal return, the pool of income against which losses can be applied is increased.

Subject to specific exceptions discussed below, the taxpayer who earns income from a business computes his or her income on an accrual basis. For example, amounts receivable would be included in income and amounts payable would be deductible from that income. The same method would be followed reporting business income on the terminal period return. However, there are some items which are treated differently for the purposes of the final return. No deductions are allowed for reserves against capital gains, profits resulting from the sale of other types of property, or commission income of insurance agents or brokers. Only reserves for doubtful accounts receivable, prepaid rents, and for amounts received before goods have been delivered or services have been performed, are allowed. See ¶510 for a discussion of where additional reserves may be permitted where the receivable subject to the reserve was transferred to a spouse or spouse trust.

Where the taxpayer operates a business as a sole proprietor, a deduction for capital cost allowance cannot be made in the terminal period since the Act deems the taxpayer to have disposed of all depreciable capital property immediately before death, leaving no assets in respect of which capital cost allowance can be claimed. (A similar result would be obtained if the deceased taxpayer owned an interest in a rental property.) If, however, this deemed disposition results in the taxpayer realizing a terminal loss at death, that loss may be deducted against any capital gains and against other income in the year of death. This is discussed in greater detail in Chapter 3 (¶300). Where the deceased taxpayer was a professional, a reserve for untaxed 1971 receivables cannot be claimed and that amount will be brought into income in the year of death pursuant to ITAR 23(4)(a). The reserve would be included on the terminal period return and not be included in a separate return filed under subsection 150(4) (Interpretation Bulletin IT-278R2, paragraph 18).

With respect to eligible capital property owned by the deceased taxpayer in respect of a business see ¶318 for a discussion on the treatment of such property.

¶220

## ¶222

## Income from a Trust

If the deceased taxpayer was an income beneficiary of a trust, the Act provides a further opportunity for splitting that income if the trust was one which was created as a result of the death of another person, i.e., a testamentary trust, and the trust does not report its income on a calendar year basis. Any income paid or payable from the trust after the end of its last completed fiscal period may be reported in a separate return, again with full personal credits and available deductions which have not been taken in other terminal returns claimed against that income. If the last complete fiscal period was in the taxation year of death, only the income for the period from the close of the trust's fiscal year to the date of death is included in the separate return (paragraph 104(23)(d)). All other income paid or payable to the deceased from the testamentary trust for the completed fiscal period is included in the terminal period return. Income from a non-testamentary trust does not qualify for this special treatment since an *inter vivos* trust may not have a fiscal year for tax purposes which is other than a calendar year (paragraph 249(1)(b), subsection 104(2)). Therefore, income from an *inter vivos* trust, which is paid or payable to a deceased as at the date of death, would be reported in the terminal period return.

If the deceased beneficiary was a beneficiary of more than one testamentary trust, it is the Canada Revenue Agency's position that the election under paragraph 104(23)(d) may be made separately in respect of benefits under each trust. However, only one paragraph 104(23)(d) return may be filed.

## ¶224

## Reserves in the Year of Death

Many of the reserves a taxpayer is entitled to deduct during his or her lifetime are no longer available in the year of death (section 72). No reserve is allowed as a deduction in the taxpayer's final year except where an amount receivable is transferred in consequence of the taxpayer's death to the taxpayer's spouse or common-law partner or to a trust for the benefit of a spouse or common-law partner and the appropriate election is made. As a result, income for which those reserves were established in prior years must be included in income in the year of death. For example, a taxpayer might establish a reserve in the year of sale of a capital property for that portion of the sale proceeds that will not be actually payable until later years. Subject to specific exceptions for spouses, common-law partners and trusts for the benefit of a spouse or common-law partner, it is not possible to defer the recognition of that income after death (see ¶510). Therefore, it is not uncommon for a large amount of income to be reported in the terminal period return with no actual receipt of cash with which to pay the additional tax liability. Reserves which will be included in income in the year of death are reserves for capital gains (subparagraph 40(1)(a)(iii)), replacement property reserves (paragraph 44(1)(e)), reserves for the p roceeds of the sale of other property (paragraph 20(1)(n)), and reserves for commission income of insurance agents or brokers (subsection 32(1)). Reserves for untaxed 1971 accounts receivable of a deceased professional must also be included in income. However, it is possible to continue to claim reserves for doubtful accounts, prepaid rents and for payments on account of goods to be delivered or services to be performed.

See ¶278 for a discussion of the treatment of a reserve on death in respect of the disposition of a non-qualifying security to certain donees after July 1997.

Where a commercial obligation (as defined in subsection 80(1)) of a taxpayer is settled without full payment, section 80 of the Act will apply. The amount of the debt forgiven reduces the taxpayer's tax attributes in the order dictated in paragraph 80(1)(c) and an income inclusion may result under subsection 80(13). A reserve may be claimed under the provisions of section 61.2 in respect of this income inclusion provided the taxpayer is an individual, other than a trust, and is resident in Canada throughout the taxation year. Any amount claimed under section 61.2 for a year is included in income in the following year under section 56.2. A reserve may again be claimed under section 61.2 in that following year. The amount of the reserve available under section 61.2 is calculated based on a formula.

Where the deceased claimed a reserve under section 61.2 in the year prior to death as a result of the application of the debt forgiveness rules, that prior year's reserve must be included in income on the deceased's terminal period return under provisions of section 56.2. In addition, a reserve may be claimed on the terminal period return under section 61.2. There is no requirement for the amount of the reserve claimed under section 61.2 in the year of death to be included in the income of the estate or any of the beneficiaries of the deceased's estate. (See Technical Interpretation 9500440 dated January 16, 1995.)

Where an individual issued a commercial obligation prior to his or her death, paragraph 80(2)(p) will apply when such an obligation is settled after the deceased's death if:

- the commercial obligation was outstanding at the time of the individual's death; and

- the individual's estate was liable for that obligation before it was settled or extinguished.

The estate will be deemed to have issued the commercial obligation at the same time and in the same circumstances as the obligation was issued by the individual.

If, however, the commercial obligation is settled by the deceased's estate within six months of the individual's death or within such longer period as is acceptable to the Minister, and the deceased's estate was liable for the obligation immediately before it was settled, paragraph 80(2)(q) provides that:

- the obligation shall be deemed to have been settled at the beginning of the day on which the individual died; and

- any amount paid by the estate on settlement or as consideration for the assumption of the debt by another person is deemed to have been paid at the beginning of the day on which the individual died.

Any interest accruing after the individual's death is ignored for purposes of computing the forgiven amount of the commercial obligation. Paragraph 80(2)(q) does not apply where any amount is included under paragraph 6(1)(a) or subsection 15(1) because of the settlement or where section 79 applies in respect of the obligation.

# ¶226

## Registered Retirement Savings Plans[9]

The income tax treatment of a Registered Retirement Savings Plan (RRSP) as a result of the death of the annuitant will depend on whether the plan is a matured or unmatured plan and the beneficiary of the plan.

An RRSP matures at the date fixed under the plan for the commencement of any retirement income, and retirement income is usually in the form of monthly annuity payments. An RRSP must mature by the end of the year in which the annuitant reaches age 69, effective for 1996 and subsequent years. For 1995 and prior years, an RRSP had to mature by the end of the year in which the annuitant reached age 71. Where the annuitant turned age 70 before 1997, the rules applicable for 1995 continued to apply, and where the annuitant turned age 69 in 1996, the RRSP had to mature by the end of 1997 (Interpretation Bulletin IT-500R, paragraph 3).

---

[9] Interpretation Bulletin IT-500R and Information Sheet RC4177 — Death of an RRSP Annuitant.

## ¶228 General Rules

In the year of death, the annuitant of an RRSP (matured or unmatured) is deemed to receive, immediately before death, a benefit under the plan (subsection 146(8.8)) and is required to include such benefit in income for the year of death (subsection 146(8)). The benefit is equal to the fair market value of all property of the plan at the date of death.

Where the deceased had no spouse or common-law partner at the date of death, paragraph 146(2)(*c.*2) requires the commutation of each annuity (matured RRSP) that becomes payable to a person other than the annuitant under the plan. The payment to that other person will be a lump sum equal to the fair market value of the annuity at the date of death of the annuitant.

Whenever an amount is deemed to have been received by the annuitant immediately before death as a benefit under an RRSP pursuant to subsection 146(8.8), an actual payment out of the RRSP, to the extent that it can reasonably be regarded as part of the amount included in the deceased's income, is not a benefit under subsection 146(1) to the person who receives it. Consequently, this amount is not income to that person under subsection 146(8). Where the amount paid out is greater than the amount deemed to have been received by the deceased annuitant, only the excess will be income to the recipient under subsection 146(8) (Interpretation Bulletin IT-500R, paragraphs 12 and 13). Where the amount paid out is less than the amount deemed to have been received by the deceased annuitant due to a loss incurred by the RRSP, there is no provision in the Act to allow the beneficiary to claim the loss or adjust the amount reported by the deceased annuitant on the terminal return.[10]

The amount of the income inclusion to the deceased under the provisions of subsection 146(8.8) can be reduced where an amount is paid to the annuitant's spouse, common-law partner or financially dependent children or grandchildren under the RRSP.

## ¶230 Refund of Premiums

In order to understand the implications to the deceased where an amount is paid under the RRSP on death to a spouse, common-law partner or financially dependent children or grandchildren, it is first necessary to review the concept of "refund of premiums". The definition of refund of premiums is relevant in determining the amount of the income inclusion for a deceased annuitant on death, the amount to be included in the income of

---

[10] See Technical Interpretation 2000-0006115 dated February 29, 2000 and 2002-0168275 dated April 1, 2003, and CRA's administrative policy that applies in limited circumstances — www.cra-arc.gc.ca/tax/registered/rrsp-e.html — 2002 RRSP Consultation Session.

a spouse, common-law partner or financially dependent children or grandchildren and the amount that can be transferred by such a beneficiary on a tax-deferred basis under paragraph 60(*l*).

Subsection 146(1) defines a refund of premiums to be:

(a) any amount paid to a spouse or common-law partner of the annuitant under an RRSP where the annuitant died *before the maturity* of the plan and that amount was paid as a consequence of the death; and

(b) any amount paid under an RRSP (*matured or unmatured*) after the annuitant died to a child or grandchild of the annuitant who was, at the time of death, financially dependent on the annuitant for support where the annuitant died after 1998.

For deaths before 1996, an amount paid under an RRSP to a financially dependent child or grandchild was considered a refund of premiums only if the annuitant had no spouse at the time of the annuitant's death. For deaths that occurred after 1995 and before 1999, an amount paid to a financially dependent child or grandchild could be considered a refund of premiums, even if the annuitant had a spouse or common-law partner at the time of death, if an election was filed with the Minister before May 2000.

For deaths after 1992, it is assumed that, unless the contrary is established, a child or grandchild was not financially dependent on the annuitant for support at the time of the annuitant's death if the income of the child or grandchild for the year preceding the year of death exceeded the basic personal amount ($8,148 for 2005). For deaths after 2002, where the child or grandchild was mentally or physically infirm, the income limit is the total of the basic personal amount ($8,148 for 2005) and disability amount ($6,596 for 2005).

A refund of premiums must be paid as a lump-sum payment.

For deaths occurring after 1992, the definition of refund of premiums will exclude any part of the amount paid to the spouse, common-law partner or financially dependent child or grandchild that is a tax-paid amount in respect of the RRSP. A tax-paid amount is generally an amount paid to a person in respect of RRSP income that is not exempt from tax under Part I because of the death of the RRSP annuitant. (See ¶238.)

In computing the income inclusion of the deceased annuitant under the provisions of subsection 146(8.8), subsection 146(8.9) permits a deduction of an amount paid to a surviving spouse or common-law partner or financially dependent child or grandchild that qualifies as a refund of premiums. The deduction under subsection 146(8.9) is determined according to a formula, and a calculation is only required when the circumstances fall outside two situations:

(a) no refunds of premiums are paid from an RRSP and therefore no deduction would be permitted under subsection 146(8.9); and

(b) when the only beneficiaries of an RRSP receive only refunds of premiums and therefore, the deduction available under subsection 146(8.9) would equal the fair market value of the RRSP at the time of death (see comment below where the RRSP incurs a loss).

The deduction under subsection 146(8.9) can be less than the amount determined under the formula. A deduction of a lesser amount would reduce the amount required to be included in the income of the beneficiaries as a benefit under an RRSP.

The deduction under subsection 146(8.9) can also be less than the amount included in the deceased annuitant's income under subsection 146(8.8). This can occur where there is a decrease in the value of the RRSP property between the date of the annuitant's death and the date the RRSP property is distributed to the beneficiaries as a refund of premiums. There is no provision in the Act whereby the beneficiary can claim the loss realized by the RRSP or adjust the amount reported by the deceased annuitant under subsection 146(8.8).[11]

## ¶232 Surviving Spouse or Common-Law Partner

*Matured RRSP*

Where the deceased annuitant had a spouse or common-law partner who at the time of the annuitant's death was designated as a beneficiary under a matured RRSP, the portion of the property in the plan which becomes receivable by the spouse or common-law partner as a consequence of the annuitant's death reduces the amount deemed to be received by the deceased immediately before death (subsection 146(8.8)). Any payments received by the surviving spouse or common-law partner under the matured RRSP would be included in the spouse's or common-law partner's income under subsection 146(8).

Where the annuitant dies and, as a consequence of the death, the legal representative of the annuitant becomes entitled to receive amounts under the matured plan for the benefit of the annuitant's spouse or common-law partner, a joint election (filed by the spouse or common-law partner and the

---

[11] See Technical Interpretation 1999-0013725 dated February 8, 2000 and 2002-0168275 dated April 1, 2003 and CRA's administrative policy that applies in limited circumstances — www.cra-arc.gc.ca/tax/registered/rrsp-e.html — 2002 RRSP Consultation Session.

legal representative) is available under subsection 146(8.91). This election deems the spouse or common-law partner to have become the annuitant under the plan. As a result of the election, the amounts that the legal representative is entitled to receive will be deemed to be receivable by the spouse or common-law partner and reduce the amount included in the deceased's income in the year of death under subsection 146(8.8). Such amounts, when paid, are deemed to be received directly by the spouse or common-law partner and are included in the spouse's or common-law partner's income under subsection 146(8). It is not necessary that the amounts received by the legal representative in fact be paid to the spouse or common-law partner in order to take advantage of this election.

Paragraph 8 of Interpretation Bulletin IT-500R outlines the circumstances in which the legal representative will be considered to receive amounts for the benefit of the spouse or common-law partner under a matured RRSP.

*Unmatured RRSP*

Where the deceased annuitant had a spouse or common-law partner at the time of death and the spouse or common-law partner is paid an amount under an unmatured RRSP, the payment will qualify as a refund of premiums. To the extent that a deduction is claimed under subsection 146(8.9) in computing the income inclusion of the deceased, the payment will be included in the spouse's or common-law partner's income under subsection 146(8).

The legal representative of the deceased may claim a deduction of less than the maximum amount calculated under subsection 146(8.9). See paragraph 9 of Interpretation Bulletin IT-500R.

When an amount is paid from an unmatured RRSP of a deceased annuitant to the annuitant's legal representative and the spouse or common-law partner is a beneficiary of the annuitant's estate, a joint election (filed by the spouse or common-law partner and the legal representative) is available under subsection 146(8.1). The election is similar to that available where an amount is paid from a matured RRSP of a deceased annuitant to the annuitant's legal representative. (See Interpretation Bulletin IT-500R, paragraphs 10 and 11.) The election must be made and filed with the Minister in prescribed form (Form T2019 — Death of an RRSP Annuitant — Refund of Premiums).

¶232

## ¶234   Financially Dependent Child/Grandchild

*Matured RRSP*

Where an annuitant dies after 1998, a payment under a matured RRSP to a financially dependent child or grandchild will qualify as a refund of premiums and may reduce the income inclusion of the deceased, as discussed above. This might include, for example, a lump-sum commuted value of any annuity payments remaining under the guaranteed term of the deceased's life annuity. (See ¶230 for the definition of refund of premiums for deaths occurring before 1999.)

Where the annuitant dies and, as a consequence of death, the legal representative of the annuitant becomes entitled to receive amounts under the matured plan for the benefit of a financially dependent child or grandchild who is a beneficiary of the annuitant's estate, a joint election (filed by the beneficiary and the legal representative) is available under subsection 146(8.1). The amount designated on the election is deemed to have been received by the dependent child or grandchild as a benefit that is a refund of premiums under an RRSP. It is not necessary that the estate actually pay the designated amounts to the child or grandchild. The election must be made and filed with the Minister in prescribed form (Form T2019 — Death of an RRSP Annuitant — Refund of Premiums).

Paragraph 11 of Interpretation Bulletin IT-500R discusses the factors to be considered by the legal representative in determining whether an amount can be designated to be a refund of premiums.

*Unmatured RRSP*

Where an annuitant dies after 1998, a payment under an unmatured RRSP to a financially dependent child or grandchild will qualify as a refund of premiums and may reduce the income inclusion of the deceased as discussed above. (See ¶230 for the definition of refund of premiums for deaths occurring before 1999.)

Where the annuitant dies and, as a consequence of the death, the legal representative of the annuitant becomes entitled to receive amounts under an unmatured RRSP for the benefit of a financially dependent child or grandchild who is a beneficiary of the annuitant's estate, an election is available similar to that discussed above in respect of amounts under a matured RRSP.

## ¶236   Rollover Provisions

Paragraph 60(*l*) permits a beneficiary who is the spouse or common-law partner of the deceased and receives a refund of premiums to defer the payment of tax on all or part of the amount included in the spouse's or common-law partner's income under subsection 146(8). The spouse or common-law partner may claim a deduction under paragraph 60(*l*) in respect of all or part of the amounts for the year they are included in the spouse's or common-law partner's income under subsection 146(8), to the extent they are paid by the spouse in the year or within 60 days after the end of the year:

(a) as a premium under an RRSP under which the spouse or common-law partner is the annuitant (provided he or she is under 69 years of age);

(b) to acquire a life annuity[12];

(c) to acquire an annuity for the spouse or common-law partner for a term equal to 90 minus the spouse's or common-law partner's age; or[12]

(d) to a carrier as consideration for a registered retirement income fund under which the spouse or common-law partner is the annuitant.

The same options are available to a refund of premiums received by a beneficiary who is a child or grandchild of the deceased annuitant and who was financially dependent at the time of death on the deceased annuitant by reason of physical or mental infirmity.[12]

If a beneficiary is a child or grandchild of the deceased annuitant who was financially dependent on the deceased, he or she can defer the payment of tax on all or part of a refund of premiums by acquiring a specific type of annuity under the provisions of paragraph 60(*l*). In order to qualify, the child, grandchild or a trust under which the child or grandchild is the sole person beneficially interested in the amounts payable under the annuity, must be the annuitant and the term of the annuity cannot exceed 18 minus the age of the child or grandchild at the time of its acquisition. The annuity must be acquired in the year of the receipt of the refund of premiums or within 60 days after the end of the year. This type of annuity can also be acquired by a child or grandchild who was financially dependent on the deceased annuitant by reason of physical or mental infirmity.

---

[12] Draft legislation released on February 27, 2004 proposes that for taxation years that end after 2000 and before 2004, a trust may be the annuitant of an annuity referred to in (b) and (c) above if the spouse, or common-law partner, child or grandchild is physically or mentally infirm and the spouse, child or grandchild is the sole person beneficially interested in amounts payable under the annuity prior to their death. For taxation years that end after 2003, the trust option will only be available if the spouse, common-law partner, child or grandchild is mentally infirm. In the February 23, 2005 federal budget the Government indicated it will review the tax rules in this area with a view to providing more flexibilty where appropriate.

## ¶238   Income Earned After Death

The rules applicable to the income earned within an unmatured RRSP after the death of the annuitant and prior to the distribution to the beneficiary will depend on the type of RRSP. To the extent that income earned after the death of the annuitant is considered to be a refund of premiums, the beneficiary will be able to take advantage of the rollover provisions of paragraph 60(*l*).

If a refund of premiums is payable out of an insured RRSP to a surviving spouse or common-law partner or financially dependent children or grandchildren, interest accrued from the date of death to the date of actual payment is treated as part of the refund of premiums. An insured RRSP is generally one issued by a person licensed to carry on in Canada an annuities business (Interpretation Bulletin IT-500R, paragraph 19).

If a refund of premiums is payable out of a depositary RRSP, income accrued up to the end of the year following the year of death is treated as a refund of premiums. Income accrued after that time will be included in the income of the person entitled to the proceeds of the RRSP and does not qualify as refund of premiums. A depositary RRSP is one which consists of deposits with a person who is a member of the Canadian Payments Association, or a credit union that is a shareholder or member of a body corporate referred to as a "central" for the purposes of the *Canadian Payments Association Act* (Interpretation Bulletin IT-500R, paragraph 20).

The entire amount in an unmatured trusteed RRSP on or before December 31 of the year following the year of the annuitant's death, representing the value of the RRSP at the date of payment, will be considered to be a refund of premiums. A trusteed RRSP is generally one issued by a corporation licensed under the laws of Canada or a province to carry on in Canada the business of offering to the public its services as trustee of any periodic or other amount as a contribution to the trust (Interpretation Bulletin IT-500R, paragraph 21).

The income of a trusteed RRSP, including the taxable portion of any capital gains and losses that accrued after December 31 of the year following the year of death, is subject to the normal trust rules pursuant to subsection 146(1). To the extent that the amount is paid to a beneficiary of the trust, the trust would be entitled to a deduction in computing its income pursuant to paragraph 104(6)(a.2) for 1996 and subsequent years. For years prior to 1996, the trust would be entitled to a deduction under paragraph 104(6)(b) to the extent that the amount was payable to a beneficiary. To the extent that the trust has taken a deduction in computing its income and the non-taxable portion of capital gains or losses accrued in the trust after December 31 of the year following the year of death are included in the beneficiary's income as a benefit from an RRSP and taxable under subsection 146(8).

Paragraphs 24 and 25 of Interpretation Bulletin IT-500R contain two examples outlining the implications on the distributions of an unmatured trusteed RRSP where the distribution occurs after December 31 of the year following the year of death. See also Information Sheet RC4177 for a chart summarizing the reporting of amounts paid out of the deceased's RRSP.

## ¶240   Joint and Several Liability

On the death of an annuitant, a person (including the estate of the deceased annuitant) who receives an amount free of tax out of or under an RRSP is jointly and severally liable with the deceased annuitant for a portion of the deceased's additional tax payable which arose because the amount was included in the deceased's income under subsection 146(8.8) (subsection 160.2(1)). This joint and several liability is equal to the proportion of such additional tax to the deceased that the recipient's tax-free share of the plan is of the total of the plan amounts included in the income of the deceased for the year of death by virtue of subsection 146(8.8).

Section 160.2 will apply only to the taxpayer (including the estate of the deceased annuitant) who, under the terms of the plan, receives tax-free funds directly from the plan upon the death of the annuitant. Therefore, in a case where tax-free plan funds are paid to the estate as a beneficiary of the plan, the estate is jointly and severally liable under section 160.2. There is no such liability on any beneficiary of that estate who may ultimately receive any of these funds.[13]

## ¶242

## Registered Retirement Income Funds[14]

The income tax treatment of a Registered Retirement Income Fund (RRIF) as a result of the death of the annuitant of the plan is similar to the treatment of an RRSP on the death of the annuitant.

## ¶244   General Rules

Where the annuitant of a RRIF dies, the annuitant is deemed to have received, immediately before death, an amount out of the plan equal to the

---

[13] Recent Ontario case, *Amherst Crane Rentals v. Perring* ([2005] 5 CTC (Ont. CA)) dealt with the treatment of RRSP proceeds following the death of the annuitant. The Ontario Court of Appeal held that RRSPs do not form part of the estate but instead devolve directly to the designated beneficiary. The Supreme Court of Canada denied leave to appeal this case.

[14] Information Sheet RC4178 — Death of a RRIF Annuitant.

fair market value of all property in the plan at the time of death (subsection 146.3(6)). This amount is required to be included in the deceased annuitant's terminal income tax return (paragraph 56(1)(*t*)).

Where the deceased has included such amounts in income, an actual payment out of the RRIF will not be subject to tax in the hands of the recipient to the extent that it can reasonably be regarded as part of the amount included in the deceased's income (paragraph 146.3(5)(*a*)). Where the amount paid out of the RRIF is less than the amount deemed to have been received by the deceased due to a loss incurred by the RRIF subsequent to the deceased's death, there is no provision in the Act to allow the recipient of the RRIF to claim the loss or adjust the amount reported by the deceased annuitant on the terminal return.[15]

The amount of the income inclusion to the deceased under the provisions of subsection 146.3(6) can be reduced where an amount is paid to the deceased's spouse, or common-law partner or financially dependent children or grandchildren.

If the deceased's spouse or common-law partner is named as the successor annuitant under the plan (by the terms of the deceased's will or by the terms of the RRIF contract), there is no income inclusion to the deceased pursuant to subsection 146.3(6). Instead, the surviving spouse or common-law partner will include the payments from the RRIF in income when actually received (subsection 146.3(5)).

If the deceased does not name the spouse or common-law partner as the successor annuitant (either in the deceased's will or in the RRIF contract), payments can continue to the surviving spouse or common-law partner provided the deceased's legal representative consents and the RRIF carrier agrees (subsection 146.3(1) "annuitant").

## ¶246 Designated Benefits

In order to understand the implications to the deceased where an amount is paid under the RRIF on death to a spouse, common-law partner or financially dependent children or grandchildren, it is necessary to review the concept of "designated benefit".

Subsection 146.3(1) defines a designated benefit of an individual to be:

(a) amounts paid under a RRIF after the death of the last annuitant, to the legal representative of the deceased, that would have been consid-

---

[15] See Technical Interpretation 2003-0004635 dated April 1, 2003 and CRA's administrative policy that applies in limited circumstances — www.cra-arc.gc.ca/tax/registered/rrsp-e.html — 2002 RRSP Consultation Session.

ered to have been refunds of premiums if the amounts had been received by the individual were the fund an unmatured RRSP, and which are designated jointly by the legal representative and that individual; and

(b) amounts paid directly to the individual under a RRIF after the death of the last annuitant that would have been refunds of premiums had the fund been an unmatured RRSP.

Therefore, an amount paid directly to the surviving spouse or common-law partner as the named beneficiary of the RRIF as a consequence of the death of the deceased, and an amount paid to the legal representative of the deceased that has been elected on, are considered to be designated benefits in respect of the surviving spouse or common-law partner.

Where an annuitant dies after 1998, an amount paid directly to financially dependent children or grandchildren as the named beneficiaries of the RRIF as a consequence of the death of the deceased, and an amount paid to the legal representative of the deceased that has been subject to an election, are considered to be designated benefits in respect of financially dependent children or grandchildren. For deaths before 1996, an amount paid under a RRIF to a financially dependent child or grandchild was considered a designated benefit only if there was no surviving spouse or common-law partner. For deaths that occurred after 1995 and before 1999, an amount paid to a financially dependent child or grandchild could be considered a designated benefit, even where there was a surviving spouse or common-law partner, if an election was filed with the Minister before May 2000. See ¶230 for a discussion of when a child or grandchild is considered financially dependent on the RRIF annuitant.

In computing the income inclusion of the deceased under the provisions of subsection 146.3(6), subsection 146.3(6.2) permits a deduction of an amount paid to a surviving spouse, common-law partner or financially dependent child or grandchild that qualifies as a designated benefit. The deduction under subsection 146.3(6.2) is similar to the deduction under subsection 146(8.9) in respect of a payment of a refund of premiums to these same types of individuals under an RRSP. The legal representative of the deceased may claim a deduction of less than the maximum amount calculated under subsection 146.3(6.2).

The same rollover options are available under paragraph 60(*l*) for a designated benefit received by a surviving spouse, common-law partner or a child or grandchild of the deceased who was financially dependent on the deceased by reason of physical or mental infirmity as applied to a refund of premiums received by these same individuals under an RRSP. (See ¶236 for a discussion of the rollover provisions under paragraph 60(*l*).) However, the amount of the designated benefit that may be transferred under paragraph 60(*l*) for such individuals is calculated under subsection 146.3(6.11), is classified as an eligible amount, and is determined with reference to the minimum amount under the RRIF for the year.

If a designated benefit is received by a child or grandchild of the deceased who was financially dependent on the deceased, the beneficiary can defer the payment of tax on the designated benefit by acquiring a specific type of annuity as provided in paragraph 60(*l*). This type of annuity can also be acquired by a child or grandchild who was financially dependent on the deceased by reason of physical or mental infirmity. See ¶236 for a description of the terms of this annuity.

## ¶247   Income Earned After Death

Similar rules apply to a RRIF in respect of income earned after death as apply to an RRSP. See ¶238 for a discussion of the rules applicable to an RRSP.

## ¶248   Joint and Several Liability

Where a person other than the annuitant of the RRIF receives a payment from the RRIF, subsection 160.2(2) ensures that the annuitant and the recipient are jointly and severally liable for the portion of the tax payable by the deceased as a result of the income inclusion pursuant to paragraph 146.3(6).

## ¶249

## Home Buyers' Plan

If the deceased participated in the Home Buyers' Plan, subsection 146.01(6) requires the deceased's remaining Home Buyers' Plan balance to be included in the terminal return. The amount of the inclusion is reduced for any RRSP contributions made before death that are designated as a Home Buyer's Plan repayment for the year of death.

If, at the time of death, the deceased had a spouse or common-law partner who was resident in Canada immediately before the taxpayer's death, the spouse or common-law partner can jointly elect with the deceased's legal representative to make the repayments under the Home Buyers' Plan and to not have the income inclusion rules apply to the deceased (subsection 146.01(7)).

The joint election can be made by a letter signed by the surviving spouse or common-law partner and the deceased's legal representative and attached to the deceased's return for the year of death. The letter should state that an election is being made to have the surviving spouse or common-law partner continue making repayments under the Home Buyers' Plan, and to not have the income-inclusion rule apply for the deceased.

## ¶250

## Lifelong Learning Plan

If the deceased made a Lifelong Learning Plan withdrawal, subsection 146.02(6) requires the deceased's remaining Lifelong Learning Plan balance to be included in the terminal return. The amount of the inclusion is reduced for any RRSP contributions made before death that are designated as a repayment under the Lifelong Learning Plan.

If, at the time of death, the deceased had a spouse or common-law partner who was resident in Canada immediately before the taxpayer's death, the spouse or common-law partner can jointly elect with the deceased's legal representative to make the repayments under the Lifelong Learning Plan and to not include the Lifelong Learning Plan balance in the terminal return (subsection 146.02(7)).

The joint election can be made by a letter signed by the surviving spouse or common-law partner and the deceased's legal representative and attached to the deceased's return for the year of death. The letter should state that an election is being made to have the surviving spouse or common-law partner continue making repayments under the Lifelong Learning Plan, and to not have the income inclusion rule apply for the deceased.

## ¶252

## Employee Profit Sharing Plans (EPSP)

An Employee Profit Sharing Plan (EPSP) is a combination of a bonus arrangement and a forced savings plan under which an employer makes payments directly to the plan. Such payments are deductible by the employer if made during the year or within 120 days thereafter (subsection 144(5)).

All amounts received by the plan during a year from the employer, together with all income earned by the plan and all capital gains realized by it for the year, must be allocated to employees who are beneficiaries of the plan (subsection 144(1) the definition of EPSP). The amounts allocated to an employee must be included in computing income for that year (paragraph

6(1)(*d*)). Dividends from taxable Canadian corporations also retain their nature and are taxed accordingly in the hands of the employees (subsection 144(8)).

A capital gain allocated to an employee is treated as a capital gain in the employee's hands (subsection 144(4)). Prior to February 23, 1994, any such capital gain allocated to an employee by the EPSP would have qualified for the capital gains exemption. If an employee had an interest in an EPSP at the end of February 22, 1994 and the interest had an accrued capital gain, the employee could have elected to "crystallize" the gain. Such an election would have created an exempt capital gains balance in respect of the employee's interest in the EPSP. To the extent that capital gains are allocated to an employee after February 22, 1994 and before 2005, the employee can draw down on any remaining exempt capital gains balance (subsection 39.1(6)). For 2005 and subsequent years, any exempt capital gains balance at January 1, 2005 would be added to the employee's adjusted cost base in respect of the EPSP interest (paragaph 53(1)(*p*)).

Since a beneficiary is taxed on the basis of allocations made by the trustee, the beneficiary is not subject to tax on payments actually received, provided they represent:

(a) payments made by the beneficiary to the trustee;

(b) net amounts that were previously allocated to the beneficiary, including losses other than capital losses;

(c) capital gains made by the trust for taxation years after 1971 to the extent they have been allocated by the trust to the beneficiary;

(d) capital gains either realized by the trust prior to 1972 or that represent appreciation in value of trust properties that occurred prior to 1972;

(e) unrealized capital gains, as of December 31, 1971, inherent in the value of property received by the beneficiary from the trustee;

(f) a dividend received by the trust from a taxable Canadian corporation, to the extent allocated to the beneficiary (a dividend under subsection 83(1) received after May 25, 1976 is excluded from this category and as a result, amounts which a trustee allocates as subsection 83(1) dividends will not be included in the sources available for tax-free distribution); or

(g) certain life insurance proceeds received by the trust upon the death of the life insured, to the extent allocated to the beneficiary (Interpretation Bulletin IT-379R, paragraph 2).

¶252

Amounts attributable to the taxpayer will have borne tax at an earlier time or will be of such a nature that no tax is payable at any time. Therefore, in the year of death, the taxpayer would be subject to tax only on the allocation made by the trustee to the taxpayer during the year, and no additional consequences would arise with respect to receipts from the EPSP. In some cases, the deceased may not receive sufficient funds from the EPSP to cover all amounts previously included in income. Since the employee will have paid tax on all amounts that were absolutely or contingently allocated to the employee in prior years, subsection 144(9) provides some relief.

Subsection 144(9) allows a deduction from income where a person ceases to be a beneficiary of the EPSP and does not receive sufficient funds (forfeiture). If forfeiture occurs prior to the death of the taxpayer, the deduction would be claimed by the deceased. If forfeiture occurs after death, the deceased's estate would be entitled to the deduction and would take into account amounts previously allocated to the employee. The deduction is equal to the total of all amounts included in computing the employee's income for the year and preceding years less:

(a) the "gross-up" for dividends from taxable Canadian corporations allocated to the employee;

(b) 25% of the total dividends from taxable Canadian corporations allocated to the employee;

(c) capital gain and loss allocations under subsection 144(4); and

(d) any amounts actually received or receivable by the employee.

# ¶254

## Deferred Profit Sharing Plans

Paragraph 56(1)(*i*) and subsection 147(10) provide that certain amounts received by a beneficiary from a trustee under a Deferred Profit Sharing Plan (DPSP) are to be included in income. The term "beneficiary", as it is used in these subsections, means any person entitled to benefits under a DPSP, including both employees and former employees of the employer making contributions to the plan, their estates and certain persons designated by these employees and former employees.

Paragraph 147(2)(*k*) requires that a DPSP must provide that all amounts vested in an employee become payable not later than the earlier of:

(a) 90 days after the earliest of

(i) the death of the employee,

(ii) the day on which the employee ceases to be employed by an employer who participates in the plan, and

(iii) the termination or winding-up of the plan; and

(b) the end of the year in which the beneficiary attains 69 years of age.

The vested amount may be paid out as a lump-sum amount, or two alternative methods of payment may be elected by the employee on all or any part of the amount payable to the employee, if provided by the plan. These alternative methods are:

(a) equal instalments payable not less frequently than annually over a period not exceeding ten years from the date the amount becomes payable (subparagraph 147(2)(*k*)(v)); or

(b) annuity payments under a qualified annuity contract commencing no later than the end of the year in which the beneficiary attains 69 years of age, the guaranteed term of which, if any, does not exceed 15 years (subparagraph 147(2)(*k*)(vi)).

Where an employee dies after having made the election under subparagraph 147(2)(*k*)(v), depending on the terms, the trustee may make the outstanding payments to the employee's beneficiary or estate throughout the period. Where an employee elects under subparagraph 147(2)(*k*)(vi) to have the trustee buy an annuity but dies before the annuity has been bought, that election necessarily becomes void since the trustee cannot buy an annuity for the employee after the employee has died. If the employee dies after the annuity has been purchased, the amounts payable to the beneficiary or estate of the employee will depend on the terms of the annuity contract.

The requirement that a vested amount becomes payable and that annuity payments must commence by the end of the year in which the employee turns 69 became effective for 1997. Prior to 1997, the vested amount had to become payable 90 days after the employee turned age 71, and the annuity payments had to commence by the employee's 71st birthday. For those employees who turned 70 in 1997, the deadline as of when vested amounts and annuities must become payable was extended to the end of 1997. For those who turned 70 before 1997, the prior year's rules applied for 1997.

Every amount received in a year by a beneficiary out of a DPSP is generally required to be included in computing the beneficiary's income under subsection 147(10).

Where a beneficiary receives a lump-sum payment or an instalment payment as described above, the amount included in computing income

¶254

may be reduced by subsection 147(11) or 147(12) if the amount received includes employee contributions or amounts in respect of which the beneficiary was previously taxed when the plan was an employee's profit sharing plan.

Subsection 147(10.1) also provides a reduction in the amount included in a beneficiary's income under subsection 147(10) if the following conditions are satisfied:

(a) the amount constitutes a single payment made to the beneficiary either upon withdrawal from the plan, retirement from employment or the death of an employee or former employee;

(b) at the time of the receipt of the single payment, the beneficiary was resident in Canada;

(c) the single payment included shares of capital stock of the corporation that was an employer who contributed to the plan, or of a corporation with which the employer did not deal at arm's length; and

(d) the beneficiary makes the required election in the manner and form prescribed by section 1503 of the Regulations. Form T2078 must be filed with the trustee of the plan within 60 days after the end of the taxation year in which the beneficiary received the payment, and with the Minister on or before the date the beneficiary must file an income tax return for the year in which the payment is received.

This election entitles the beneficiary to exclude from income the excess of the fair market value of the employer shares received over their cost to the plan. Where this election has been made, subsection 147(10.4) provides that, where in a taxation year the beneficiary exchanges or disposes of the shares or ceases to be a resident of Canada, the beneficiary must include in income for that year the excess of the fair market value of the shares at the time acquired over their cost.

As a result, the deemed dispositions which occur at the date of death would give rise to tax on any appreciation in value in the deceased's terminal return. In order to recognize the taxation of employment benefits represented by capital gains on employer shares accruing while they were held in a DPSP, only a portion of that excess is taxed. This is due to the deduction permitted in computing the beneficiary's taxable income equal to one-half of the amount included in income under subsection 147(10.4) for dispositions occurring after October 17, 2000 (paragraph 110(1)(d.3)). For dispositions occurring before February 28, 2000, the deduction was one-quarter of the income inclusion; for dispositions occurring after February 27, 2000 and

¶254

before October 18, 2000, the deduction was one-third. Capital gains accruing on those shares during the period they are held by the beneficiary and realized on the disposition of the shares may be eligible for the capital gains exemption. See ¶258 for a discussion of the changes to the capital gains exemption provisions for 1994 and subsequent years (Interpretation Bulletins (archived) IT-281R2 and IT-363R2). Where a lump-sum amount is paid to an individual who was the employee's spouse or common-law partner at the date of the employee's death, the amount can be transferred directly to a registered pension plan (RPP), the individual's RRSP or another DPSP for the individual's benefit (subsection 147(19) and Interpretation Bulletin IT-528, paragraphs 1 to 4).[16]

## ¶256
## Registered Pension Plans

Under the provisions of paragraph 56(1)(*a*), any amount received out of a superannuation or pension fund is included in the income of the recipient. Therefore, the deceased does not include such amounts in the terminal return. Instead, the beneficiary of the plan is subject to tax on the receipt.

The Canada Revenue Agency takes the position that the fact that contributions to a particular fund or plan were not deductible for tax purposes does not change the income status of the payments received from it. Furthermore, the taxable nature of these payments is not affected by the fact that the particular superannuation or pension fund or plan has not been registered by the Canada Revenue Agency. However, since unregistered pension plans may come within the definition of "employee benefit plan", payments out of such plans are taxable under subparagraph 56(1)(*a*)(i) only to the extent that they are not taxed under paragraph 6(1)(*g*) and do not represent a return of contributions to such a plan as described in subparagraph 6(1)(*g*)(ii).

A pension payment which is taxable under subparagraph 56(1)(*a*)(i) of the Act cannot, either by will or otherwise, be changed into a capital receipt. The full amount received is always classed as a superannuation or pension benefit and not as an annuity payment. Consequently, no deduction is allowable in respect of what might otherwise be considered the capital element of an amount received.

Where an employee dies and as a consequence of the employee's death a spouse, common-law partner or former spouse or common-law partner becomes entitled to a lump-sum amount from the pension plan, the amount may be transferred to the RRSP, RRIF or another RPP of the spouse,

---

[16] The February 27, 2004 draft legislation proposes to permit a transfer to a RRIF under which the individual is the annuitant for transfers made after March 20, 2003.

common-law partner or former spouse or common-law partner. The transfer must be a direct transfer (subsection 147.3(7)).

When an employee dies and a pension plan specifically provides for a lump-sum payment to be made to a minor child or grandchild of the employee, the payment may be used to purchase a qualifying annuity pursuant to paragraph 60(*l*). The annuity must have a term not exceeding 18 minus the child's or grandchild's age at the time of purchase. To the extent a qualifying annuity is purchased in the year the lump-sum payment is received, or within 60 days after the end of the year, the child or grandchild will be permitted a deduction under paragraph 60(*l*). Similar treatment is available for such payments received through a testamentary trust (paragraph 104(27)(*e*)).

Where a lump-sum payment is made to a child or grandchild who was financially dependent on the deceased employee for support because of mental or physical infirmity, the payment may be rolled over to the child's or grandchild's RRSP, RRIF or to acquire a specified annuity. The provision applies for deaths that occur after 2002. See ¶236 for a detailed discussion of the provisions of paragaph 60(*l*).

When a taxpayer has included an amount in income under paragraph 56(1)(a)(i), paragraph 60(*j*) permits a taxpayer to transfer certain amounts to a registered pension fund or plan or to an RRSP of which the taxpayer is the annuitant, and to deduct the amount transferred in computing income. There is no provision made for transfers to an RRSP of which the taxpayer's spouse is the annuitant.

The income receipts that qualify for a paragraph 60(*j*) deduction include a lump-sum payment from a non-registered plan where the payment is attributable to services rendered while the taxpayer or taxpayer's spouse was not resident in Canada, certain RPP and DPSP payments received through a testamentary trust and certain lump-sum payments for U.S. Individual Retirement Accounts.

The amount that may be deducted under paragraph 60(*j*) is limited to the taxpayer's contributions made to a registered pension fund or plan and premiums paid to an RRSP during the year or within 60 days thereafter. Also, the amount to be deducted under paragraph 60(*j*) must be designated in the income tax return for the year in which the deduction is claimed.

If prior to death, an individual made contributions to a registered pension plan in respect of pre-1990 service while not a contributor to the plan, or in respect of pre-1990 service while a contributor to the plan, subsection 147.2(4) limits the amount that can be claimed in a taxation year. For taxpayers who die after 1992, subsection 147.2(6) provides that the amount

¶256

deducted under subsection 147.2(4) for the year of death and the immediately preceding year will be computed without reference to these limits.

## ¶258

## The Capital Gains Exemption

The February 22, 1994 federal Budget eliminated the $100,000 capital gains exemption. for capital gains realized subsequent to February 22, 1994. The enhanced capital gains exemption of $500,000 with respect to shares of a qualified small business or qualified farm property was not repealed.

## ¶260   1994 Capital Gains Exemption Election

If a taxpayer owned capital property at the end of February 22, 1994 with an accrued capital gain, an election could have been filed to "crystallize" these gains on a property-by-property basis to the extent that the taxpayer had not fully utilized the $100,000 capital gains exemption. The election would result in a deemed disposition of the capital property and the taxpayer could designate the proceeds of disposition at an amount between the property's adjusted cost base and its fair market value ("FMV") at the end of February 22, 1994 that was sufficient to trigger the desired amount of capital gain.

For most capital property, other than real property, eligible capital property and investments in "flow-through entities", the designated proceeds of disposition became the new adjusted cost base of the property for subsequent dispositions.

With respect to real property, the new adjusted cost base is the designated proceeds of disposition less the portion of the capital gain not eligible for the capital gains exemption.

If the taxpayer owned eligible capital property in respect of a business and an election was made in respect of an accrued capital gain on February 22, 1994, there was no increase in the cumulative eligible capital balance. The capital gain triggered as a result of the election was credited to an exempt gains balance in respect of the business. The exempt gains balance can be used to shelter gains realized on a subsequent disposition of eligible capital property of the business.

For purposes of the capital gains exemption election, certain investments were designated "flow-through entities" and include investments in:

- an investment corporation;

- a mortgage investment corporation;

- a mutual fund corporation;

- a mutual fund trust;

- a partnership;

- a related segregated fund trust;

- a trust governed by an employee profit sharing plan;

- a trust created to hold shares of the capital stock of a corporation for the benefit of its employees;

- a trust established for the benefit of creditors in order to secure certain debt obligations; and

- a trust established to hold shares of the capital stock of a corporation in order to exercise the voting rights attached to such shares.

For these types of investments, there was no adjustment to the adjusted cost base of the investment as a result of the election. Instead, the capital gain triggered as a result of the election was credited to an exempt capital gains balance for that particular investment. The exempt capital gains balance can be used to shelter any capital gains that flow out to the taxpayer from the flow-through entity after February 22, 1994, or that are realized on a subsequent disposition of the investment. If the taxpayer sells all the interests in the flow-through investment prior to 2005, any remaining exempt capital gains balance is added to the adjusted cost base of investment. If after 2004 the taxpayer has an exempt capital gains balance in respect of a flow-through investment that the taxpayer still owns, the balance will be added to the adjusted cost base of the investment.

Generally, the election (Form T664) was to be filed by April 30, 1995. However, if the taxpayer owned eligible capital property and the fiscal period of the taxpayer's business that included February 22, 1994 ended after 1994, the election in respect of this property was due by April 30, 1996.

The election could have been late-filed up to two years from its due date provided a penalty was paid at the time of filing the election.

The election could have been amended or cancelled prior to 1998.

## ¶262  Enhanced Capital Gains Exemption

As noted above, the enhanced capital gains exemption is still available with respect to shares of a qualified small business corporation and qualified farm property.

¶262

In any particular taxation year the taxpayer is entitled to claim a deduction from income to arrive at taxable income of no more than the unused enhanced capital gains exemption. The unused capital gains exemption is $250,000 less the amounts actually claimed in prior years, adjusted for changes to the capital gains inclusion rate. The yearly entitlement to the enhanced capital gains exemption for 1995 and subsequent years is determined as the least of three amounts:

(1) the unused lifetime exemption as defined above;

(2) the annual gains limit which is defined to be the net taxable capital gains from the disposition of qualified farm property and shares of a qualified small business corporation for the year less net allowable capital losses realized from disposition of other properties for the year, less net capital loss carryovers claimed in the year, less allowable business investment losses incurred in the year, whether or not they have been claimed in income;

(3) the cumulative gains limit which is calculated to be the aggregate of the annual gains limit computed for years that end after 1984, less the capital gains exemption claimed in prior years and the cumulative net investment loss (CNIL) account.

The cumulative net investment loss (CNIL) account only applies to 1988 and subsequent taxation years. The computation is the excess, if any, of the individual's investment expenses over investment income (as defined in section 110.6).

The definition of "shares of a qualified small business corporation" is provided in subsection 110.6(1). In general terms, in order to be a share of a qualified small business corporation:

(a) the share must be a share of a small business corporation at the time of its disposition. A small business corporation is defined in subsection 248(1) and means a Canadian-controlled private corporation in which 90% or more of the value of the corporation's assets are used in an active business carried on primarily in Canada. This provision is modified in the case of death by paragraph 110.6(14)(*g*). In particular, if the 90% test is not met immediately before death, the share will still qualify if it was a share of a qualified small business corporation at any time in the 12-month period immediately preceding death. Shares and debts in certain other small business corporations can qualify as assets used in an active business.

¶262

(b) throughout the 24-month period preceding the date of disposition of the share, the share must not have been owned by anyone other than the taxpayer or a person related to the taxpayer.

(c) throughout the 24-month period preceding the date of disposition while the share is owned by the taxpayer or a person related to the taxpayer, more than 50% of the value of the corporation's assets must have been used principally in an active business carried on primarily in Canada or invested in shares and debts of certain other small business corporations.

See ¶808 for a discussion of the definition of qualified farm property.

## ¶264   Miscellaneous Provisions

The enhanced capital gains exemption is an optional deduction and a taxpayer is not required to claim the exemption in a particular year. However, since the benefits of the exemption are not transferable, the terminal tax return of the deceased should generally take advantage of the capital gains exemption to the extent possible. This may not be the case where the deceased has otherwise transferred his or her capital assets (consisting of qualified farm property or shares of a qualified small business corporation) to a spouse, common-law partner or a qualifying trust for a spouse or common-law partner. In order to create a capital gain against which to claim the capital gains exemption, the personal representative may make an election pursuant to subsection 70(6.2) (see ¶506) electing out of the rollover. This would create an immediate capital gain in the terminal return of the deceased. If the election would result in a capital gain in excess of the available exemption, the personal representative may choose not to use up the available exemption but instead take advantage of a possible long-term deferral in the hands of the spouse or the trust for the benefit of the spouse or common-law partner. Where the deceased owned shares of a qualified small business corporation, each share is considered to be a separate property of which an election under subsection 70(6.2) may be made. The personal representative may make an election under subsection 70(6.2) only in respect of some of the shares such that an excess capital gain is not created.

To be eligible to claim the enhanced capital gains exemption, the individual must be a resident of Canada throughout the year. In the year of death, the taxpayer will have met these qualifications if he or she was a resident of Canada at any time during the period commencing on January 1 and ending on the date of death, and throughout the immediately preceding taxation year (subsection 110.6(5)).

Where a taxpayer dies after 1984, the total net capital losses that can be deducted in the year of death and in the immediately preceding year from sources of income other than capital gains are reduced to the extent that the taxpayer has claimed any capital gains exemption in the taxpayer's lifetime (subsection 111(2)). (See ¶302 for a discussion on the utilization of net capital losses on death.)

Where the personal representative has elected to file separate returns for business or trust income, or rights or things, paragraph 10 of Interpretation Bulletin IT-326R3 outlines that, for deductions allowed under section 111 for non-capital, net capital, restricted farm, farm and limited partnership loss carryforwards, the capital gains deduction (section 110.6) and northern residents deductions (section 110.7) may not be claimed on those returns as they represent the return of another person.

## ¶266

## Other Deductions

Pursuant to section 114.2, the aggregate of certain deductions that may be claimed on all of the income tax returns filed on behalf of the deceased taxpayer may not exceed the amount that would have been deducted if only one return had been filed (Interpretation Bulletin IT-326R3, paragraph 2). The deductions to which section 114.2 is applicable are:

- employee stock option deduction (paragraphs 110(1)(*d*), (*d*.1)),

- charitable donation of employee option securities for 2000 and later taxation years (paragraph 110(1)(*d*.01)),

- prospector's and grubstaker's shares deduction (paragraph 110(1)(*d*.2)),

- DPSP shares deduction (paragraph 110(1)(*d*.3)),

- certain tax-exempt receipts (paragraph 110(1)(*f*)),

- home relocation loans (paragraph 110(1)(*j*)), and

- deduction for vow of perpetual poverty (subsection 110(2)).

The deductions noted above relate to a particular source of income and therefore it is the position of the Canada Revenue Agency that the deduction can be claimed in a given return only to the extent of the income from the particular source reported in that return (Interpretation Bulletin IT-326R3, paragraph 3).

## ¶268

## Personal Tax Credits

In preparing the terminal returns of a deceased taxpayer, full personal tax credits may be claimed without proration regardless of when the taxpayer died during the year. In addition, if an election has been made to file separate returns for each of business, trust or rights or things income, the same personal tax credits may also be claimed on those returns (see Interpretation Bulletin IT-326R3). These personal tax credits would include the basic personal amount, the age credit, spousal or common-law partner credit, wholly dependant ("equivalent-to-spouse") credit and the infirm dependant credit.

The amount of the allowable spousal or common-law partner credit is calculated (for taxation years after 1985) by taking into consideration the income of the spouse or common-law partner for the entire calendar year (paragraph 118(1)(a), Interpretation Bulletin IT-513R, paragraph 4). Also, the spouse's or common-law partner's tax payable for the full calendar year must be considered when determining the amount of tax credit which may be transferred to the deceased in respect of the spouse's or common-law partner's tuition, education, age, pension or mental or physical impairment credits (section 118.8). This credit can only be claimed on the ordinary return of the deceased filed under subsection 70(1). In the case of any other dependants for whom a credit is being claimed, including the equivalent-to-spouse credit under paragraph 118(1)(b), the amount of the credit is also determined with reference to the dependant's income for the full calendar year.

## ¶270

## Medical Expense Tax Credit

In ordinary circumstances, the taxpayer may claim medical expenses for a twelve-month period ending in the taxation year for which they are claimed. In the case of a deceased taxpayer, subsection 118.2(1) permits the inclusion of expenses paid within any 24-month period that includes the day of death. The normal restrictions with respect to claiming medical expenses otherwise apply except for the limit on the amount paid as remuneration for attendant care under paragraph 118.2(2)(b.1). The limit is increased to $20,000 in the year of death for 1997 and subsequent years ($10,000 for 1996 and prior years).

If not all medical expenses can be ascertained at the time of filing the terminal period return, it is understood that the Canada Revenue Agency will allow that return to be amended to include additional outlays (Interpretation Bulletin IT-519R2, paragraph 17).

For 1997 and subsequent years, a refundable medical expense tax credit is available under subsection 122.51(2) to certain individuals who have net income of at least $2,500 from employment or business. The credit is reduced as the individual's and the individual's spouse's or common-law partner's net income exceeds a specified threshold. The credit cannot be claimed on the separate returns filed under subsection 70(2), 150(4) or paragraph 104(23)(*d*).

# ¶272

## Charitable Donations Tax Credit

A tax credit in respect of charitable donations may be claimed on any of the returns filed in respect of a deceased taxpayer. The donations may be made prior to the deceased's death or pursuant to the deceased's will to a registered charity and other donees listed in subsection 118.1(1) under the definition of total charitable gifts. Effective for 1996 and subsequent years, the amount that can be claimed for these donations is 100% of the deceased's net income for the year of death. For 1995 and prior years, the limit was 20% of the deceased's net income for the year of death for donations to a registered charity and other donees. A gift to Her Majesty in right of Canada or a province ("Crown gift"), a gift of cultural property and a gift of ecologically sensitive land are also eligible as a donation and are not subject to the above limits.

The deceased taxpayer is allowed to calculate the tax credit in respect of donations made in the year and those made in the five immediately preceding taxation years to the extent that a tax-credit claim has not been taken in respect of that donation in a prior taxation year. Where the deceased taxpayer has made charitable bequests in the will, the donation is deemed to have been made by the taxpayer immediately before the taxpayer died, effective for gifts made after July 1997 (subsection 118.1(5)). For gifts made prior to August 1997, the donation is deemed to have been made by the taxpayer in the taxation year in which the individual died.

Subsection 118.1(4) deems a gift made by the individual in the year of death to have been made by that individual in the immediately preceding year to the extent the amount of the gift was not claimed for purposes of computing a tax credit in the year of death. To the extent that the gift cannot be used in the year of death, the donation can be carried back and claimed as a donation in the immediately preceding taxation year. Effective for deaths occurring in 1996 and subsequent years, the limit for donations in the tax year immediately preceding death is 100% of net income for that year.

If donations are made by the taxpayer in excess of those which can be deducted in the year of death or the year immediately preceding death, there is no provision allowing any excess to be carried forward and claimed by the estate of the deceased taxpayer.

## ¶273    Gifts of Insurance Policies, RRSPs and RRIFs

For deaths occurring prior to 1999, where a charity was designated as the beneficiary under a life insurance policy or under an RRSP or RRIF, the payout to the charity on death was not considered to be a gift made by the individual's will. As a consequence, no donation credit was available for the year of death.

For deaths occurring after 1998, subsection 118.1(5.2) deems a gift to have been made to a charity designated as a beneficiary under a life insurance policy immediately before the individual's death where the conditions of subsection 118.1(5.1) are satisfied. The conditions of subsection 118.1(5.1) are:

- the individual's life was insured under the life insurance policy immediately before the individual's death;

- the transfer of funds was made from the insurer to a qualified donee as a consequence of the individual's death and solely because of an obligation under the policy;

- immediately before the individual's death, the individual's consent would have been required to change the beneficiary;[17]

- immediately before the individual's death, the donee was neither a policyholder nor an assignee of the individual's interest under the policy; and

- the transfer occurs within 36 months from the date of death (or such longer period with the consent of the Minister).

For deaths occurring after 1998, new subsection 118.1(5.3) deems a gift of an RRSP or RRIF to have been made immediately before an individual's death where:

---

[17] See Canada Revenue Agency document 2004-0065451C6 dated May 4, 2004 for comments with respect to where the charity is named as an irrevocable beneficiary under a life insurance policy.

¶273

- a transfer is made from an RRSP or RRIF to a qualified donee solely because of the donee's interest as a beneficiary under the RRSP or RRIF;

- the individual was the annuitant under the RRSP or RRIF immediately before the individual's death; and

- the transfer occurs within 36 months from the date of death (or such longer period with the consent of the Minister).

The amount of the gift is deemed to be the fair market value of the RRSP or RRIF at the time of the individual's death.

## ¶274   Bequest of Capital Property — Election

If a taxpayer has made a bequest by will of capital property to a charity or to the Crown, the taxpayer is considered for income tax purposes to have received proceeds of disposition equal to the fair market value of the property at the date of death. A capital gain or loss may be realized on the disposition, depending on the adjusted cost base of the capital property and/ or recapture in case of depreciable property.

Where the fair market value of the property exceeds its adjusted cost base, a special election is available to the personal representative in the terminal period return (subsection 118.1(6)). Where a taxpayer has created a work of art which is classified as inventory and the individual gifts the work to charity or the Crown, the special election is also available (subsection 118.1(7)). For 2000 and subsequent years, the special election under subsection 118.1(7) will apply to artwork donated by an individual who acquired it in circumstances where subsection 70(3) applied (as a right or thing under the artist's will).

The personal representative may designate the value of the gift at an amount between the adjusted cost base of the property and its fair market value. The February 27, 2004 draft legislation proposes to amend subsection 118.1(6) for gifts made after 1999 such that the special election will be changed where the property is depreciable property. The special election will be available where the fair market value of the property exceeds the lesser of the undepreciated capital cost of the class and the adjusted cost base of the property. The personal representative may designate the value of the gift between the lesser of these two amounts and the fair market value of the property.

The elected amount is then considered to be the amount of the donation as well as the deceased's proceeds of disposition for the purpose of computing any business income, resulting capital gains or recapture in the respect of depreciable property. However, with the increase in the charitable limit for donations in the year of death and the immediately preceding year, the personal representative may find that such an election is no longer beneficial.

## ¶276   Bequest of Certain Capital Property

Effective for dispositions of certain capital property to charities (other than private foundations) after February 18, 1997, only 50% of the taxable capital gain realized is included in the donor's income. This special provision applies to:

- a share, debt obligation or right that is listed on a prescribed stock exchange;
- a share of the capital stock of a mutual fund corporation;
- a unit of a mutual fund trust;
- an interest in a related segregated fund trust; and
- a prescribed debt obligation.

This rule will apply where the taxpayer has made a bequest by will to such a charity and the bequest is satisfied by such property (paragraph 38(a.1)). Consequently, only 50% of any taxable capital gain calculated on such a bequest will be included in the terminal period return.[18]

## ¶278   Bequest of Non-Qualifying Securities

Where, after July 1997, a taxpayer makes a gift of "non-qualifying securities" (including a gift by a will) and the gift is not an excepted gift, it is deemed not to have been made at that time (subsection 118.1(13)). A non-qualified security is defined in subsection 118.1(18) to mean:

- an obligation (other than an obligation of a financial institution to repay an amount deposited with the institution or an obligation listed on a prescribed stock exchange) of the taxpayer, the taxpayer's estate or a non-arm's-length person;
- a share (other than a share listed on a prescribed stock exchange) of the capital stock of a non-arm's-length corporation; or
- any other security (other than a security listed on a prescribed stock exchange) issued by the individual or a non-arm's-length person.

Subsection 118.1(19) provides that a gift is an excepted gift if:

- the security is a share;

---

[18] Reference should be made to Technical Interpretations 2000-0011755, 2000-0015105 and 2000-0015215 dated January 11, 2001.

- the donee is not a private foundation;
- the taxpayer deals at arm's length with the donee; and
- where the donee is a charitable organization or a public foundation, the taxpayer deals at arm's length with each director, trustee, officer and like official of the donee.

If the donee disposes of the security within 60 months after the gift, or the security ceases to be a non-qualifying security within the same time period, the taxpayer is deemed to have made a gift to the donee at that subsequent time. The amount of the gift is deemed to be the lesser of the fair market value of the security at the time of disposition, or the fair market value of the security at the time the security ceases to be a non-qualifying security, and if the property is subject to an election under subsection 118.1(6), the amount designated in the election.

Although the taxpayer is not considered to have made a gift at the time of the donation as noted above, the taxpayer is considered to have disposed of the security. However, the taxpayer may claim a reserve in respect of any capital gain realized on the disposition of the non-qualifying security (subsection 40(1.01)). The taxpayer cannot claim the reserve if the taxpayer is deemed to have made a gift as a result of the donee disposing of the security or the security ceasing to be a non-qualifying security within the time period referred to above. The reserve will not be included in the taxpayer's income if the security remains a non-qualifying security beyond the 60 month period referred to above or is not disposed of by the donee within the same time period (see Technical Interpretation 2002-0128485 dated April 26, 2002).

If the taxpayer makes a donation of a non-qualifying security in the year of death (including a donation by will), no reserve may be claimed under subsection 40(1.01) in the terminal period return of the deceased (paragraph 72(1)(c)).

If the taxpayer makes a donation of a non-qualifying security prior to the date of death or a donation by will, and the non-qualifying security is disposed of within the 60-month period or ceased to be a non-qualifying security within the same time period, subsection 118.1(15) deems the donation to have been made in the taxation year in which the individual died.

## ¶280   Gifts of Cultural Property

If a taxpayer makes a gift of cultural property by will, the deceased may claim a tax credit in respect of the donation. In order to be considered as a gift of cultural property, the property must be an object that the Canadian Cultural Property Export Review Board has determined meets the criteria set out in paragraphs 29(3)(b) and (c) of the *Cultural Property Export and Import Act.* The property must also be gifted to an institution or public authority in Canada that was, at the time the gift was made, designated under subsection 32(2) of the *Cultural Property Export and Import Act* either generally or for a specified purpose related to that object (Interpretation Bulletin IT-407R4).

If the taxpayer makes a gift by will of such property, no tax will be payable in respect of any capital gain realized on the disposition of the property. In order to qualify for this treatment, the disposition of the property to the institution or Canadian public authority must occur within 36 months after the death of the donor (or such longer period as is determined to be reasonable in the circumstances) (subparagraph 39(1)(a)(i.1)).

## ¶281
## Gifts of Ecologically Sensitive Land

If a taxpayer makes a gift of ecologically sensitive land by will, the deceased may claim a tax credit in respect of the donation. The taxpayer is considered to have received proceeds of disposition equal to the fair market value of the property at the date of death. A capital gain or loss may be realized on the disposition, depending on the adjusted cost base of the property. For gifts made after February 27, 2000 of such property only 50% of the taxable capital gain realized on the disposition is required to be included in the taxpayer's income.

A gift of land (including a covenant or an easement to which land is subject) will qualify as an ecological gift if:

- the fair market value of the gift is certified by the Minister of the Environment;

- the land is certified by the Minister of the Environment to be ecologically sensitive land, the conservation and protection of which is important to the preservation of Canada's environmental heritage; and

- the gift was made to Her Majesty in the right of Canada or of a province, a municipality in Canada, a municipal or public body performing a function of government in Canada or a registered charity one of the main purposes of which is the conservation and protection of Canada's environment heritage and that is approved by the Minister of the Environment.

Reference should be made to subsection 118.1(12) for the determination of the fair market value of the gifted land or the gift of an easement that is an ecological gift. The provisions of subsection 43(2) apply for purposes of determining the adjusted cost base of a gift of such an easement.

## ¶282

## Tax Credits — Separate Returns

Pursuant to section 118.93, the aggregate of tax credits that may be claimed with respect to certain items on all of the returns filed on behalf of the deceased taxpayer cannot exceed the amount that would be deducted under those provisions if no separate returns were filed. The tax credits which would be affected by section 118.93 would be the pension tax credit (subsection 118(3)), charitable donation tax credit (section 118.1), medical expense tax credit (section 118.2), mental and physical impairment tax credit (section 118.3), tuition tax credit (section 118.5), education tax credit (section 118.6), EI and CPP tax credit (section 118.7), and transfer of education or tuition tax credits from a child or grandchild (section 118.9) (Interpretation Bulletin IT-326R3, paragraph 5). These credits may be allocated among the various separate returns regardless of the type of income on the return, except for the tax credits in respect of EI and CPP and the pension credit, which can be claimed only in the return in which the income relating to the credit is reported.

## ¶284

## Alternative Minimum Tax

As outlined in section 127.55 of the Act, the obligation to pay minimum tax does not apply to a taxpayer's terminal return as filed under subsection 70(1). Additional taxes from prior years (minimum tax credits) which were incurred as a result of the minimum tax provisions may be utilized in this terminal return if the normal tax exceeds the minimum tax amount in the year. To the extent there are utilized minimum tax credits, there is no relief for 1988 and subsequent taxation years.

In addition, the minimum tax provisions will not have application to any of the separate elective tax returns of the taxpayer filed pursuant to subsection 70(2) (rights or things), paragraph 104(23)(*d*) (income beneficiary of a testamentary trust) or subsection 150(4) (proprietorship or partnership income). Since minimum tax does not apply to these returns, the minimum tax carryover provisions also do not have application (subsection 120.2(4)).

## ¶286

## Payment of Tax

Provided the personal representative of the deceased taxpayer furnishes acceptable security to the Minister, the personal representative may file an election on Form T2075 (Regulation 1001) to pay by instalments tax arising on death (subsection 159(5)). Security may be in the form of a charge on the property of the deceased taxpayer, or a letter of guarantee from a bank. A maximum of ten equal consecutive annual payments are allowed, with interest payable from the day the tax would otherwise have been payable on the balance of tax outstanding, at the prescribed rate, at the time the election is made (subsection 159(7)). It is unlikely that interest paid would be an allowable deduction to the estate since it is not paid for the purpose of earning or producing income. At the time of filing the election, the personal representative must stipulate the number of instalments in which tax will be paid.

Amounts which qualify for instalment payments include rights or things included in the deceased's income regardless of whether the personal representative has elected to file a separate return for those items, recapture of capital cost allowance in excess of terminal losses which arise as a result of the deemed disposition of depreciable property, capital gains in excess of capital losses which arise as a result of the deemed disposition of non-depreciable property, deemed dispositions of resource property and land inventory, and untaxed 1971 receivables of a deceased professional. Tax imposed in the year of death on all other sources of income may not be paid by instalment.

The instalment base is determined by subtracting from the amount of tax payable on the terminal period return the amount of tax that would have been payable if those amounts specified in subsection 159(5) had not been included in income. The first instalment is due on or before the day tax, in respect of those amounts, would be payable were it not for the election. Each subsequent payment is due on the same date as that of the initial payment over a maximum of nine years, and an instalment must be made every year.

¶286

# 3

# Taxation of Property Held at Death

---

## ¶300

### Introduction

The introduction of a tax on capital gains in 1972, and the corresponding repeal of the federal *Estate Tax Act,* gave rise to specific provisions in the Act to deal with the taxation of capital property owned by a taxpayer at death. Subsection 70(5) was introduced to provide a series of rules which apply to deem a taxpayer to realize all accrued gains and losses in respect of capital property, both depreciable and non-depreciable, owned immediately before death.

## ¶301

### Capital Property

### ¶302    General Rules

Paragraph 70(5)(*a*) provides that, immediately before death, a deceased is deemed to have disposed of each capital property owned at that time. The deemed proceeds of disposition for each property is its fair market value at the time of the deemed disposition. This rule applies to both depreciable and non-depreciable property.

Paragraph 70(5)(*b*) provides that a person, who as a consequence of the taxpayer's death acquires capital property of the deceased, is deemed to have acquired it at the time of death at a cost equal to its deemed fair market value immediately before death. Accordingly, subject to specified exceptions discussed below, all accrued capital gains and losses, terminal losses and recapture on capital property of the deceased up to the time of death are realized on death.

Taxable Canadian property (paragraph 115(1)(*b*)) owned by a non-resident is also deemed to be disposed of immediately before death (Interpretation Bulletin IT-420R3).

The valuation of capital properties deemed to be disposed of on death is subject to the same rules as for *inter vivos* dispositions. If the capital property was purchased after 1971, its adjusted cost base would be its actual cost to the taxpayer subject to specific adjustments as provided in subsections 53(1) and (2) of the Act. The deemed capital gain or loss is the difference between the adjusted cost base of the property and its fair market value immediately before death. The taxable gain or allowable loss is one-half of this amount for dispositions after October 17, 2000, two-thirds of this amount for dispositions after February 27, 2000 and before October 18, 2000, and three-quarters of this amount for dispositions before February 28, 2000.

If the capital property was acquired prior to 1972, the value of the property would be determined in accordance with the transitional rules under the median or tax-free zone method (ITAR 26(3)). That is, the cost of the property for the purposes of calculating the gain or loss is deemed to be the middle amount of the actual cost of the property to the taxpayer, the fair market value of the property on December 31, 1971 (V-Day), and the deemed proceeds of disposition subject to specified adjustments, pursuant to section 53. The effect of this provision is to tax only those gains arising after the commencement of tax on capital gains, to the extent that those gains exceed the actual cost of the property, and to allow only those capital losses arising after V-Day.

Alternatively, the personal representative may file an election, pursuant to the transitional rules, deeming the cost of capital property acquired by the deceased prior to 1972 to be the fair market value of that property on V-Day (ITAR 26(7), Form T2076). However, if during the years prior to death but after 1971 the taxpayer disposed of capital property acquired prior to 1972, and reported the gain or loss from that disposition based either on the tax-free zone method or elected the fair market value at V-Day, the same method must be followed for all dispositions of pre-1972 properties, including deemed dispositions at death. In order for the election to be valid, the return in which the election is made must be filed within the specified time limits.

¶302

## ¶303   Payment of Tax

If the total deemed taxable capital gains exceed the total deemed allowable capital losses, the tax liability for those gains may be paid in up to ten equal consecutive annual instalments, subject to the personal representative furnishing security acceptable to the Minister and filing the requisite election prior to the first instalment falling due (subsection 159(5), Form T2075). The first instalment must be paid by the day on which the tax would otherwise have been payable had the election not been made. Each subsequent instalment must be paid on or before the next following anniversary date. Interest at the prescribed rate is charged on the outstanding balance of tax owing. This is discussed in greater detail in the section dealing with payment of tax (¶286).

## ¶304   Utilization of Losses

If the total deemed and actual allowable capital losses exceed the taxable capital gains, the excess may be applied against all other income reported on the terminal period return (less the actual amount of capital gains exemptions previously claimed by the taxpayer — see ¶258, subsection 111(2)).

If there is insufficient income in the terminal period to absorb the net capital losses, they may be carried back against income from all sources in the taxation year prior to the year of death, again subject to an adjustment for the capital gains exemptions previously claimed (Form T1-A must be used to carry back the losses). Any excess net capital losses unapplied in those two taxation years cannot be used to reduce income from any other taxation year of the deceased taxpayer, nor can those capital losses be transferred to the estate or to a beneficiary directly.

If the deceased had net capital losses in the year of death, those losses could also be carried back and applied to reduce taxable capital gains realized in the preceding three years. Any unapplied net capital losses could then be used to reduce income from any source for the year of death or year immediately preceding death (subject to an adjustment for the capital gains exemptions previously claimed). There is no requirement that the net capital losses must first be applied to reduce taxable capital gains of previous years before they are used to reduce income from any source.

In addition to the unlimited application of net capital losses realized in the year of death, any net capital losses carried forward from prior years may be claimed against other income in the year of death and in the year prior to death without any restriction on the amount of the loss which may be claimed (subject to an adjustment for the capital gains exemptions previously claimed) (subsection 111(2), Interpretation Bulletin IT-232R3). Where the capital gains inclusion rate for the years in which the loss carryforwards were realized is different from that in the year of death, the loss carryforwards will have to be adjusted to reflect the capital gains inclusion rate for the year of death. There is no similar adjustment to the amount of the capital gains exemption claimed in previous years.

Where there is a large loss carryforward available, it may be advantageous for the personal representative to include as much income as possible in the terminal period return in order to utilize those losses. For example, the personal representative might elect under subsection 70(6.2) to transfer appreciated capital property to a spouse, common-law partner or a trust for the benefit of the spouse or common-law partner at its fair market value at death to trigger a capital gain in the terminal period. As a result, capital gains for the year of death would be offset by capital losses carried forward. The adjusted cost base of the property to the spouse, common-law partner or the trust would be its fair market value immediately before the taxpayer's death. Subsection 70(6.2) does not allow an election at an amount between the adjusted cost base and fair market value. The election results in a deemed disposition at fair market value of the property subject to the election. Accordingly, an election under subsection 70(6.2) could give rise to a gain in excess of that required to offset any available losses. This is discussed further in Chapter 5.

## ¶305

## Depreciable Capital Property

The deemed disposition of depreciable property may give rise to recapture and capital gains, or could result in a terminal loss (paragraph 70(5)(a)). Capital cost allowance cannot be claimed in the terminal period return since the Act deems the taxpayer to have disposed of all depreciable and non-depreciable capital property immediately before death (see *Katz Estate v. The Queen*, 76 DTC 6377 (F.C.T.D.)). Consequently, by virtue of this deeming provision, the taxpayer would not own any depreciable property at the time of death. In order to be entitled to claim capital cost allowance, the taxpayer must own the subject property at the end of the taxation year (subsection 13(21), paragraph 20(1)(a), and regulation 1100(1)(a)).

If the fair market value of the property at the time of the deemed disposition is greater than its undepreciated capital cost, recapture of capital cost allowance will result which will be included in the deceased taxpayer's income for the year of death. If the fair market value is less than the undepreciated capital cost, the resultant terminal loss may be deducted in computing income of the terminal period. If the deemed proceeds of disposition exceed the adjusted cost base of the property, a capital gain will result, one-half of which will be included in income reported in the terminal period return for dispositions after October 17, 2000 (two-thirds for dispositions after February 27, 2000 and before October 18, 2000, and three-quarters for dispositions before February 28, 2000).

Where depreciable property was owned by the deceased on December 31, 1971 (V-Day), and the capital cost of the property to the deceased was less than its fair market value on V-Day and less than the deemed proceeds of disposition, the deceased's proceeds of disposition would be the capital cost plus the amount by which the deemed proceeds exceed the fair market value of the property on V-Day (ITAR 20(1)(a)). The net effect of this computation is that any portion of the capital gain which accrued prior to January 1, 1972 will not be taxed.

If, instead, the V-Day value was less than the original cost, the deemed proceeds (ITAR 20(1)(a)) would not apply and the ordinary rules in subsection 40(1) would apply to determine any capital gain. Similarly, if the deemed proceeds were less than cost, a terminal loss may result depending on the amount of capital cost allowance previously claimed. ITAR 20(1)(a) may apply to a beneficiary who inherits depreciable property after 1971 (ITAR 20(1.2), Interpretation Bulletin (Archived) IT-217R and special release thereto.) An actual disposition of depreciable property does not give rise to a capital loss since the cost of depreciable property can only be deducted as capital cost allowance or a terminal loss.

*Example (ITAR 20(1)(a))*

| | |
|---|---|
| Cost ........................................................... | $100,000 |
| F.M.V. at Valuation Day (V-day) ................................. | $120,000 |
| Deemed proceeds at death....................................... | $130,000 |

Deemed proceeds

= cost + (deemed proceeds - V-day)

= $100,000 + ($130,000 - $120,000)

= <u>$110,000</u>

The deemed proceeds of disposition of depreciable capital property are considered to be the cost of that property to the recipient estate and beneficiary, except where the deceased's capital cost exceeds the deemed capital cost of the property to the beneficiary as determined pursuant to paragraph 70(5)(b). For the purposes of sections 13 and 20 dealing with depreciable property and capital cost allowance, the beneficiary's capital cost is deemed to be the same as that of the deceased taxpayer (paragraph 70(5)(c)). The difference between the deceased's cost and the deemed proceeds of disposition is deemed to be capital cost allowance already allowed to the benefi-

¶305

ciary. If there is a subsequent sale for proceeds in excess of the deemed undepreciated capital cost, the beneficiary vendor would incur recapture up to the amount of the deemed capital cost. Eventually, all of the recapture may be taxed at such time as the property is disposed of, or deemed to be disposed of, for proceeds in excess of the undepreciated capital cost to the beneficiary.

*Example*

A taxpayer acquired a depreciable property of class 8 in 1990 at a cost of $100,000. She has claimed capital cost allowance so that at her death the undepreciated capital cost is $60,000. The fair market value at death is $90,000. The taxpayer dies, leaving the property to a child.

| | |
|---|---:|
| Deemed proceeds to deceased (paragraph 70(5)(a)) | $ 90,000 |
| Recapture to deceased | $ 30,000 |
| Cost to child (paragraph 70(5)(b)) | $ 90,000 |
| Deemed capital cost to child (subparagraph 70(5)(c)(i)) | $100,000 |
| Deemed allowed to child (subparagraph 70(5)(c)(ii)) $100,000 - $90,000 | $ 10,000 |
| Undepreciated capital cost to child for purposes of capital cost allowance | $ 90,000 |

If the child were to sell the property for $100,000, the following would result:

| | |
|---|---:|
| Capital cost | $100,000 |
| Proceeds | $100,000 |
| Undepreciated capital cost | $90,000 |
| Capital cost allowance recapture | $10,000 |

Separate rules apply if the deceased owned both land and building and the proceeds of disposition are determined pursuant to subsection 13(21.1) (paragraph 70(5)(d)). Subsection 13(21.1) provides for the reallocation of the proceeds of disposition between land and building in circumstances where the original allocation would give rise to a capital gain on the land and a terminal loss on the building. As a result, the terminal loss otherwise determined is applied to reduce the proceeds of disposition of the land, thereby reducing the amount of the capital gain which would be realized on the land. The proceeds of disposition of the building are correspondingly increased, thereby reducing to nil the amount of the terminal loss which would be realized on the building.

In these circumstances, by virtue of paragraph 70(5)(d), the beneficiary of the land is considered to acquire the land at a cost equal to the proceeds as reduced by subsection 13(21.1). The building is deemed to be acquired at a capital cost equal to that of the deceased, and the beneficiary is deemed to have claimed capital cost allowance equal to the difference between the cost

¶305

to the deceased and the deemed proceeds — again as adjusted pursuant to subsection 13(21.1).

For example, assume that the adjusted cost base of the land to the deceased was $20,000 and that the capital cost of the building was $100,000. At the time of death, the undepreciated capital cost of the building is $20,000. The deemed proceeds of disposition on death are allocated on the basis of $50,000 to the land and nothing to the building, resulting in a $30,000 capital gain on the land and a terminal loss of $20,000 on the building.

Subsection 13(21.1) would reallocate the deemed proceeds to increase the deemed proceeds on the building to $20,000, thereby reducing the terminal loss to nil. The deemed proceeds on the land would be reduced to $30,000, thereby reducing the capital gain by $20,000. Finally, by reason of paragraph 70(5)(d), the deemed cost of the land to the beneficiary would be $30,000. In addition, the beneficiary would be deemed to have acquired the building for $100,000 and to have claimed $80,000 as capital cost allowance. Accordingly, if the beneficiary were to dispose of the building and realized proceeds of disposition in excess of $20,000, the beneficiary would be taxable on the excess as recapture.

Tax on the recapture of capital cost allowance may be paid in up to ten equal consecutive annual instalments subject to interest at the prescribed rate being charged on the outstanding balance (see ¶286 for details).

## ¶306

## Shareholdings and Death

If the deceased taxpayer was the controlling shareholder of a corporation, death could affect the ability of the corporation to claim losses carried forward. The Act provides that a corporation is not allowed to deduct any part of net capital losses for a preceding year if control of the company has been acquired during the year, subject to specific exceptions (subsection 111(4)). Similarly, no deduction will be allowed in respect of non-capital losses if there is an acquisition of control and specific tests regarding the carrying on of the business are not met (subsection 111(5)). Paragraph 111(5)(a) of the Act provides tests for the utilization of non-capital losses of a corporation which are incurred in carrying on a particular business. After control changes, any non-capital loss of the corporation incurred in a prior taxation year may be claimed only to the extent of the corporation's income from the same business or, in certain circumstances, from a substantially similar business. In addition, the business must be carried on for profit or with a reasonable expectation of profit throughout the particular year.

Where these conditions are met, losses incurred prior to the change of control may be deducted to the extent of the aggregate of the two amounts described in subparagraph 111(5)(a)(ii). The first amount is the corporation's income for the year from that business. The second amount is the income from a business of which substantially all of the income is from activities of a similar nature to those of that particular business. The Canada Revenue Agency views the words "substantially all" to mean not less than 90%.

If on the death of a shareholder controlling shares pass either to the estate or to related beneficiaries, there is deemed to be no change of control of the company and loss carryforwards will continue to be available (subparagraph 256(7)(a)(i)). However, distribution of a controlling interest to any other parties, including unrelated shareholders pursuant to a buy-sell arrangement, would result in an acquisition of corporate control and any net, non-capital loss or farm loss carryforwards may no longer be available.

Paragraph 111(5)(b) provides similar rules with regard to the carryback of non-capital losses occurring in taxation years following the change in control to taxation years before the change in control.

Valuation of the shares of a closely held private corporation poses another problem on the death of a shareholder. Shares which are capital property of a taxpayer are deemed to be disposed of at their fair market value immediately before death. If the shareholders have entered into a buy-sell agreement providing for the optional or compulsory sale of the shares by the estate to the remaining shareholders, presumably the formula as determined in the agreement would represent the fair market value of the property. This is generally defined as the price which a willing purchaser would pay to a willing vendor in an open and unrestricted market.

The Canada Revenue Agency makes the following statements in IT-140R3 as to the effect of a buy-sell agreement on the value of corporate shares:

> When determining the proceeds deemed to have been received by the deceased pursuant to subsection 70(5), the fair market value of the property subject to the buy-sell agreement must be determined at the time immediately before death. The Department's view is that, where the deceased and the surviving party to the buy-sell agreement (survivor) did not deal at arm's length, it is a question of fact whether the fair market value for the purpose of subsection 70(5) will be determined with reference to the buy-sell agreement.

> Where the deceased and a survivor did not deal at arm's length at the time the agreement was made, the Department's view is that paragraph 69(1)(b) applies when the estate sells the property to the survivor pursuant to the agreement and that it is a question of fact whether fair market value under paragraph 69(1)(b) will be determined with reference to the buy-sell agreement.

¶306

The effect of a corporation owning life insurance on the life of a share-holder has also posed a problem in determining the value of those shares on deemed disposition. In *The Queen v. Mastronardi*, 77 DTC 5217 (F.C.A.), the court held that life insurance proceeds received by the company should not affect the value of shares held at death. Presumably, the basis for this position is that shares were deemed to be disposed of immediately before death, and at that time the company was not entitled to the proceeds of the life insurance. Subsequent to the *Mastronardi* case and for deaths occurring after December 1, 1982, subsection 70(5.3) provides that for purposes of subsection 70(5), the value of a life insurance policy under which the deceased was the person whose life was insured shall be its cash surrender value. For dispositions after October 1, 1996, subsection 70(5.3) was amended such that it applies for the purposes of subsections 70(5) and 104(4), and section 128.1, and for the purposes of determining the value of any property, not just shares of a corporation.

Therefore, both the existence of a buy-sell agreement and of corporate-owned life insurance should be carefully considered in establishing the fair market value of shares subject to a deemed disposition on death.

# ¶307   Stop-Loss Rules

Where the deceased owned shares of a private corporation, these shares may be redeemed by the deceased's estate. The redemption may result in a capital loss to the estate that may be used to offset a deemed capital gain on death.

In determining whether a capital loss has been realized by the estate, the provisions of subsection 40(3.6) must be considered. For dispositions after April 26, 1995, where a taxpayer disposes of shares to a corporation that is affiliated with the taxpayer immediately after the disposition, the loss on the disposition is deemed to be nil. The deemed loss (otherwise calculated without reference to subsection 40(3.6) and paragraph 40(2)(g)) is added to the adjusted cost base of any remaining shares of the corporation owned by the taxpayer.

Subsection 251.1(1) defines affiliated persons or persons affiliated with each other. An estate would be affiliated with a corporation if the estate controlled the corporation. Under new paragraph 251.1(1)(g), effective after March 22, 2004, a trust and a person would be affiliated if the person was a majority interest beneficiary of the trust. Majority interest beneficiary is defined in new subsection 251.1(3). Therefore, if a majority interest beneficiary controls the corporation after the redemption of the estate's shares, the estate would be affiliated with the corporation.

New subsection 40(3.61) provides that for losses from dispositions after March 22, 2004, subsection 40(3.6) will not apply to the extent an election is made under subsection 164(6).

## ¶308   Corporate-Owned Life Insurance

As noted above, frequently the shares of a private corporation acquired by an estate or beneficiary as a consequence of the death of a shareholder are redeemed by the corporation, generally giving rise to a capital loss to offset a deemed capital gain on death.

Subsection 89(1) of the Act provides that, where a private corporation, on or before June 28, 1982 or after May 23, 1985, becomes a beneficiary under a corporate-owned policy, it includes in its capital dividend account the life insurance proceeds it receives on the death of a person to the extent that the proceeds exceed the corporation's adjusted cost basis of the policy (as defined in subsection 148(9)). Proceeds of insurance received between June 28, 1982 and May 23, 1985 were included in a separate account referred to as the life insurance capital dividend account. With the repeal of this provision, the proceeds of this account are now included in the capital dividend account (subsection 89(1)). On the redemption of shares held by the deceased's estate, the company may elect, pursuant to subsection 83(2), that any resulting dividend under subsection 84(3) be paid as a tax-free capital dividend.

*Redemptions Prior to April 27, 1995*

The adjusted cost base of the shares to the estate is equal to the fair market value of the shares immediately before death. On a share redemption, a deemed dividend would be realized, equal to the difference between the proceeds of redemption and the paid-up capital of the shares. An actual disposition would also result from the redemption. For the purposes of determining any gain or loss on the actual disposition, the proceeds of disposition excluded any amount considered to be a dividend, thereby reducing the proceeds. Consequently, a capital loss would often result in the redemption of the shares, since the shares held by the estate would have a high adjusted cost base and low proceeds of disposition. This capital loss was first used to reduce other capital gains realized by the estate. Any remaining net capital loss could be used by the estate to recover tax paid in the deceased's final taxation year by reason of the deemed disposition on death if the capital loss was realized in the first taxation year of the estate (subsection 164(6)). Where subsection 164(6) applied, the personal representative of the deceased would file an amended terminal period return. Any capital losses subject to the election would reduce the amount of capital gains exemption. Any resulting tax refund would either be paid to the estate or applied to amounts owing by the estate. Amounts subject to the subsection 164(6) election were deductible only in the subsection 70(1) return for the year of death.

*Redemptions Occurring After April 26, 1995*

Where shares owned by an estate are redeemed after April 26, 1995, and the company elects any resulting dividend under subsection 84(3) be paid as a tax-free capital dividend, the provisions of subsection 112(3.2) will reduce the capital loss realized on the shares by the estate. In computing the realized capital loss, the loss denial rules of subsection 40(3.6) must be considered. If the capital loss is not denied under subsection 40(3.6), the reduction of the capital loss to the estate under subsection 112(3.2) will be:

The lesser of

(i) the total capital dividends received by the estate in respect the shares, and

(ii) the capital loss of the estate determined without reference to this subsection less any taxable dividends received by the estate on the shares,

less, where the estate acquired the share as a consequence of death of the deceased and the disposition occurs during the estate's first taxation year, one-half of the lesser of

(iii) the capital loss of the estate determined without reference to this subsection, and

(iv) the deceased's capital gain from the disposition of the shares immediately before the individual's death.

(For dispositions after February 27, 2000 and before October 18, 2000, the fraction referred to above is changed to one-third, and for dispositions before February 28, 2000, it is changed to one-quarter.)

Subsection 112(3.2) applies to dispositions of shares by the deceased's estate that occur after April 26, 1995. However, the pre-April 27, 1995 rules will continue to apply to dispositions after April 26, 1995 in certain grandfathered circumstances.

## ¶309 Employee Stock Options

Employee stock options owned by a taxpayer at death will result in an employment income inclusion on the terminal period return (paragraph 7(1)(e)). The amount of the income inclusion is the difference between the value of the right to purchase the shares immediately after the taxpayer's death and the amount paid by the taxpayer to acquire the right. A deduction of one-half of the income inclusion (for dispositions after October 17, 2000, one-third for dispositions after February 27, 2000 and before October 18, 2000, and one-quarter for dispositions before February 28, 2000) may be available on the terminal period return under paragraph 110 (1)(*d*) if certain conditions are met. If the stock option is cancelled as a result of the employee's death, there will be no income inclusion.

The deceased's estate will acquire the stock options and the provisions of section 49 will apply to the exercise, disposition and expiry of the option by the estate as the stock options will generally be considered to be capital property to the estate. The estate will be considered to have acquired the stock options at the fair market value of the options immediately after the taxpayer's death (paragraph 69(1)(*c*) — see also CRA documents 9504325 dated March 30, 1995 and 9510190 dated May 10, 1995).

If the stock option expires, is exercised or disposed of by the estate within the first taxation year of the estate, and the value at the time of exercise or disposition has decreased, the benefit actually received by the estate may in fact be less than the amount included in income on the terminal period return. Subsection 164(6.1) allows the personal representative to elect to treat the difference as a loss from employment for the year of death. The amount of the loss is the employment income benefit deemed to have been received by the taxpayer less the total of:

(a) the excess of the value of the option immediately before the time it was exercised or disposed of over the amount paid by the deceased to acquire the option; and

(b) if a deduction was claimed on the terminal period return by reason of paragraph 110(1)(*d*), one-half of the amount calculated in (a) for deaths that occur after October 17, 2000 (one-third for deaths that occur after February 27, 2000 and before October 18, 2000 and one-quarter for deaths that occur before February 28, 2000).

If the estate elects under subsection 164(6.1), the adjusted cost base to the estate of the option is reduced by the amount of the loss calculated without reference to (b) of the formula noted above (paragraph 164(6.1)(*b*) and paragraph 53(2)(*t*)).

¶309

Example:

| | |
|---|---|
| Cost to purchase option to employee | $Nil |
| Exercise price | $ 10 |
| Fair market value of share at the time of the grant of the option | $ 10 |
| Fair market value of share immediately after death | $ 16 |
| Fair market value of option immediately after death | $ 6 |
| 7(1)(e) benefit | $ 6 |

Assume the option was exercised by the estate in its first taxation year and:

| | |
|---|---|
| Value of share at the time of exercise by the estate | $ 13 |
| Value of the option immediately before it was exercised by the estate | $ 3 |

Employment loss under subsection 164(6.1)=$6-3=$3. If a paragraph 110(1)(d) deduction of $3 was claimed on the terminal period return, the employment loss would be $6-($3+$1.50)=$1.50. The adjusted cost base of the option to the estate would be reduced by $3.

The election is available only if made within the first taxation year of the estate. An option which expires within the first year is deemed to have been disposed of for the purposes of this provision. In order to claim the loss, an amended return for the year of death must be filed no later than the last day for filing the terminal period return or elective return for the year of death, and the last day for filing the return for the first taxation year of the estate (regulation 1000(2)).

## ¶310  Employee Stock Option Shares

When an employee acquires shares under a stock option, subsection 7(1.1) (for shares of certain Canadian-controlled private corporations) and subsection 7(8) (for shares of certain non-CCPC acquired after February 27, 2000) allow the recognition of the stock option benefit to be deferred until the shares are disposed of provided certain conditions are satisfied. A stock option benefit will arise where the amount paid by the employee to acquire the shares is less than the fair market value of the shares at the time the option is exercised.

As subsections 70(5) and (6) deem the taxpayer to have disposed of the shares on death, any deferred stock option benefit will be required to be included in the deceased's terminal return under subsection 70(1). A deduction in computing taxable income of one-half of the stock option benefit (for dispositions after October 17, 2000, one-third for dispositions after February 27, 2000 and before October 18, 2000, and one-quarter for dispositions before February 28, 2000) may be available under paragraphs 110(1)(*d*) or 110(1)(*d*.1) if certain conditions are met.

## ¶311   Rollover of Shares in a Small Business Corporation

Former subsections 70(9.4) and (9.5) provided for the rollover of shares in a small business corporation where the shares were transferred to a child (as defined) of a deceased on the death of the deceased, or as a consequence of the death of the spouse who was the beneficiary of a spouse trust established by the deceased, where such transfer was after May 25, 1978 and before 1988.

The rollover was available with respect to share dispositions which occurred on the taxpayer's death, provided the recipients of the shares were Canadian residents immediately prior to the transfer. As a result, the realization of capital gains for income tax purposes could be postponed until the children disposed or were deemed to dispose of the shares, unless such subsequent disposition also qualified for rollover treatment. This tax deferral was in addition to the lifetime capital gains exemption otherwise available.

The rollovers under former subsections 70(9.4) and (9.5) were closely related to a similar rollover available under former subsection 73(5) in respect of an *inter vivos* transfer of shares of a small business corporation to a child. The maximum capital gain that could be deferred under all three provisions on pre-1988 transfers was $200,000 (pre-1988 taxable capital gain of $100,000) and the maximum deferral on any transaction to which a rollover applied was reduced by the amount of capital gain deferred on previous transfers to which these provisions applied.

As a consequence of these inter-generational share rollovers, the recipient would acquire shares with a potentially high fair market value and nominal adjusted cost base. The inherent gain in respect of these shares could present a liquidity problem if a recipient were deemed to dispose of those shares on death.

## ¶318

## Eligible Capital Property

An eligible capital property is an intangible capital property which has an indefinite legal life and which is associated with a business. It does not include shares, bonds and other such financial assets. Eligible capital properties include goodwill, and franchises and concessions with no fixed term. For dispositions after 1987, an amount equal to three-quarters of the cost of an eligible capital property is added to cumulative eligible capital (subsection 14(5) "cumulative eligible capital"). An amount equal to three-quarters of the proceeds of sale of an eligible capital property is deducted from cumulative eligible capital. If a deduction creates a negative balance of cumulative eligible capital, that negative balance is included in the taxpayer's business income (subsection 14(1)).

The income inclusion for the negative balance has two components. First, the portion of the negative balance representing recapture of previous deductions claimed pursuant to paragraph 20(1)(*b*) is included in income. Second, the remaining negative balance (reduced by any exempt gains balance of the taxpayer in respect of the business) is included in income as follows. For taxation years ending after October 17, 2000, two-thirds of the net amount would be included in income. For taxation years that end after February 27, 2000 and before October 18, 2000, eight-ninths of the net amount would be included in income, and for taxation years that ended before February 28, 2000, the entire net amount would be included in income. For fiscal periods that end after February 22, 1994, subsection 14(1.1) deems the net amount in respect of eligible capital property attributable to qualified farm property to be a taxable capital gain for purposes of the enhanced capital gains exemption. (See ¶808 for a discussion of the enhanced capital gains exemption in relation to qualified farm property.)

Subsection 14(1.01) provides an election for dispositions of eligible capital property in taxation years that end after February 27, 2000. A taxpayer may elect to report a capital gain on the disposition of eligible capital property (other than goodwill) of which the taxpayer can identify the cost.

Cumulative eligible capital can be amortized by the 7% declining balance method (paragraph 20(1)(*b*)). Normally, the full unamortized balance of cumulative eligible capital associated with a business can be deducted from income when the taxpayer ceases to carry on the business.

Subsection 70(5.1) provides that where a person dies owning eligible capital property in respect of a business, and someone other than a spouse or common-law partner or corporation to which subsection 24(2) applies acquires it, the deceased is deemed to have disposed of such property immediately before death for proceeds equal to four-thirds of the taxpayer's cumulative eligible capital in respect of the business. Three-quarters of the deemed proceeds would be deducted from the taxpayer's cumulative eligible capital, thereby reducing it to zero (Interpretation Bulletin IT-313R2).

The beneficiary is deemed to have acquired that property immediately after the death of the taxpayer at an amount equal to the deemed proceeds. If the beneficiary continues to carry on the business of the deceased to which

¶318

the eligible capital property relates, the beneficiary is deemed to have made an expenditure in respect of the eligible capital property equal to the aggregate of the taxpayer's cumulative eligible capital and the deductions under paragraph 20(1)(*b*) previously taken by the taxpayer in respect of the eligible capital property which have not been recaptured. The beneficiary is also deemed to have claimed paragraph 20(1)(*b*) deductions equal to the unrecaptured deductions. Accordingly, recapture of the deductions is not avoided in a transfer which is subject to subsection 70(5.1). The beneficiary may amortize three-quarters of that deemed cost of acquisition as cumulative eligible capital on a 7% declining-balance basis.

If the beneficiary does not continue to carry on the deceased's business, the eligible capital property is deemed to be an ordinary capital property. When the beneficiary later disposes of the property, a capital gain or loss will be determined using the deceased's deemed proceeds of disposition as the adjusted cost base of the property.

These provisions apply only when an eligible capital property is acquired as a consequence of the death of a taxpayer. If such property is not transferred upon the death of a taxpayer, the balance of the cumulative eligible capital is written off against income for the year of death since the taxpayer ceased carrying on business on death (subsection 24(1)).

If the deceased had an exempt gains balance as a result of making an election under subsection 110.6(19), the balance disappears on death.

If the deceased has no cumulative eligible capital in respect of a business, there are no deemed proceeds of disposition on death.

The provisions dealing with the transfer of eligible capital properties on death assume that the deceased has only one eligible capital property per business. However, the taxpayer may have more than one such property in any one business. For example, the taxpayer could have owned two or more open-ended franchises in one business. If the provisions are strictly followed, the deceased is deemed to have disposed of each property for proceeds equal to four-thirds the cumulative eligible capital accumulated through the acquisition of all such properties, and an income inclusion in respect of eligible capital expenditures may result. The beneficiary or beneficiaries would write off three-quarters of those increased proceeds. It is open to question whether the Canada Revenue Agency would strictly enforce these provisions or acknowledge that each franchise was a separate business.

Where the deceased's business passes to a spouse or common-law partner, the rollover is effected by subsection 24(2) and not subsection 70(5.1). This rollover applies only where the spouse or common-law partner

¶318

acquires all eligible capital property, other than such property having no value. The effect of the two provisions is identical.

The rules in ITAR 21, which phase in the taxability of the proceeds of disposition of an eligible capital property, do not apply to a deemed disposition on death. In addition, there is no intimation that the beneficiary is deemed to have carried on the business on that date. Instead, the beneficiary always deducts from cumulative eligible capital the full proceeds of disposition of any eligible capital property inherited from the deceased.

Eligible capital property is not a right or thing for the purposes of subsection 70(2) (subsection 70(3.1)).

## ¶320

## Canadian and Foreign Resource Properties

A Canadian resource property is defined in subsection 66(15) of the Act. It includes any property acquired after 1971 that is:

(1) any right, licence or privilege to explore for, drill for, or take petroleum, natural gas or other related hydrocarbons in Canada;

(2) any right, licence or privilege to prospect, explore, drill or mine for minerals in a mineral resource in Canada;

(3) any right, licence or privilege to store underground petroleum, natural gas or related hydrocarbons in Canada;

(4) any oil or gas well situated in Canada or any real property in Canada the principal value of which depends on its petroleum or natural gas content (but not including any depreciable property);

(5) any rental or royalty computed by reference to the amount or value of production from an oil or gas well, a mineral resource or a natural accumulation of petroleum or natural gas in Canada;[19]

(6) any real property situated in Canada, the principal value of which depends upon its mineral resource content (but not including any depreciable property); or

---

[19] The February 27, 2004 draft legislation proposes to amend the definition of Canadian resource property for property acquired after December 20, 2002 such that a rental or royalty will only qualify if the person paying the rent or royalty has an interest in the property and 90% or more of the rent or royalty is payable out of or from the proceeds of production from the well or accumulation.

(7) any right to or interest in any property (other than a right by virtue of being a beneficiary of a trust or a member of a partnership) described in (1) to (6) above.

Canadian resource properties include oil, gas and mineral rights in Canada, including royalty interests therein. Foreign resource properties correspond to Canadian resource properties except that the properties in question must be located outside Canada (subsection 66(15)).

Immediately before death, the deceased is deemed to have disposed of all Canadian and foreign resource properties for their fair market value at that time (paragraph 70(5.2)(*a*)). There is an exception if the properties are left to a surviving spouse or common-law partner or to a trust for the benefit of a spouse or common-law partner, as discussed in Chapter 5.

Accordingly, the income of the deceased for the year of death includes the amount that would have been included in computing income had the taxpayer disposed of the properties at their fair market value immediately before death.

Canadian and foreign resource properties are not rights or things (subsection 70(3.1)). Accordingly, their value cannot be reported in a separate return pursuant to subsection 70(2). It is possible to pay the tax in respect of their deemed disposition by equal consecutive annual instalments, plus interest at the prescribed rate over a period of up to ten years (subsection 159(5)). Acceptable security arrangements must be made with the Minister in order to pay by instalment.

The following outlines very briefly the application of the resource provisions on the purchase or sale (or deemed sale) of resource properties. The various costs incurred are collected in the following pools for purposes of determining how quickly those costs can be written off against income.

❑ CEE — Canadian Exploration Expenses generally include the cost of finding oil or gas or minerals in Canada and these costs can be written off at the rate of 100% against any type of income (subsection 66.1(3)).

❑ CDE — Canadian Development Expenses generally include the cost of further developing a known oil or gas or mineral body in Canada. These costs include the cost of mining rights in Canada plus the cost of oil and gas rights incurred before December 12, 1979. These costs can be written off at a rate of 30% per annum against any type of income (subsection 66.2(2)).

❑ COGPE — Canadian Oil and Gas Property Expenses generally include the cost of oil and gas rights in Canada if purchased after

December 11, 1979. These costs can be written off at the rate of 10% per annum against any type of income (subsection 66.4(2)).

When an individual dies:

(a) The deceased is deemed to dispose of all foreign resource properties and Canadian resource properties immediately before death and to have received proceeds of disposition equal to their fair market value at that time (paragraph 70(5.2)(a)).

(b) Any person who as a consequence of the deceased's death acquires a foreign resource property or Canadian resource property that is subject to paragraph 70(5.2)(a) is deemed to have acquired the property at a cost equal to the fair market value immediately before death (paragraph 70(5.2)(a.1)).

(c) The proceeds of disposition of a foreign resource property are included in income as calculated in subsection 59(1).

(d) The deemed proceeds of disposition of a Canadian oil and gas property are deducted from the deceased's COGPE pool. Any negative balance in that pool is deducted from the deceased's CCDE pool (subsection 66.4(1)).

(e) The deemed proceeds of disposition of Canadian mining properties are deducted from the deceased's CCDE pool. Any negative balance in that pool is included in income (subsection 66.2(1)).

(f) If the deemed disposition of a resource property on death has directly or indirectly caused an inclusion in the deceased's income, the deceased could fully offset this income inclusion with any balance in the CEE pool. Up to 25% of the income inclusion from the deemed disposition of resource properties can be offset with any earned depletion pool of the deceased. Up to 25% of such income inclusion can be offset by any supplementary depletion of pool the deceased. Any unclaimed balance in the deceased's Frontier Exploration Allowance pool or CEE pool can be claimed fully against any type of income.

Any unclaimed balances after the year of death in CEE, CCDE, COGPE, Earned Depletion, Supplementary Depletion, or Frontier Exploration Allowance is lost to the deceased, the estate and the beneficiaries.

¶320

## ¶322

## Land Inventory

Immediately before death, the deceased is deemed to have disposed of any land which is part of an inventory of a business for proceeds equal to its fair market value at the time of death (paragraph 70(5.2)(c)). There is an exception for land transferred to the deceased's spouse, common-law partner or to a trust for the benefit of a spouse or common-law partner as discussed in Chapter 5.

Land inventory includes properties held for resale or on speculation, as opposed to land held for the production of rental income or for use as a business location. Land includes fixtures on land, such as buildings and leasehold interests in land.

The entire gain realized on the deemed disposition is included in income as business income. If the land was held as part of a business proprietorship whose fiscal year-end closed in the deceased's taxation year but prior to death, the income from the deemed disposition could be reported on a separate tax return. Business income from the end of that fiscal year to the date of death would be reported on that separate return (subsection 150(4)). This option would only be available if the deceased had filed an election to use an off-calendar fiscal year end. (See ¶220.)

Land included in inventory of a business is not a right or thing (subsection 70(3.1), Interpretation Bulletin IT-212R3, paragraph 17). Accordingly, income realized on a deemed disposition cannot be reported on a separate tax return for rights or things. Cash-basis inventory which is not land is a right or thing for the purposes of subsection 70(2) (Interpretation Bulletin IT-212R3, paragraphs 2 and 6).

Where the will is not specific, the executors might distribute the land *in specie* to the beneficiary, rather than dispose of it during the estate administration period. By reason of subsection 23(1), a disposal by the estate during the administration period would be considered to have been made in the course of carrying on the taxpayer's business. As a result, the gain accruing from the death of the deceased until the sale of the property would be taxed as business income rather than as a capital gain (assuming it would otherwise be held by the beneficiary as capital property). This difference could be significant.

## ¶324

## Principal Residence

Like other capital properties, the deceased's principal residence is deemed to be disposed of immediately before death at its fair market value. However, the usual exemption from tax for gains on disposition of principal residences applies.

Section 54 of the Act provides that, after 1981, a family unit may treat only one residence as its principal residence for a taxation year. Subsection 40(6) of the Act provides transitional rules where more than one principal residence was owned by members of a family unit at the end of 1981. This subsection in effect provides that the capital gain realized after 1981 on the disposal of a principal residence will be split into a pre-1982 and post-1981 part. Thus, if the residence of a taxpayer qualified as a principal residence at the end of 1981 but did not qualify after that date, only the portion of the gain that accrued before 1982 may qualify for the principal residence exemption. This situation may occur, for example, where, prior to 1982, the taxpayer and the taxpayer's spouse or common-law partner each owned a residence, both of which qualified as a principal residence in a taxation year. After 1981, only one such home may qualify as a principal residence in a taxation year. (See Interpretation Bulletin IT-120R6.)

# 4

# Executors, Administrators and Trusts

---

## ¶400

### General

The estate of a deceased person is a trust for both legal and tax purposes and is often referred to as a testementary trust as discussed below. Subject to specific exceptions as provided in the Act, including the applicable rates of tax (subsection 104(1), 117(2) and 122(1)), the estate is governed by the same provisions as an *inter vivos* trust which is a trust created during the lifetime of an individual and not as a consequence of death. The affairs of the estate are directed by the legal representative of the deceased as defined in subsection 248(1). If the deceased died having prepared a will, the legal representative would generally be the executor or executors appointed in the will. If the deceased did not have a will and died intestate, the deceased's legal representative would be the administrator or administrators appointed by and subject to the supervision of the courts for the purpose of managing and distributing the deceased's property in accordance with the relevant provincial laws. In either case, the appointee in the capacity of safeguarding and administering the property of the estate would be considered a trustee, or the person in whom legal ownership of the assets of the estate vests. The trustee holds and controls the property of the estate on behalf of those persons having a beneficial interest in the estate's assets (the beneficiaries of the estate) until the obligations of the deceased are satisfied and the property of the estate is finally distributed.

## ¶401

## Testamentary Trust

A testamentary trust is defined in subsection 108(1) as a trust or estate that arose on and as a consequence of the death of an individual, including a trust created under the terms of an individual's will or by reason of a court order relating to an estate for the relief or support of dependants as provided in subsection 248(9.1). However, a testamentary trust does not include:

(a) a trust created by a person other than the individual;

(b) a trust created after November 13, 1981, if before the end of the taxation year property has been contributed to the trust other than by an individual on or after death and as a consequence of death;

(c) a trust created before November 13, 1981 if after June 28, 1982 property has been contributed to the trust, other than by an individual on or after death and as a consequence of death, or where more than half of the fair market value of the property owned by the trust has been contributed to the trust other than by an individual as a consequence of death;

(d) by reason of a proposed addition to the definition, a trust which after December 20, 2002 and before the end of the taxation year incurs a debt or other obligation to pay an amount to, or guaranteed by, a beneficiary or a person with whom the beneficiary does not deal at arm's length. However, this would not include an amount payable to the beneficiary as part of their entitlement under the trust, an amount payable by reason of services rendered to the trust, or an amount payable to the beneficiary by reason of a payment made by the beneficiary on behalf of the trust, for example, funeral expenses paid by the beneficiary on behalf of the deceased. In the latter case, the trust must reimburse the beneficiary for such amounts within a year of the beneficiary making such payment (or such longer period as the Minister considers reasonable) and it must be reasonable to conclude that the person would have been willing to make such payment had they been dealing with the trust at arm's length.

These restrictions are an anti-avoidance provision to deter the ability to take advantage of the low rates of tax of a testamentary trust on fund loaned or otherwise advanced to an estate or trust.

# ¶402

## Residence of an Estate[20]

An estate is taxable in Canada if it is a resident of Canada for tax purposes, carries on business in Canada, or disposes of taxable Canadian property as defined in subsection 248(1). The Act provides that reference to a trust or estate shall be read as a reference to the trustee or the executor, administrator, heir or other legal representative having ownership or control of the trust property (subsection 104(1)). A trust is generally deemed not to include an arrangement where the trust can reasonably be considered to act as agent for all of the beneficiaries under the trust with respect to dealing with trust property (subsection 104(1)). The residence of a trust is a question of fact and is determined on the basis of the relevant circumstances in each case. In the absence of any specific provisions in the Act pertaining to the residence of a trust, it is generally accepted that an estate or trust is resident where the trustee, or the majority of trustees who manage or control the assets of the trust, resides. In the case of an estate, one would look to the residence of the executor(s) or administrator(s) of that estate.

The Canada Revenue Agency, in Interpretation Bulletin IT-447 at paragraph 2, has indicated that the following would be relevant in determining which trustee in fact has control or management of the trust:

- ability to control changes in the trust's investment portfolio,
- responsibility for management of business or property owned by the trust,
- responsibility for banking and financing arrangements for the trust,
- control over any other trust assets,
- ultimate responsibility for preparation of trust accounts and reporting to beneficiaries of the trust, and
- power to contract and deal with trust advisors.

The residence of the trustee who exercises the preponderance of management and control will determine the residence of the trust. If there are two or more trustees who are relatively equal in exercising management and control, and trustees exercising in excess of 50% of management and control reside in one jurisdiction, their residence will determine the residence of the trust.

---

[20] See Green, R. A., "The Residence of Trusts for Income Tax Purposes", (1973) 21 *Canadian Tax Journal* 217; Interpretation Bulletin IT-447.

If the residence of the trust cannot be determined based on the foregoing, the Canada Revenue Agency will look to other factors, including the location where the legal rights in respect of the trust assets are enforceable and the location of the assets of the trust. The residence of the beneficiary of an estate would be relevant only if the beneficiary had substantial control over and power to manage trust assets.

A non-resident testamentary trust arising as a consequence of the death of an individual after 1975 may also be deemed to be a resident of Canada in respect of its Canadian source and foreign accrual property income where a beneficiary of the trust is a Canadian resident at any time in the taxation year of the trust, and the trust falls within the other rules governing foreign accrual property income (clause 94(1)(b)(i)(D))[21]. In order for a trust to be deemed a Canadian resident, the distribution of the income or capital of the trust must depend upon the exercise by or failure to exercise a discretionary power, and the trust must have acquired property from a person who was:

- a beneficiary, a person related to the beneficiary, or an aunt, uncle, niece or nephew of a beneficiary;

- resident in Canada at any time in the 18-month period prior to death; and

- resident in Canada for an aggregate period or periods totalling more than 60 months prior to the end of the year in question.

# ¶404

## Filing Tax Returns for a Trust

When a taxpayer dies, the legal representative assumes responsibility for the supervision, management and distribution of the assets and liabilities held or incurred by the taxpayer during the taxpayer's lifetime. For income tax purposes, the death of a taxpayer not only terminates the deceased's final taxation year, but also marks the opening of the first taxation year of the estate.

The duty of the legal representative to file any outstanding tax returns on behalf of the deceased, including the tax return for the abbreviated terminal period, is discussed in Chapter 2, ¶202. In addition, the legal representative must file a T3 Trust Information and Income Tax Return for income, including capital gains, of the estate. This return must be filed annually within 90 days of the end of each taxation year of the estate. Any

---

[21] The federal government has proposed extensive changes to the taxation of non-resident trusts. At the date of writing, the proposed amendments to section 94 remain in draft form and have not been enacted.

tax owing must be paid at that time (regulations 204(1) and (2), Information Circular 78-14R3, Form T3). If the estate is wound up after the end of its usual taxation year, a return must be filed for the usual taxation year within the 90-day limit, as well as for the stub period within 90 days after the final distribution on winding up. If the estate is wound up within the first taxation year after death, the personal representative must file a T3 return within the prescribed time for the period of administration. According to the administrative policy of the Canada Revenue Agency, a return for the estate does not have to be filed where the trust receives income that is allocated to one or more beneficiaries and the total income, including capital gains and losses, received by the legal representative does not exceed $500, the income taxable to any single beneficiary does not exceed $100, none of the income is taxable to the estate and none of the income is allocated to a non-resident.

The purpose of the return is to report income of the trust and to provide information with respect to any distributions to beneficiaries. Unless a copy of the will was filed with the terminal period return, it should be included with the first T3 return for the estate. In addition, beneficiaries of the estate to whom income is paid or payable must be provided T3 Supplementary forms indicating the quantum and source of income which they are required to report on their personal returns. Income from an estate or trust which is paid or payable to a non-resident beneficiary is subject to 25% non-resident withholding tax, unless reduced by treaty (paragraph 212(1)(c)). Withholding tax also applies to a distribution of capital where the distribution may be reasonably considered to relate to a capital dividend received by the trust (subparagraph 212(1)(c)(ii)). Form NR4 Supplementary must be issued to the non-resident beneficiary from whom tax is withheld. Amounts paid to a non-resident do not retain their nature, but are considered to be paid or credited as income from a trust regardless of the source of that income to the estate or trust (subsection 212(11)).

No withholding tax is payable on amounts paid out of an estate or trust where the source of the amounts to the estate or trust is:

- dividends or interest received by the estate from a non-resident-owned investment corporation (as defined in paragraph 133(8)(d) of the Act),

- copyright royalties related to literary, dramatic, musical or artistic works, but excluding film and television royalties, or

- interest allocated to a non-resident beneficiary that is received by a mutual fund trust maintained primarily for the benefit of non-resident beneficiaries,

¶404

if tax would not otherwise have been payable had the amounts been paid by the non-resident-owned investment corporation, person paying the copyright royalties or mutual fund trust to the non-resident rather than to the trustee (subsection 212(9), Interpretation Bulletin IT-465R).

If the T3 trust return is not filed by the prescribed due date, a penalty of between 5% and 17% of unpaid tax (5%, plus 1% for each complete month not exceeding 12 that the return is late), may be levied against the estate (subsections 162(1)). A trustee who fails to file a return as required by subsection 150(3) is liable to a penalty of $10 per day of default but not exceeding $50 (subsection 162(3)). Interest at the rate prescribed by the Canada Revenue Agency is also charged on outstanding tax (subsection 161(1)) and compounded daily (subsection 248(11)).

Once the returns for the estate have been filed and the tax liability has been satisfied, the Canada Revenue Agency will issue a clearance certificate (as discussed in Chapter 2 (¶204)) allowing the legal representative to wind up the estate and distribute its assets without the personal representative incurring any personal liability for unpaid tax (subsections 159(2) and (3)). However, even though clearance certificates have been issued to an executor or trustee, the estate may still be liable for tax (*Boger Estate v. The Queen*, 93 DTC 5276 (F.C.A.)). To the extent that the executors or trustees distribute any property of the estate without first obtaining the relevant clearance certificate, they may be held personally liable for any tax owing by either the deceased or the estate (subsection 159(3)). Accordingly, the personal representative should require personal indemnities from the beneficiaries of the estate prior to making distributions to the beneficiaries. The personal representative should also consider holding back part of the final distributions for a reasonable period of time as a contingency fund.

## ¶406

## Fiscal Period of the Estate

A trust is required by the Act to report its income on a calendar year basis (subsection 104(2), paragraph 249(1)(*b*)). However, the legal representative of a testamentary trust, as defined in subsection 108(1), may choose a fiscal period for reporting the estate's income subject to the limitation that a fiscal period may not exceed 12 months (paragraph 104(23)(*a*)). It is also acceptable for the opening and closing fiscal periods of the estate to be less than 12 months. In some cases the legal representative may choose to report estate income on a calendar year basis. However, to facilitate maximum deferral of tax and as a matter of convenience it is more common for the fiscal year to be based on the 12-month period commencing on the date of death. All subsequent fiscal years would follow this same pattern and each would close on the anniversary of the taxpayer's death. For reasons of accounting convenience or timing of income, a legal representative might want to select some other 12-month fiscal period. For example, the estate may be entitled to a lump-sum income receipt at a certain time during the first year of the estate. In order to obtain maximum tax deferral, the legal representative might choose a year end immediately before the income receipt. Since the tax would not be payable until 90 days after the end of the estate's fiscal year, the payment of tax on that amount could be deferred for up to 15 months. However, once the fiscal year of the estate is established, it cannot be changed without the concurrence of the Minister (paragraph 104(23)(a), Interpretation Bulletin IT-179R). If the sole reason for the change is to save or defer taxes, consent will not be granted.

## ¶408

## Income Recognition by Beneficiaries

A beneficiary must include in income any amount which is paid or payable to the beneficiary during the year from the estate, together with the value of all benefits other than capital distributions and amounts paid by the trust for the upkeep of property maintained for a beneficiary as are reasonable in the circumstances (subsection 104(13), section 105). An amount is deemed to be payable by the estate if it is actually paid to the beneficiary or if the beneficiary is entitled to enforce payment of the amount (subsection 104(24)). A beneficiary is taxable in respect of income from or benefits under a trust in the beneficiary's taxation year in which the trust's year ended (paragraph 104(23)(c)). For example, if a trust having a March 31 fiscal year end pays income earned by the trust to a beneficiary in October 2005, that income would not be required to be reported by the beneficiary until the 2006 taxation year (which would generally be filed by April 30, 2007) since the beneficiary is not considered to have earned that income until the March 31, 2006 year end of the trust. If the estate reported income on a calendar year basis, the beneficiary would report income in the calendar year when it became payable from the estate. Therefore, if the estate has a non-calendar year end, the beneficiary may have the opportunity to defer tax liability for one year.

This could also work to the detriment of the beneficiary if insufficient consideration were given to the date of winding-up the estate. For example, if an estate with a March 31 year end were wound up in November, the estate would have two fiscal year ends in the same calendar year, and the beneficiary would be required to report in the same calendar year the income from both the first completed period and the final stub period of the estate. This could be avoided if the estate were wound up after the end of the particular calendar year, for example, January instead of November.

As noted above, if the legal representative anticipates the receipt of a lump-sum income amount in addition to the ordinary income receipts of the estate, a fiscal period closing immediately prior to the lump-sum income receipt could be chosen in order to defer tax liability on that amount until the second fiscal period of the estate. If, during that second period, the income is distributed to the beneficiaries of the estate, liability for tax on that income will shift from the estate to the beneficiaries. Assuming that the fiscal year of the estate closes after the end of the calendar year, tax on the lump-sum amount could be deferred even further. For example, if the taxpayer died on September 1, 2005 and a large income amount were to be received February 15, 2006, the trustee might select a fiscal period which would end on January 31. The initial stub period for the estate would be September 1, 2005 to January 31, 2006 and the large receipt would be included in the income of the estate for the period ending January 31, 2007. If such income is paid or payable to the beneficiaries during the second fiscal period, they would be required to report the amount in their personal income tax return for the calendar year ending December 31, 2007, which would generally be filed April 30, 2008.

## ¶410

## Computation of Income of an Estate

The Act taxes the income of an estate or testamentary trust in the same manner as for an individual, and the marginal rates applicable to an individual are applied to the income earned by the estate (subsections 104(1) and 117(2)). An estate is not entitled to personal credits under section 118 (subsection 122(1.1)) although it could claim a tax credit for specific charitable donations made by the estate (section 118.1). The general rule is that gifts made by will are treated as having been made in the year of death (subsection 118.1(5)). If the will provides for ongoing periodic gifts to a charity, the charity is treated as an income beneficiary of the estate. The estate could also deduct fees charged by executors and trustees for their work in administering and managing investments of the estate, to the extent that those fees apply to earning the income of the estate, provided the executor's principal business includes such activity (paragraph 20(1)(*bb*) and Interpretation Bulletin IT-238R2, paragraph 4), or executors' fees for managing rental property or carrying on a business for the trust.[22] Since trustee fees are taxable to the recipient, the estate is required to issue a T4 Supplementary to the executor or trustee for those amounts and withhold the requisite tax and CPP.

---

[22] See *Bardsley Trust v. M.N.R*, 82 DTC 1659 (T.R.B.).

If the estate incurs interest expense for the purpose of investing in income- producing property (for example, bonds, shares or rental property), interest paid in respect of borrowed funds will be deductible from the income of the estate (paragraph 20(1)(*c*)). (The trustees should ensure that they have the requisite power under the will authorizing them to borrow on behalf of the estate.) In addition, the estate may deduct fees paid for the management of the investments of the estate including investment counsel fees (paragraph 20(1)(*bb*)), for safety deposit box rental or for accounting fees paid for recording income. Only those expenses which have been incurred for the purposes of earning income of the estate are deductible. Amounts which relate to capital assets of the estate or to the personal expenses of the beneficiaries or trustees are not properly deductible to the estate. In the case of capital property held by the estate, expenses relating to those properties (for example, brokerage fees on the sale of securities) might be capitalized as either an addition to the cost base of property which is acquired, as a deduction from the proceeds of disposition on the sale of the property, or treated as a cost of disposition of the property.

The Act provides that a trust is taxed as an individual (subsection 104(1)). However, the Canada Revenue Agency has taken the position that, if pursuant to a separation agreement or domestic contract, the estate were required to continue to pay alimony or maintenance to a former spouse or common-law partner, such amount would not be deductible to the estate in that an estate is not a natural person and has neither a spouse nor a child. Consequently, the conditions in paragraphs 56(1)(*b*) and (*c*) cannot be satisfied.

Income of an estate or trust which is paid or payable to its beneficiaries in the taxation year of the estate or trust in accordance with the provisions of the will, or under the provisions of the applicable provincial law where the deceased died intestate, may be deducted from the income of the estate (subsections 104(6), (13) and (24)). However, no deduction is allowed for such payments to non-resident beneficiaries unless the trust is resident in Canada throughout the particular year (subsection 104(7)).[23]

In certain circumstances trust income will be considered payable in a year to a beneficiary even though it is subject to some restriction (subsection 104(18)). In particular, income will be considered payable where:

---

[23] The federal government has proposed extensive changes to the taxation of non-resident trusts and the addition of proposed subsection 104(7.01) for trusts — which are deemed to be resident in Canada. If enacted, the ability of a trust to deduct amounts paid or payable to its beneficiaries would be subject to the provisions of subsection 104(7.01). As at the date of writing, the proposed amendments have not been enacted.

- the beneficiary has not attained the age of 21 years before the end of the year;

- the beneficiary's right to the income is vested by the end of the year;

- the right to trust income did not become vested because of the exercise or non-exercise of a discretionary power; and

- the right to income is not subject to any future condition, other than a condition that the individual survive to an age not exceeding 40 years.

Consequently, since an amount which satisfied these conditions would be considered payable to a beneficiary, it would be deductible to the estate pursuant to subsections 104(6) and (13). This provision overrides subsection 104(24), which would otherwise provide that income not paid out in a taxation year is not considered to be payable to a beneficiary.

In some circumstances, the legal representative may be required to hold and maintain property of the estate for the use of a life tenant or beneficiary. Income of the estate which is used to maintain the property or applied towards the property taxes is considered to be income of the beneficiary to the extent that it is considered reasonable in the circumstances (subsection 105(2)). Such amounts may be deducted in computing the income of the estate (paragraph 104(6)(*b*)). The value of any other benefits, other than capital distributions, to the taxpayer during the year from or under the trust are included in the beneficiary's income for that year, but no corresponding deduction is allowed to the estate (subsections 105(1), 104(6)).

## ¶411

## The 21-Year Revaluation Rule

This rule is often referred to as the "21-year deemed disposition rule" for trusts and is found in subsections 104(4) and (5). Under subsection 104(4), non-depreciable capital property, resource property and land inventory are deemed disposed of and reacquired immediately thereafter by the trust at fair market value. Under subsection 104(5), depreciable property is deemed disposed of and reacquired immediately thereafter by the trust at its fair market value.

The date of the deemed disposition is as follows:

(a) for a qualifying trust for the benefit of a spouse or common-law partner, at the time of the spouse's death and every 21 years thereafter, and

(b) for all other trusts (except alter ego and joint partner trusts created after 1999), every 21 years beginning the later of January 1, 1972 and the date the trust was created (paragraphs 104(4)(*b*) and (*c*)).

This will result in the trust realizing accrued gains or losses and recaptured depreciation on those specified dates.

Planning in anticipation of a deemed disposition is important because many trusts have non-liquid assets and will realize accrued gains and recapture without having funds to pay the tax liability which may arise. In anticipation of death, one may plan by acquiring insurance to fund any tax liability arising. However, for an estate which may be subject to this rule, this is not possible.

Planning might include terminating the trust prior to the deemed disposition date under subsection 107(2) by distributing the assets of the trust to the beneficiaries on a tax-deferred basis. However, consideration must be given to the terms of the trust (in the testator's will), the interests of the beneficiaries, the residency of the beneficiaries, the nature of the assets and any special circumstances. Without the power to terminate the trust prior to its termination date (otherwise provided for in the creating instrument), the exercise of a broad discretionary power of encroachment should be considered.

In some circumstances, an application to the court for an order varying the terms of the trust may be undertaken.

Under subsection 107(2), it must be determined if this provision is applicable to the particular situation. Also, attention must be paid to any income interests which may be disposed of on a termination of the trust and the tax consequences which flow in that event. It is suggested the testator's will should provide for the beneficiaries' interests to be satisfied by a distribution of capital.

In 1991, amendments were made to the Act permitting an extension of the 21-year rule and the postponement of capital gains taxation on trust property until the death of the last "exempt beneficiary" as defined in the Act. Later amendments resulted in the elimination of this election. If a trust elected to postpone tax on deemed capital gains, it was subject to a deemed realization of the trust assets at fair market value as at January 1, 1999, unless the trust property was distributed to beneficiaries before that date.

¶411

## ¶412

## Interest on Inheritance Taxes

An estate or a beneficiary of an estate may deduct, from income interest accruing with respect to succession duties, inheritance taxes or estate taxes, including foreign death duties (paragraph 60(*d*)). Entitlement to the deduction depends on who is liable for the payment of tax. Although the federal *Estate Tax Act* was repealed as to deaths occurring after 1971, and succession duty legislation has been repealed in every Canadian province, it is possible that the liability for estate taxes and other death duties may have been spread over several years so that some estates may still owe interest on outstanding taxes. Where the estate claims this interest deduction and has insufficient income in a taxation year against which to offset all of the accruing interest, the result is a non-capital loss which may be carried back against estate income for three years and carried forward for seven years (paragraph 111(1)(*a*)). Losses of an estate or trust cannot be allocated to the beneficiaries of the estate.

If the beneficiary claims the deduction for the interest, the deduction may be claimed against income from the estate, against other personal income or against a combination of the two (Interpretation Bulletin IT-203 (archived)). If the deduction is claimed against other personal income, the amount of deductible interest is calculated according to the amount of interest accrued in the calendar year and the amount of death duties for which the beneficiary is liable.

If money is borrowed to pay death taxes, interest paid on the borrowed funds would not generally be deductible since it would not be paid for the purpose of earning or producing income.

Where an estate or beneficiary is required to include in income amounts derived from superannuation or pension plans, death benefits, registered retirement savings plans, deferred profit sharing plans or income-averaging annuity contracts which were held by the deceased, the estate or beneficiary is entitled to a deduction to the extent of succession duties or estate taxes relating to those amounts (paragraphs 60(*m*), (*m*.1)).

## ¶414

## Dispositions of Property by a Legal Representative

In the absence of a rollover to a spouse or common-law partner or to a qualifying trust for the benefit of such person, the estate of the deceased taxpayer is deemed to have acquired both the depreciable and non-depreciable capital property of a deceased taxpayer at its fair market value immediately prior to the taxpayer's death (subsection 70(5)). If the estate sells that property, it could realize either a capital gain or loss in the case of non-depreciable capital property, or recapture, capital gain or a terminal loss in the case of depreciable property.

If the disposition takes place in the first taxation year of the estate and as a result the estate realizes a capital or terminal loss, the legal representative of the deceased may elect to have those losses treated as capital losses or terminal losses of the deceased for the terminal period (subsection 164(6)).

In circumstances where a disposition is considered to be made to an affiliated person, the capital loss which might otherwise arise will be denied (subsection 40(3.6)). By reason of the expanded definition of affiliated persons in amendments to section 251.1, an estate would be considered to be affiliated with a beneficiary who was considered to have a majority interest in the income or capital of the estate. Similarily, spouses are considered to be affiliated. However, subsection 40(3.61) would not deny the application of losses pursuant to subsection 164(6) in such circumstances.

When the legal representative makes the election, an amended income tax return for the terminal period must be filed, and the capital losses or terminal losses realized by the estate in its first taxation year reported as losses for the terminal period. The effect of the election is to adjust any capital gains exemption claimed pursuant to section 110.6 for the year of death. That is, the exemption may only be claimed in respect of taxable capital gains net of allowable capital losses and allowable business investment losses for the year, and net capital losses of other years. Where an election is made under subsection 164(6), any capital gains exemption claimed for the year of death may be reduced or completely denied.

The amended return for the year of death must be filed on or before the later of:

(a) the last day for filing a regular or elective return for the year of death, and

(b) the date when the return for the first taxation year of the estate is due.

The election under subsection 164(6) must be filed on or before the later of those two dates (regulation 1000(2)).

The election must include the following:

- a letter indicating that part of the excess capital losses or terminal losses of the estate in respect of which the election is made;

- a schedule of capital losses and gains, if applicable;

¶414

- a schedule of undepreciated capital costs, if applicable; and

- a statement of the non-capital loss and farm loss of the estate for its first taxation year, calculated as if the election had not been made.

Where a tax refund arises as a consequence of making the election, that amount is either paid to the estate or applied against taxes owing for the first year of the estate. An amount subject to the election may be deducted only against income of the terminal period and may not be deducted for any year preceding the year of death (paragraph 164(6)(f)).

Subsection 164(6) would not apply to a qualifying spouse trust or common-law partner trust where losses on dispositions of capital assets arise within the first year after the death of the surviving spouse or common-law partner beneficiary, unless the surviving beneficiary were to die within one year of the first death. Any capital losses arising in the spouse trust or common-law partner trust after the survivor's death could, however, be carried back for three years to offset any capital gains realized by the spouse or common-law partner trust. In particular, on the death of the surviving spouse or common-law partner, the trust would be deemed to have disposed of all of its capital property at its fair market value at that time. By reason of the deemed disposition, the trust may realize a capital gain, depending on the adjusted cost base to the spouse trust or common-law partner trust of its property. Any losses realized by the trust in the three taxation years following the death of the surviving spouse or common-law partner could be carried back to offset capital gains on the deemed disposition. In order to take advantage of this ability to offset, the will or trust should provide sufficient flexibility to allow the estate or trust to continue for at least three years after the death of the surviving spouse or common-law partner.

# ¶416

## Taxation of Distributions and Allocations to a Beneficiary

Distributions and allocations of the capital and income of an estate to its beneficiaries are made either in accordance with the provisions of the will or other testamentary instrument (where the individual died testate) or in accordance with the applicable federal and provincial laws (where the individual died intestate).

Income of the estate which is paid or payable to a beneficiary is taxed in the hands of that beneficiary at the beneficiary's personal marginal rates (subsection 104(13)). Similarly, the value of all benefits, except for distributions of capital, to a taxpayer from or under a trust are included in the income of the taxpayer, as are amounts paid out of the income of a trust for the upkeep, maintenance or taxes in respect of property held by the trust or estate for the use of the beneficiary (subsections 105(1), (2)). In order to prevent double taxation of such income, subject to the provisions of subsection 104(7) and proposed subsection 104(7.01) which relate to non-resident beneficiaries and non-resident trusts which are deemed to be resident in Canada, the estate is allowed to deduct from its income the amounts which are taxable to the beneficiary, other than amounts included in the beneficiary's income under subsection 105(1) as benefits to the taxpayer from or under the estate or trust (subsection 104(6)). As a result, in some cases the estate may never have income subject to tax.

In computing the income of a trust, less than the entire amount paid or payable to a beneficiary may be deducted (paragraph 104(6)(*b*)). This may be restricted for amounts payable to a non-resident beneficiary if the trust is not resident in Canada throughout the year (subsection 104(7)). The purpose of this provision is to enable a trust to use its losses from other years which cannot be allocated to beneficiaries in circumstances where this trust would otherwise be obliged to pay or allocate all of its income to its beneficiaries. It also allows testamentary trusts to choose to be taxed at the trust level rather than at the beneficiary level.

The amount of income designated by the trust not to have been paid is calculated under subsection 104(13.1). Capital gains may also be designated as retained by the trust and the amount deemed not to have been paid to the beneficiary is determined under subsection 104(13.2).

The amount designated under these provisions may still be paid to the beneficiaries but will not be included in computing the beneficiary's income from the trust. This may give rise to planning opportunities for testamentary trusts which are taxed at personal marginal rates. Where the beneficiaries of a testamentary trust are taxed at a higher rate than the trust, the trust could designate some or all of the trust income not to be paid to a beneficiary in the year and have this amount taxed in the trust at a lower rate.

A testator might maximize the opportunities this affords by establishing multiple testamentary trusts within the will for the benefit of different beneficiaries, subject to the possible application of subsection 104(2) which could deem the trusts to be taxed as one.

Amounts are considered to be paid or payable to a beneficiary when actually paid to the beneficiary or when the beneficiary is entitled to enforce the payment of an amount from the trust (subsection 104(24)). If the beneficiary is taxed on an amount which is payable but not yet received, there is no additional tax when the amount is actually received. In general, the time when an income beneficiary is entitled to enforce payment is easily ascertained since the terms of payment are usually directed by the will, whether on a periodic basis or at the discretion of the personal representative.

In the case of the residue of the estate, until that amount has been determined and the property of the estate has been distributed, the income of the estate during the period of administration is not payable to the residuary beneficiary.[24] For that reason, income earned on the residue of the estate is taxable in the estate in the absence of the actual payment of that income to the estate's beneficiaries.

Certain difficulties may arise when the estate realizes capital gains in respect of property held by the estate. It is not uncommon for a will to provide that the income of the estate is to be paid to some of the beneficiaries while the capital of the estate is held for the residuary beneficiaries, with specific restrictions on the time at which the corpus may be distributed. Capital gains in the estate represent an accretion to its capital property and are not paid or payable to the income beneficiaries unless otherwise specified in the will. Since capital gains may be required to be retained by the estate, it is the estate which is liable for tax on those gains subject to the following exception.

Where an amount paid or payable to a beneficiary includes a taxable capital gain which is traceable to a capital disposition by the estate (resident in Canada throughout the year), the amount of the capital gain may be designated by the legal representative as a capital gain in the hands of the beneficiary (subsection 104(21)). Accordingly, the gain is taxable to the beneficiary at the beneficiary's marginal rate and is not taxed as a gain to the estate provided the beneficiary is not a non-resident (subsection 104(6)). For this provision to apply, the amount designated must reasonably be considered to be part of the amount included in computing the income of the particular beneficiary by virtue of subsection 104(13) or (14). In making this determination, regard must be had to all the circumstances, including the terms and conditions of the will or testamentary trust. For example, if the will allows the legal representative to encroach on capital in favour of the beneficiary, this would support the reasonableness of the designation.

An estate or trust may claim the capital gains exemption under section 110.6 only if it is a qualifying spouse trust or common-law partner trust and only for the taxation year of death of the beneficiary spouse or common-law partner. However, capital gains allocated by the estate or trust to a beneficiary or beneficiaries would be included in the income of such beneficiary and could be reduced by the available capital gains exemption of the particular beneficiary, provided the beneficiary is otherwise eligible to claim the

---

[24] Sheppard, A. F., "Income Tax Planning in the Administration of Estates", *1976 Conference Reports*, Canadian Tax Foundation, pp. 762-95, at 793.

exemption. Subsection 104(21.2) provides that, where a capital gain has been designated by an estate or trust to a beneficiary, the estate or trust must also designate a proportionate amount of its eligible taxable capital gains to the beneficiary (paragraph 104(21.2)(*a*)). The eligible taxable capital gain is, generally speaking, the taxable capital gains of the estate or trust minus its allowable capital losses. If the trust has no such losses, the full amount of the taxable capital gain would be the eligible capital gain.

The lifetime capital gains exemption limit applies only to the individual beneficiaries and not to the estate or trust. As a result, the estate or trust is not limited in the amount of eligible taxable capital gains which it may designate to the beneficiaries. The extent to which the capital gains exemption may be claimed by the beneficiaries is limited only at the beneficiary level and is dependent upon the number of Canadian resident individual beneficiaries of the estate or trust. For example, if an estate realized a $2,000,000 eligible taxable capital gain which was allocated to four beneficiaries, each of whom had the full $500,000 capital gains exemption available, the full $2,000,000 gain could be sheltered.

See ¶258 for a discussion of the capital gains exemption.

At trust law, the proceeds of disposition of a capital property would generally form part of the capital of the estate and would be distributable to only the capital beneficiaries in accordance with the terms of the will or testamentary instrument, or, in the absence of a will, in accordance with the relevant statutory provisions. If the capital is not currently distributable, it may be necessary for the taxable capital gain to be subject to the preferred beneficiary election, if available. Otherwise the gain may be taxed only in the estate, depending on the terms of the will.

Net capital losses of an estate in excess of taxable capital gains may not be allocated to its beneficiaries but are subject to the usual carryover rules against capital gains realized by the estate. Accordingly, unless the estate realizes a capital gain to offset its losses, subject to the application of subsection 164(6) discussed above, the estate may have unusable losses (paragraph 104(6)(*b*), subsection 104(21), Interpretation Bulletin IT-381R3).

## ¶418 Preferred Beneficiary Election[25]

*Taxation Years Beginning Before 1996*

For taxation years beginning before 1996, the trustees of an estate were able to avoid paying tax on the accumulating income of an estate by making a preferred beneficiary election jointly with its preferred beneficiary or bene-

---

[25] For a more detailed discussion see Bernstein, Jack and Suzanne I. R. Hanson, "The Taxation of Accumulating Income of Trusts", (1980) 28 *Canadian Tax Journal* 715.

ficiaries, as defined. This is a statutory election which was made jointly by the estate and the beneficiary within 90 days of the estate's year end (subsection 104(14), regulation 2800(1)). Subject to a possible application made pursuant to the fairness rules, there was no provision which would allow a preferred beneficiary election to be late-filed. Accordingly, if an election were not filed within the 90-day period, the accumulating income of the estate or trust would be taxable in the estate or trust and could not otherwise be taxed to the beneficiary. The election designated the amount subject to the election and the computation of that amount, as well as details of the trust. This election made it possible for specified beneficiaries, including a spouse or former spouse and the children, grandchildren and great-grandchildren (as well as the spouses of such persons) of the deceased, to choose to include in their personal income an amount equal to their share of the accumulating income of the estate as defined in subsection 108(1). A preferred beneficiary had to be a Canadian resident. The amount elected was generally computed in relation to the preferred beneficiary's percentage share of the residue of the estate.

Where the trust was a qualifying spouse trust, the spouse beneficiary's share of the accumulating income of the trust was considered to be all of the accumulating income. If the trust was not a spouse trust but a non-discretionary trust, the preferred beneficiary's share of the accumulating income was generally considered to be the beneficiary's proportionate share. In the case of a discretionary trust, the preferred beneficiary's share was as set out in regulation 2800(3)(*e*) which provided that where the surviving spouse was entitled to share in the accumulating income, then all of the accumulating income was attributed to the spouse. Where there was no surviving spouse, the preferred beneficiary's share was determined by dividing the amount of the accumulating income of the trust by the number of preferred beneficiaries alive at the end of the year who may be entitled to share in that income (regulation 2800(3)(*f*)).

The estate was not liable for tax on those amounts deemed to be included in the income of a preferred beneficiary. In addition, no amount had to be paid or made payable from the estate.[26] When the amounts in respect of which the election was made were received by the beneficiary at some future time, there was no additional tax on that amount. As discussed in the section dealing with the fiscal period of an estate, amounts paid, payable or elected to be included in the income of the beneficiary, are reported by the beneficiary in the taxation year of the beneficiary in which the estate's taxation year ends.

---

[26] However, see *Sachs v. The Queen*, 80 DTC 6291 (F.C.A.) and the discussion in Jack Bernstein and Suzanne I. R. Hanson, *supra*, at page 745.

A preferred beneficiary election would be advantageous where, for example, the marginal rate of the beneficiary was lower than that of the estate. However, the preferred beneficiary election might not always produce the best results for the beneficiary involved. If, for example, the beneficiary's right to participate in the distribution of the estate was conditional upon certain events occurring, as in the case where the beneficiary must reach a certain age specified by the will, it would be possible that the beneficiary would pay tax on an amount which might never be received. It is also possible that the beneficiary's interest in the estate could be diluted at some future time if, for example, there was a provision in the will for the unborn issue of certain persons to be included within the class of beneficiaries. That is, the beneficiary may have a one-quarter interest in the estate at the time of paying tax pursuant to the election, but on actual distribution of the estate, the beneficiary's proportionate share may have been diluted to, say, one-twelfth. To the extent that the beneficiary made an out-of-pocket payment to satisfy the tax without otherwise receiving any amount from the estate, the preferred beneficiaries might be advised to seek independent legal advice.

*Taxation Years Beginning After 1995*

For taxation years of a trust or estate which commence after 1995, the preferred beneficiary election is restricted to apply only to those beneficiaries who are entitled to a tax credit for mental or physical impairment, or who would be entitled to that credit if no deductions were claimed for remuneration of an attendant or for care in a nursing home. In the case of a testamentary trust having a non-calendar year, this test will be satisfied if the beneficiary was entitled to the tax credit for the taxation year of the beneficiary that ends in the year of the trust.

In order to qualify, the beneficiary must be resident in Canada. In addition, the beneficiary must be the settlor of the trust, the spouse or common-law partner, or former spouse or common-law partner of the settlor, a child, grandchild or great-grandchild of the settlor, or the spouse or common-law partner of such person (subsection 108(1) "preferred beneficiary"). An adult beneficiary who is dependent on others by reason of mental or physical infirmity, and in respect of whom the handicapped dependant credit can be claimed, may also qualify as a preferred beneficiary. In this case, the adult beneficiary's income for the year that ends in the trust year cannot exceed a threshold amount, as indexed (i.e. the same income limit used for the purposes of the personal tax credit in subsection 118(1)). The income limit is computed excluding any amount designated under a preferred beneficiary election and allocated to the adult beneficiary.

¶418

The preferred beneficiary's share in the accumulating income of a trust is referred to as the allocable amount for the preferred beneficiary. The allocable amount for a preferred beneficiary is the accumulating income of the trust for the year, provided the beneficiary has a right of any type to any portion of that income. The right to income cannot be entirely contingent on the death of another beneficiary who has a capital interest in the trust and does not have an income interest in the trust. Otherwise, the allocable amount is nil (subsection 104(15)).

For trust taxation years ending after February 22, 1994, the filing deadline for a preferred beneficiary election is extended and may be amended or revoked where the late, amended or revoked election is made solely because of a late or amended capital gains election, or the revocation of a capital gains election (subsections 104(14.01), (14.02)). As such, the extension coincides with the filing of the late or amended capital gains election or revocation. An election or amended election made pursuant to this provision is considered to have been made within the prescribed time set out in subsection 104(14), and a revoked election is considered never to have been made.

## ¶420
## The Estate or Trust as a Conduit

In the absence of specific flow-through or conduit provisions contained in the Act, sources of income paid or payable to a beneficiary would lose their original character in the estate and would be received by the beneficiary as ordinary income. The conduit principle applies to dividends from taxable Canadian corporations (subsection 104(19)), special tax-free and capital dividends that are designated by the trust (subsections 104(20)), foreign business and non-business income and foreign tax credits (subsection 104(22), 104(22.1), 104(22.2), 104(22.3) and 104(22.4)), taxable capital gains (subsections 104(21), (21.1), (21.2) and (21.3)), pension income (subsection 104(27)), deferred profit sharing plan benefits (subsection 104(27.1)), death benefits (subsection 104(28)) and resource income (subsection 104(29)). However, any allowable capital losses in excess of taxable capital gains realized by the estate cannot flow through to the beneficiaries. Any excess may be carried back three years and forward indefinitely, and applied against income of the trust (paragraph 111(1)(b), Interpretation Bulletin IT-381R3). The Act contemplates that the legal representative of the deceased must make a reasonable allocation of amounts eligible for flow-through from the trust and designate them in respect of the beneficiaries and the estate itself.

Subsection 104(19) ensures that dividends designated by the trust are treated as being received by the beneficiary on the share of the capital stock of the corporation on which the trust received the dividend.

# 5

# Spouses, Common-Law Partners and Qualifying Trusts*

## ¶500

### Capital Properties

Chapter 3 (¶300) reviewed those provisions of the Act dealing with the deemed disposition of capital property held at death. However, as noted in that chapter, the rules regarding the deemed realization of capital gains and recapture on death are modified where the capital property owned by the deceased passes to a spouse or a spouse trust. In that case, the Act provides for a rollover of the cost of the capital property from the deceased to the spouse or to a qualifying spouse trust with the result that tax on capital gains and recapture is deferred until the surviving spouse dies or otherwise disposes or is deemed to dispose of the property — for example, on becoming a non-resident of Canada.

---

* Effective in 1993, subsection 252(4) provided that words referring to a spouse of a taxpayer include the person of the opposite sex who cohabits at that time with the taxpayer in a conjugal relationship and

  • has cohabited with the taxpayer throughout a 12-month period, or

  • would be a parent of a child of whom the taxpayer would be a parent.

Subsection 252(4) was repealed effective for 2001 and later years as a result of the definition of common-law partner being added in subsection 248(1). The definition of common-law partner is similar to the extended definition of spouse contained in subsection 252(4) but has been extended to cover same-sex partners.

Throughout this chapter a reference to spouse and spouse trust should be construed as meaning a spouse or common-law partner and spouse trust or common-law partner trust for 2001 and subsequent years.

In order for the spousal rollover provisions to apply, the following four criteria must be satisfied:

1. the deceased must be a resident of Canada immediately before death;

2. the spouse must be a Canadian resident immediately prior to the death of the deceased taxpayer, or if the property passes to a qualifying spouse trust, the trust must be resident in Canada immediately after the property vested indefeasibly in the trust;

3. the property must pass to the spouse or spouse trust as a consequence of the death of the deceased; and

4. it can be established within 36 months from the date of death, or where the legal representative has made written application to the Minister within that period, within such longer period as the Minister considers reasonable in the circumstances, that the property has become vested indefeasibly in the spouse or spouse trust. Property passing to a spouse on intestacy would also qualify for the rollover provisions (subsection 70(6)).

Interpretation Bulletin (archived) IT-449R discusses the Canada Revenue Agency's interpretation of what is meant by "vested indefeasibly". Subsection 248(9.2) provides that property shall be deemed not to have vested indefeasibly:

- in a qualifying spouse trust unless the property vested indefeasibly in the trust before the death of the spouse; and

- in an individual (other than a trust) unless the property vested indefeasibly in the individual before the individual's death.

Interpretation Bulletin IT-305R in paragraphs 9 to 12 discusses the provisions of subsection 248(8), 248(9) and 248(9.1) with regards to when property is considered to have been transferred to a spouse trust as a consequence of the death of a taxpayer.

## ¶502 What Constitutes a Qualifying Spouse Trust

A qualifying spouse trust may be created either during the life of a taxpayer or by the taxpayer's will. A qualifying spouse trust will be considered to be created by a taxpayer's will if it is established under the will or by a court order in relation to the estate made pursuant to an Act providing for the relief or support of dependants (subsection 248(9.1), Interpretation Bulletin IT-305R4).[27] A spouse trust does not include an agreement by the beneficiaries which is made under variation of trusts legislation.

The fact that the personal representative may be empowered by the will to allocate properties to be transferred to the spouse trust will not disqualify the trust as a spouse trust. For example, the will might direct the executors to allocate to the trust those assets which have a fair market value in excess of their tax cost so as to take advantage of the available tax deferral. This is also the case where the will fails to provide specific directions to the personal representative and an allocation is made in accordance with the relevant laws of the jurisdiction (Interpretation Bulletin IT-305R4).

In order to qualify as a spouse trust, the trust must provide that the deceased's spouse is entitled to receive all of the income from the trust property while the spouse is alive, and that prior to the death of the spouse, no one other than the spouse may receive or obtain the use of any of the income or the capital of the trust (paragraph 70(6)(b)). A trust will qualify as a spouse trust where the deceased's spouse is entitled to receive all the income from the trust during his/her lifetime and there is no power to encroach on the capital of trust. Where the testator provides for income of the trust to be paid to some other person on the condition that such income is to be used for the benefit of the spouse, it is the Canada Customs and Revenue Agency's position that such provision would not disqualify an otherwise qualifying spouse trust (Interpretation Bulletin IT-305R4, paragraph 15).

Where the terms of the trust provide that during the lifetime of the spouse, loans can be made to persons other than the spouse, on non-commercial terms, the trust will not qualify as a spousal trust. Reference should be made to Interpretation Bulletin IT-305R4, paragraph 16 and Technical Interpretations 2002-0127075 dated March 15, 2002 and 2003-0019235 dated July 25, 2003.

The fact that a testator has provided for the income or capital of the trust to be used to pay any death duties payable as a consequence of the death of the taxpayer, or to pay any income or profits tax on the income of the trust, will not disqualify the trust as a spouse trust (subsection 108(4), Interpretation Bulletin IT-305R4). However, if the testator has provided that a personal representative may draw upon the income and assets of the trust to pay any other debts which might arise, the trust will be considered tainted for the purposes of the Act and will therefore not qualify for the purposes of the rollover provisions.

---

[27] See *Winnifred M. Hillis and Irvin Hillis, Administrators of the Estate of William Edward Hillis v. The Queen*, 83 DTC 5365 (F.C.A.), where the court held that vesting in the spouse did not occur within the required time period as a result of disclaimers by the other beneficiaries. Therefore, no spousal roll over was available.

Once a qualifying spouse trust is established, it remains subject to the provisions of the Act governing such trusts, regardless of whether it becomes tainted or circumstances otherwise change. For example, the trust might be changed by statutory variation or the spouse might disclaim or renounce his or her interest in the trust in favour of other beneficiaries. Regardless of such actions, the trust would be deemed to have disposed of its property for fair market value proceeds on the death of the surviving spouse. Further, even after the death of the surviving spouse, the trust would continue to be characterized as a qualifying spouse trust for the purposes of the Act until the trust was fully distributed.

## ¶504   Untainting a Spouse Trust

If the trust funds may be used to satisfy only testamentary debts, it is possible for the personal representative to untaint the trust by making a special election (subsection 70(7), Interpretation Bulletin IT-305R4). Testamentary debts are defined by the Act as debts owing by or obligations of the deceased taxpayer which were outstanding immediately before the taxpayer's death, and debts for which the estate is liable as a consequence of the taxpayer's death, such as funeral expenses and expenses incurred in the care and management of the assets of the estate, but excluding amounts owing to any beneficiary of the estate (paragraph 70(8)(c)). Also included are liabilities for income taxes payable for taxation years up to and including the year of death, and any succession, estate or other death duties payable in consequence of the taxpayer's death.

In order for the personal representative of the deceased to untaint the trust, the representative must determine the total amount of testamentary debts of the trust and deduct from that amount the total death duties payable in respect of the property in the trust, as well as any debts secured by mortgage or hypothec on the deceased's property. The difference is considered to be non-qualifying debt (paragraph 70(8)(b)). If the personal representative wishes to untaint the trust, he or she must elect in the terminal period return that the trust is to be treated as a spouse trust and must submit a list of those properties (other than a net income stabilization account) transferred to the trust which have a fair market value of not less than the total of the non-qualifying debts. The list may include money. The Department has outlined its administrative practice with respect to the valuation of the specified properties and non-qualifying debts in Interpretation Bulletin IT-305R4, paragraph 25. It is the Department's position that where the legal representative has exercised reasonable efforts to compute the non-qualifying debts and the fair market value of specified properties as accurately as possible from the available facts, and those values are subsequently determined to be incorrect, an adjustment will be available in certain instances. Where the value of the specified properties is actually less than the total of the non-qualifying debts, it is the practice of the Department to permit additional properties to be specified at that later time in order that the provisions of subsection 70(6) may still apply to the unspecified properties of the trust.

As a consequence of this election deeming the trust to be a spouse trust, the listed properties offsetting the non-qualifying debt are deemed to be disposed of at their fair market value, and any resulting gains, income or losses are realized in the terminal period return of the deceased. The tax cost of the property to the trust is increased accordingly. All of the remaining property transferred to the trust would be deemed to rollover to the spouse trust at the deceased's adjusted cost base.

If the fair market value of the specified properties exceeds the total non-qualifying debts, and the legal representative has specified one non-depreciable capital property to exclude from the spousal rollover, the deceased is deemed to realize only a portion of the accrued capital gain or loss on that property. Interpretation Bulletin IT-305R4 in paragraph 22 illustrates the calculation of the capital gain or loss on that property under the provisions of subparagraph 70(7)(*b*)(iii).

If the personal representative elects to untaint the trust, the properties which are listed in the election do not have to be actually disposed of in order to pay the non-qualifying debts. The personal representative may draw on any available funds in order to satisfy those debts (Interpretation Bulletin IT-305R4, paragraph 24).

When the provisions in subsection 70(7) have been used to untaint a spouse trust, the filing deadline for the terminal return of the taxpayer is extended. Pursuant to paragraph 70(7)(*a*), the legal representative has up to 18 months from the date of death to file this return. This is the case whether or not the trust is successfully untainted. It is the position of the Department that this extended time for filing also applies to special returns that may be available pursuant to subsection 150(4) and paragraph 104(23)(*d*). The deadline for filing the deceased's rights or things return (subsection 70(2)) may be indirectly extended since the notice of assessment with respect to the terminal return may be received later. However, the normal rules (later of one year from the date of death and 90 days after receipt of notice of assessment) continue to apply. The extended filing deadline does not apply to returns of the deceased for years prior to the year of death. These returns must be filed the later of six months from the date of death and the day on which the return would otherwise be required to be filed (see ¶200). The time extension provided in paragraph 70(7)(*a*) does not apply for purposes of section 161. As a result, interest at the prescribed rate will accrue with respect to any

¶504

unpaid tax from either April 30 of the year following the date of death if the taxpayer died between January 1 and October 31, or from six months after the date of death if the taxpayer died between November 1 and December 31 (see ¶200 for a discussion of the interest provisions).

The extensions provided pursuant to paragraph 70(7)(*a*) are only available if the tainted spouse trust is capable of being untainted. Therefore, it is important to note the opening words of subsection 70(7) to determine its applicability. The trust must be created by the taxpayer's will (or by court order, subsection 248(9.1)) and, except for the payment of (or provision for payment of) any particular testamentary debts in respect of the taxpayer, it would otherwise be classified as a qualifying spouse trust as previously described in ¶502. For example, if the trust were required to fund obligations out of its assets which did not represent testamentary debts or were not for the benefit of the spouse, the trust would not be eligible for the provisions of subsection 70(7). Accordingly, the legal representative would not be able to make the election pursuant to paragraph 70(7)(*b*), and the extended filing deadlines outlined in paragraph 70(7)(*a*) would not be applicable.

Reference should be made to Interpretation Bulletin IT-305R4 paragraph 26 for a discussion on two interpretations as to the manner in which a spouse trust is created that are acceptable to the Canada Revenue Agency and the options available to the personal representative.

## ¶506   Application of Rollover Provisions

The rollover provisions apply automatically whenever there is a distribution of capital property to a spouse or qualifying spouse trust. However, the personal representative may elect in the tax return for the year of death for any property to be transferred as an ordinary distribution — that is, at its fair market value in the case of capital property (subsections 70(5), (6.2)).[28] A separate election may be made for each capital property owned by the deceased at death. The election must be made in the terminal return filed pursuant to subsection 70(1). Where this election is made with respect to property transferred to a qualifying spouse trust, there will be a deemed disposition at fair market value of property held by the trust on the death of the surviving spouse as would be the case if the election were not made (subsection 104(4)).

## ¶508   Reasons for Avoiding Rollover Provisions

It may be desirable to avoid the rollover provisions for a variety of reasons. Since allowable capital losses incurred by the taxpayer cannot be

[28] For transfers occurring prior to 1993, depreciable property would be deemed to be disposed of at a point midway between its fair market value and undepreciated capital cost.

carried over and claimed by the estate or surviving spouse, it may be advantageous to trigger accrued gains for capital property owned by the deceased against which those losses may be applied. The spouse or spouse trust will be deemed to acquire the property for an amount equal to the deemed proceeds of disposition to the deceased. This means that the adjusted cost base of the property is stepped up for the purposes of determining future gains realized by the spouse or spouse trust.

If at the time of death the taxpayer owned shares of a qualified small business corporation or qualified farm property and had unused capital gains exemption, it may be possible to realize sufficient capital gains on death to offset the available exemption. See ¶258 for a discussion of the changes to the capital gains exemption provisions for 1994 and subsequent years.

If a taxpayer filed an election under subsection 110.6(19) with his or her 1994 personal income tax return, and has a remaining exempt capital gains balance (for taxation years prior to 2005) in respect of an interest in a flow-through entity (e.g., mutual fund units) at the time of death, an election pursuant to subsection 70(6.2) could result in sufficient capital gains being realized to utilize the remaining balance.

However, since the election pursuant to subsection 70(6.2) results in a deemed disposition at the fair market value for capital property, it is possible that the election could result in a deemed capital gain in excess of the available exemption or other shelter and a tax liability may arise. The personal representative in such circumstances must compare the disadvantage of triggering an immediate tax liability by using the available capital gains exemption or other shelter against the value of a possible long-term tax deferral under the spousal rollover provisions.

Where the deceased owned shares of a corporation that are considered to be capital property, each share is considered to be a separate property of which an election under subsection 70(6.2) may be made. The personal representative may make an election under subsection 70(6.2) only in respect of some of the shares such that an excess capital gain is not created.

Conversely, if property owned by the deceased has an accrued capital loss, it may be preferable to realize those losses at death by electing a fair market value transfer. Net capital losses realized in the year of death may be carried back and claimed against taxable capital gains realized in the three preceding taxation years. Where the capital gains inclusion rate in the year of death is different from the rate used in the three preceding taxation years, the net capital loss that may be claimed will have to be adjusted.

Subsection 111(2) provides special rules for the deduction of net capital losses under paragraph 111(1)(b) in the year in which a taxpayer dies. Losses

¶508

carried forward from a prior taxation year and any unused net capital losses realized in the year of death are deductible in the year of death and the immediately preceding year. Firstly, the net capital loss carryforward balance is deductible to the extent of taxable capital gains of those years. Secondly, the amount deductible includes the excess of the net capital losses available for carryforward under paragraph 111(1)(b) over the total aggregate of:

(a) the amount of net capital losses claimed to shelter taxable capital gains in the two years; and

(b) previous capital gains exemptions claimed.

The balance of net capital losses, as computed above, is deductible in full against other income in the year of death and the preceding year. Where the capital gains inclusion rate for the years in which the loss carryforwards were realized is different from that in the year of death, the loss carryforwards will have to be adjusted to reflect the capital gains inclusion rate for the year of death. There is no similar adjustment to the amount of the capital gains exemption claimed in previous years. (See also ¶304 — Utilization of Losses.)

In the absence of the election, that property would pass to the spouse or spouse trust at its high adjusted cost base and, on a subsequent disposal, the loss would be realized according to the ordinary provisions unless at the time of the disposition the property had appreciated to a value in excess of that tax cost.

Generally, where property has been transferred to a spousal trust, the property is deemed to be disposed of at fair market value on the death of the surviving spouse (paragraph 104(4)(a)). As a result, the tax deferral with respect to such property will cease at the date of death of the spouse unless the property has been disposed of by the trust before that time. Some relief may be available pursuant to subsection 110.6(12), wherein the spousal trust is permitted to claim the capital gains exemption which the deceased spouse has not utilized as at the date of death. This provision effectively produces the same result as if the trust had disposed of the property immediately before the surviving spouse's death and the trust had designated the gain to be taxed in the hands of the spouse (subsections 104(21), (21.1), (21.2) and (21.3)). Due to the repeal of the $100,000 capital gains exemption, the deduction under subsection 110.6(12) is limited to the spouse's unused capital gains exemption in respect of qualified farm property and qualified small business corporation shares, effective for taxation years ending after February 22, 1994. However, for taxation years of the trust that ended after February 22, 1994 and before 1997, the trust could have claimed the spouse's unused $100,000 capital gains exemption in respect of taxable capital gains realized prior to February 22, 1994, and accrued to February 22, 1994 where

¶508

the trust elected under subsection 110.6(19). See ¶258 for a discussion of the changes to the capital gains exemption provisions for 1994 and subsequent years.

# ¶510

## Reserves

As discussed in Chapter 2 (¶224), the personal representative of a deceased taxpayer may not claim a reserve in the year of death for property sold in the course of a business, for unearned insurance commissions or for capital property. However, provided the deceased taxpayer was a Canadian resident immediately before death, and the receivable subject to the reserve was transferred to a spouse or spouse trust on the death of the taxpayer and as a consequence of death, special provisions apply (subsection 72(2)). The personal representative and the spouse or spouse trust may file a joint election (Form T2069) whereby a reserve may be claimed in the terminal return of the deceased against amounts claimed as a reserve in the preceding year which are included in income in the terminal period. The amount of the reserve claimed in the terminal period must then be included in the income of the spouse or spouse trust in the first taxation year of the spouse or spouse trust, as the case may be, ending after the death of the taxpayer. However, the spouse or spouse trust may claim a reserve in future taxation years in respect of those receivables. Paragraph 72(2)(c) restricts the maximum period of the time for which reserves may be claimed.

The spouse or spouse trust must compute the available reserve as if the property were disposed of by them at the time it was disposed of by the deceased taxpayer. This ensures the spouse or spouse trust claims the reserve only to the extent the taxpayer could have claimed it had the death not occurred. Reserves that relate to dispositions of qualified farm property and qualified small business corporation shares after 1984 and are included in income, will be eligible for the enhanced capital gains exemption for 1988 and subsequent years (see Interpretation Bulletin (archived) IT-236R4, paragraph 14).

In order for the spouse or spouse trust to be entitled to claim the reserves, the right to receive the amount must be transferred to the spouse or spouse trust. This might be in the form of a mortgage, debt instrument, conditional sale agreement, etc. This may be accomplished by direct transfer pursuant to the terms of a will or, where the personal representative is so empowered, by allocation of that property right by the representative.

## ¶512

## Land Inventory

If land inventory of the deceased taxpayer's business is transferred on death and as a consequence of death to a spouse or a spouse trust, both the deemed realization of the property and the tax liability can be deferred until some future time. The deceased is deemed to have disposed of the land inventory immediately prior to death for proceeds equal to the cost amount of the property to the taxpayer immediately before death, being the lesser of the deceased taxpayer's cost of the property and its fair market value (paragraph 70(5.2)(*d*), subsection 10(1)). The deemed proceeds to the deceased taxpayer are also the deemed cost to the spouse or spouse trust.

The deferral of income recognition is available only if the deceased and the surviving spouse were residents of Canada immediately prior to the death of the deceased taxpayer, or in the case of a testamentary qualifying spouse trust, if the trust was resident in Canada immediately after the land inventory vested in the trust (paragraphs 70(5.2)(*d*), 70(6)(*b*)). In addition, it must be established within 36 months after the death or, where written application has been made to the Minister of National Revenue by the taxpayer's legal representative, such longer period as the Minister considers reasonable in the circumstances, that indefeasible vesting of the land inventory in the spouse or spouse trust has occurred.

It has been suggested that provided the spouse or qualifying spouse trust is not a trader in land, the land which was considered to be inventory to the deceased may be converted to a capital property.[29] Hence the spouse or spouse trust would be liable for tax on only a portion of the gain on actual or deemed disposition of the land instead of on the total amount of the gain. This preferential taxation would be accorded to the gain which accrued up to the time of the deceased's death as well as to the gain which accrued afterwards.

In some circumstances, the rollover may not result in a benefit. The deceased may have loss carryovers which may not be used if there is no income against which to offset them. The rollover is automatic so that if land which is inventory is transferred to the deceased's spouse or spouse trust, no income will be recognized. The election under subsection 70(6.2) which would accommodate a fair market value realization at death, regardless of the transfer of property to a spouse or spouse trust, does not apply to land inventory. However, if a spouse trust is created under the will and the trustee has the power to allocate assets to the trust, the trustee may choose not to

---

[29] Sheppard, A. F., *Income Tax Planning in the Administration of Estates*, 1976 C.R. 762 at p. 778.

allocate land inventory to the trust and therefore have the provisions of paragraph 70(5.2)(c) apply. In this manner, it may be possible to realize sufficient income on the death in order to utilize the available loss carry-overs.

## ¶514

## Resource Properties

Where a deceased taxpayer dies owning Canadian and foreign resource properties, he or she is deemed to have disposed of those properties immediately prior to death for proceeds equal to their fair market value (paragraph 70(5.2)(a)). As is the case with land inventory, it is possible to avoid the inclusion of the deemed proceeds of disposition in the income of the deceased if such property is transferred as a consequence of death to a spouse or qualifying spouse trust (paragraph 70(5.2)(b)). Once again, preferential tax treatment is conditional on both the deceased and spouse being Canadian residents immediately prior to the death of the deceased taxpayer or, where the transfer is to a spouse trust, that the trust is a resident of Canada immediately after the resource property is vested in the trust. Vesting must be established within 36 months of death or, upon written application to the Minister, such longer period as the Minister considers reasonable in the circumstances.

Provided that these conditions are satisfied, the personal representative of the deceased may designate in the terminal period return of the deceased the proceeds for which the property is deemed to be transferred. Those deemed proceeds may not be greater than the fair market value of the property immediately prior to death. The spouse or spouse trust is deemed to acquire the property at a cost equal to the amount which was included in the deceased's income as a result of the designation by the personal representative. However, if there remains a balance in the pools for exploration and development expenses after reducing for the deemed proceeds, a claim may be made on the deceased's terminal return in the normal manner. No further deduction is allowed for any remaining unclaimed balance by the deceased or surviving spouse or spouse trust (Interpretation Bulletin IT-125R4, paragraphs 15 to 18).

## ¶516

## Principal Residence[30]

The principal residence of a taxpayer is one of the few properties which is excluded from tax on capital gains. If a taxpayer dies owning a principal residence, he or she will be deemed to have disposed of that property immediately before death for proceeds equal to the fair market value of the property. However, if the property is designated in the terminal period return as a principal residence, the amount of the gain otherwise determined will be reduced by the proportion of the gain that one plus the number of years during which the property was a principal residence and during which the deceased was a Canadian resident, is of the number of years during which the deceased owned the property either jointly or otherwise. Accordingly, if the property were a principal residence during the full period of ownership, there would be a full reduction of the gain otherwise determined.

The rules relating to the principal residence exemption provide that, with respect to capital gains which accrue after 1981, a family unit (taxpayer, spouse, and minor children) may treat only one residence as its principal residence for a taxation year. Subsection 40(6) of the Act provides transitional rules where more than one principal residence was owned by members of a family unit at the end of 1981. This subsection provides that the capital gain realized after 1981 on the disposition of a principal residence cannot exceed the amount of the gain calculated as if it were determined in two parts — that part of the gain calculated to the end of 1981, and that part calculated on the basis of the new rules. Therefore, if the residence of a taxpayer qualified as a principal residence at the end of 1981, but did not so qualify after that date, only the portion of the gain that accrued before 1982 may qualify for the principal residence exemption. This situation could occur where, for example, the taxpayer and the taxpayer's spouse each owned a residence before 1982, each of which qualified as a principal residence in a taxation year. After 1981, only one property may qualify as a principal residence in a taxation year.

If the deceased taxpayer bequeaths or otherwise disposes of a principal residence to a spouse (for example, by operation of law in the case of a joint tenancy) or to a spouse trust in circumstances where subsection 70(6) applies, the transferee is deemed to have owned that property as their principal residence throughout the period when the deceased owned it, and the property is deemed to be the principal residence of the transferee for any taxation year for which it would have been the principal residence of the

---

[30] Interpretation Bulletin IT-120R6 — Principal Residence.

deceased had it been so designated (subsection 40(4)). If the transferee is a spouse trust, the trust is deemed to have been resident in Canada for each taxation year during which the deceased was resident in Canada.

As a result, no capital gain will be realized on that property at the death of the taxpayer, nor on subsequent disposition of the property by the spouse or spouse trust, provided the full principal residence exemption is available. In the case of a spouse trust, the principal residence exemption will be available for the period that the property is held by the spouse trust, provided the property is ordinarily inhabited by the surviving spouse, a spouse or former spouse of the surviving spouse or a child of the spouse, and was designated as the principal residence by the trust. If the surviving spouse, a spouse of the surviving spouse, or minor child ("family unit") designates another property as a principal residence, subparagraph (c.1)(iv) of the definition of "principal residence" in section 54 would preclude the spouse trust from making a principal residence designation in respect of the property owned by the trust.

Where subsection 40(4) deems the principal residence of the deceased to be that of the transferee during the entire period when that property was the principal residence of the deceased, this would not restrict the spouse from designating another property owned at December 31, 1981 (for example, a summer cottage) as a principal residence for the years prior to 1982.[31]

Where a spouse trust owns a residence for which an election under subsection 45(2) has been made and the spouse trust designates the residence as a principal residence for any of the four years after the election is made, all of the beneficiaries (not just the spouse) and their family units would be precluded from designating another property as their principal residence for any of those four years designated by the spouse trust (see Technical Interpretation 2003-0034095 dated November 21, 2003).

## ¶518

## Death Benefits

Death benefits are included in income and taxable to the recipient pursuant to subparagraph 56(1)(a)(iii). A death benefit is defined in subsection 248(1) and generally includes an amount received in the year by any person upon or after the death of an employee in recognition of the employee's service in an office or employment.

---

[31] See discussion in Technical Interpretation 2004-0075051E5 dated November 3, 2004 of such an example.

The following payments are considered to be death benefits:

(a) payments in recognition of the employee's service even though the payments continue for a long time on a periodic basis, or for the lifetime of the recipient, if they were made under an employer's fund or plan that is distinctly separate from certain plans such as a superannuation or pension fund or plan, a salary deferral arrangement, or a retirement compensation arrangement; and

(b) payments in recognition of service of an employee who dies prior to retirement that represent a settlement of his or her accumulated sick leave credits to which the employee was entitled under the terms of the office or employment.

Interpretation Bulletin IT-508R, in paragraphs 4 to 8, outlines the types of payments which are not considered to be death benefits.

Where an amount is received by a surviving spouse of the taxpayer and the spouse is the only person who received such an amount, the taxable amount is reduced by the lesser of:

(a) the gross amount received in the year by the surviving spouse; and

(b) the amount, if any, by which $10,000 exceeds the total of all amounts received by the surviving spouse in preceding taxation years on or after the death of the employee.

For example, if a surviving spouse were to receive $7,000 from the deceased's employer and no other amounts were paid to any other person, no amount would be taxable to the spouse.

For the purpose of the death benefit definition in subsection 248(1), a person is considered a surviving spouse of the deceased employee only if that person is an individual who:

(a) is a spouse of the deceased employee; and

(b) is the only person who has received a gross amount of a death benefit in respect of the employee.

Where more than one spouse has received an amount, the $10,000 reduction is divided between the spouses in proportion to the amount each spouse receives. This reflects the fact that due to the extended definition of spouse in subsection 252(4) for years after 1992 and before 2000, and the new definition of common-law partner in subsection 248(1) for 2001 and later years, a taxpayer could have more than one surviving spouse.

¶518

If an amount is received by a taxpayer who is not the spouse and there is only one spouse who is in receipt of a death benefit, the taxable amount to the taxpayer is reduced by the lesser of:

(a) the gross amount received by the taxpayer in the taxation year; or

(b) $10,000 minus any amount received by the surviving spouse.

Where more than one taxpayer other than the surviving spouse receives a benefit, the deduction is prorated based upon the proportion that the amount received by the taxpayer is of the aggregate of all gross amounts received at any time by all taxpayers other than the surviving spouse. The maximum benefit is $10,000 and is available to other taxpayers only to the extent it is not utilized by the surviving spouse. Therefore, if an amount is deducted by another taxpayer in a taxation year, this taxpayer will be required to revise the claim if in a subsequent year the surviving spouse receives an additional amount such that the total claim would exceed $10,000 (Interpretation Bulletin IT-508R, paragraph 14).

Where more than one spouse and an individual other than a spouse have received an amount, the $10,000 reduction is divided between the recipients in proportion to the amount each received.

# 6

# Some Income Tax Aspects of the Ontario Family Law Act*

## ¶600

### Framework of the Ontario Family Law Act

The estate planning process has been significantly impacted in Ontario by the *Family Law Act* (R.S.O. 1990, c. F3) (the "FLA") which was proclaimed in force in Ontario on March 1, 1986. The FLA introduced two critical changes to the law, namely,

1. the concept that on marriage breakdown the spouses should share equally in the appreciated *value* of all assets acquired during the marriage; and

2. the application of the concept of equal sharing of *value* on death of the first spouse to die.

The concept of family assets under the predecessor family-law legislation in Ontario has been replaced by the concept of net family property. Subject to specific exceptions, the net value of all assets acquired after the date of marriage is required to be shared equally between spouses. An equalization claim may be made either on marriage breakdown or on death. In addition, an application may be made under the FLA in circumstances where spouses are still cohabiting if there is a serious danger that one spouse may improvidently deplete the net family property. Although the FLA does

* The authors wish to acknowledge with gratitude the assistance of Mary Louise Dickson, Q.C. and Llana Nakonechny of Dickson, MacGregor, Appell, Toronto, in reviewing and updating the materials in this chapter.

not create an equal interest in property, it allows a spouse to require the equalization of the value of assets on a marriage breakdown or on death.

The FLA applies where the person died after March 1, 1986 leaving a surviving spouse owning net family property having a value less than that of the deceased. This assumes that the spouses had not contracted out the provisions of the FLA.

Subsection 5(2) of the FLA provides that when a spouse dies, if the net family property of the deceased spouse exceeds the net family property of the surviving spouse, the surviving spouse is entitled to one-half the difference between those amounts. It is only the surviving spouse and not the estate of the deceased spouse which can make a claim for equalization and only where the value of the net family property of the survivor is less than that of the deceased (*Re Rosenberg and Romberg* (1989), 70 O.R. (2d) 146; *Panangaden v. Panangaden Estate* (1991), 4 O.R. (3d) 332)). An equalization claim cannot be made where the net family property of the survivor is greater than that of the deceased. A person acting under a power of attorney for an incapacitated spouse could make an election for the incapacitated surviving spouse.

In *Re Weinstein and Litigation Guardian of Weinstein* (1997), 35 O.R. (3d) 229 (Ont. Ct. Gen. Div.), the court held that property owned by a mental incompetent that had been left by the mental incompetent to her grandchildren under a valid codicil could not be subject to a claim brought by her husband for an equalization. The court indicated that the grandchildren had a vested interest in the property at the time of the application because the grandmother could not change her will.

Property is defined in the FLA as "any interest, present or future, vested or contingent, in real or personal property . . ." and specifically includes an employer's contribution to a spouse's pension plan. Because of the broad manner in which property is defined, it has been suggested that even a licence to practise a profession may be considered property for the purposes of the FLA. The value of such property could be subject to dispute since the licence is specific to the person who has it and is based on the qualifications entitling the person to such licence. However, it now appears settled (*Linton v. Linton* (1988), 64 O.R. (2d) 18; *Caratun v. Caratun* (1992), 47 E.T.R. 234) that professional degrees or licences are not to be treated as property under the FLA. Accordingly, a spouse's contribution in assisting or enabling the other spouse to obtain the personal right that goes with the degree or licence is dealt with as a matter of spousal support rather than equalization.

Net family property means the value of property after deducting debts, other liabilities and excluded property under subsection 4(2) of the FLA, and

¶600

after deducting the net value of property which was brought into the marriage, other than a matrimonial home. There may be more than one matrimonial home for the purposes of the FLA, and each spouse continues to be entitled to an equal right of possession of the matrimonial home, regardless of how title to the property is registered. There is no definition of debts or liabilities, nor is there a definition of value. Accordingly, the FLA does leave some uncertainty in making the relevant calculations.

On the occurrence of a triggering event, which would include the death of a spouse, the value of all of each spouse's property, including excluded property, is determined as at the relevant date. The value of excluded property is then taken out. In the case of death, the relevant date is the day immediately prior to the date of death. The debts and liabilities of each spouse at the relevant date are also determined and deducted from the total. Also deducted is the value of all property brought into the marriage with the exception of the matrimonial home net of debts existing at the date of marriage (*Black v. Black* (1988), 66 O.R. (2d) 643). The result is the net family property. Excluded from net family property for the purposes of equalization is the value of the following property which exists at the date of separation or death, or property into which such property can be traced:

- property, other than the matrimonial home, that was acquired by gift or inheritance from a third person after the date of marriage;

- income from such property if the donor or testator of the property has expressly stated that income from the property is to be excluded from the net family property of the beneficiary;

- damages or rights to damages for personal injuries including nervous shock, mental distress or loss of guidance, care and companionship or part of a settlement representing those damages;

- proceeds or a right to proceeds from a life insurance policy;

- property, other than the matrimonial home, into which the above property can be traced; and

- any property that the spouses have agreed, by domestic contract, not to be included in the spouses' net family property.

## ¶602

## Estate Considerations

Subsection 6(1) of the FLA provides that when a spouse dies leaving a will, the surviving spouse may either take under the will or elect to receive the equalization entitlement under section 5 of the FLA. If the spouse dies intestate, the surviving spouse would either elect to receive the net family property entitlement under the FLA, or take under Part II of the *Succession Law Reform Act* which provides for distribution on intestacy. Where the spouse chooses to inherit under the will or take a distribution as on intestacy, any other property which passes to the surviving spouse outside the estate, including proceeds of a life insurance policy where the survivor is the designated beneficiary or a survivor's pension, will also form part of the entitlement of the surviving spouse. However, if the surviving spouse elects to take under the FLA, the FLA provides that all gifts to the surviving spouse in the will are revoked, and the surviving spouse is deemed to have disclaimed the right to receive payment under an insurance policy or a pension plan unless the deceased has expressly provided that such payments are in addition to the entitlement under the net family property regime (subsections 6(8), (9)).

The election must be filed with the Clerk of the Ontario Court (General Division) Estates within six months after the death of the deceased spouse. If no election is filed within that time, the survivor is deemed to have taken entitlement under the will or as on intestacy, as the case may be (subsection 6(10)). An election once made cannot be withdrawn or revoked (*Re Bolfan Estate* (1992), 87 D.L.R. (4th) 119). In limited circumstances, the time for making the election may be extended by the Court.

In order to assist the administration of the estate and to assist the spouse to determine whether to elect under the FLA, it is prudent for each spouse to have kept careful records. Such accounting records would include the value of the spouse's assets and liabilities as at the date of marriage and transactions occurring during marriage. Therefore, a historical perspective will have been gained together with the tracing of the sources and application of assets and monies of each spouse. This will also provide a basis from which the spouses may wish to undertake estate planning and assess the possibility of the surviving spouse making the FLA equalization election in light of the existing property held by each, and the potential for an increase in the value of the property until the death of the spouse.

An executor or administrator may not make a distribution of the deceased spouse's estate within six months of the death unless the surviving spouse gives written consent to the distribution or distribution is authorized by the Court, although the personal representative could make reasonable advances to dependants of the deceased spouse for support (subsections 6(14), (15), (17)). Otherwise, to the extent that distributions are made by the personal representative within the six-month period, the personal representative may be personally liable to the surviving spouse for amounts distributed in contravention of the FLA (subsection 6(19)).

¶602

The FLA represents a significant impediment to achieving a degree of certainty in the estate planning process. Unless the spouses have agreed by domestic contract not to make a claim under the FLA for equalization, the deceased's planning may essentially be rewritten by reason of the surviving spouse electing under the FLA. Some of the more significant tax-related concerns are summarized below.

# ¶604

## Filing Income Tax Returns

The *Income Tax Act* provides that, when the person has died without filing an income tax return for a taxation year for which tax is owing, the legal representative must file the return within six months from the day of death. Administratively, it has been the position of the Canada Revenue Agency that the tax return must be filed by the later of six months following the date of death or April 30th of the year following death. Paragraph 150(1)(*b*) applies only in respect of returns for a year where a taxpayer dies after October 1 in the year, and before May 1 of the following year. In such circumstances, the personal representative has six months from the date of death to file a return for the year of death. For taxpayers who die in the first ten months of the year, the filing deadline is April 30 or the filing due date of the following year.

In the case of *May, Executor of Koziej v. M.N.R.*, 85 DTC 690 (T.C.C.), which was decided before the statutory amendments to the filing deadlines, the court upheld penalties for late filing of the terminal period return. In that case, the testator died on January 9, 1979 naming the appellant as executor of his estate. The appellant applied for letters probate and subsequently the testator's estranged wife, who was left out of the will, filed a caveat. The appellant was appointed administrator *pendante lite* on September 4, 1979, but probate was not granted until February 5, 1981. The terminal period tax return was filed by the appellant on August 4, 1982. In that case, the Minister's position was that a return should have been filed by July 9, 1979, which was six months from the date of death, and imposed statutory penalties on that basis. The argument made by the appellant was that he was not the legal representative until probate was granted and that he was therefore under no obligation to file a return within six months of the death.

The court held that the appellant derived his title from the will which spoke from the date of death. The granting of probate merely proved the will as it had existed at all times and that the appellant was in fact the legal representative of the deceased from the date of death. Although the legal argument is important, of greater interest to the practitioner is the uncertainty as to how the Canada Revenue Agency was administratively assessing the return for the terminal period. Based on the administrative position of the Canada Revenue Agency, the latest date for filing the return would have been April 30, 1980, or approximately 16 months after the date of death. In the decision, the administrative position of the Canada Revenue Agency was not raised in support of a reduction in the penalty. (Where the property is allocated to a tainted spouse trust, to which subsection 70(7) applies in order to qualify the trust for the spousal rollover, the deadline for filing is 18 months following the date of death, although interest on unpaid taxes will be payable from the six-month date (paragraph 70(7)(a)).)

Since the surviving spouse has up to six months from the date of death to elect to take their entitlement under the FLA, a legal representative may have some difficulty in filing the terminal period return on time. In addition, it may be that the six-month period under the FLA may be extended by the court. This might arise, for example, where there is a dispute as to value or determination of assets and an extension is allowed to provide the surviving spouse additional time to determine values and make an appropriate election. In order to avoid a late-filing penalty, it may be prudent for the legal representative to file the return as if the property were to pass under the will and to pay any outstanding taxes owing at that time. If the surviving spouse does elect to claim under the FLA, it would likely be necessary to file an amended return to report any additional tax liability by reason of the claim being made, or possibly claim a refund of tax previously paid based on the provisions of the will. However, by filing within the six-month period, the executor may be able to avoid a late-filing penalty.

## ¶606

## Qualifying Spouse Trust

In circumstances where the deceased has provided for property to pass to a qualifying spouse trust, with or without power to encroach, in favour of the beneficiary spouse, the spouse's equalization under the FLA may in fact be greater than the present value of the life interest in the trust and an election under the FLA may be made.

Where property passes to a qualifying spouse trust created by the will, a rollover would be available and no tax would be payable on the death of the deceased spouse in respect of those assets allocated to the qualifying spouse trust. However, by electing under the FLA, depending on the manner in which the equalization is satisfied, some tax liability may arise in respect of appreciated assets not allocated to the surviving spouse in satisfaction of the equalization entitlement. As a result, the balance of assets remaining after the equalization entitlement will pass to the residuary beneficiaries of the estate, and capital assets not transferred to the spouse will be deemed to have been disposed of at their fair market value.

In order to satisfy the tax liability arising on the equalization, it may be necessary for the estate to borrow funds or liquidate other assets. For example, if the spouse were equalized by receiving the matrimonial home together with the cash received under the insurance policy, those assets would have no inherent tax liability. If, at the time of death, the deceased also owned a rental property and had a registered retirement savings plan which were not allocated to the spouse in satisfaction of the equalization entitlement, the rental real estate would be deemed to have been disposed of at fair market value immediately before death and recapture and/or a capital gain could result. The refund of premiums under the RRSP would be taxable in the terminal period and the ability to shelter the tax by having the refund of premiums paid to the spouse and transferred to the spouse's RRSP would be lost.

Similarly, the use of a qualifying spouse trust together with a post mortem estate freeze offers the further deferral of capital gains by directing any additional growth away from the surviving spouse and in favour of the testator's next generation.

In order to alleviate the potential disruption to an estate plan by reason of an equalization claim, the spouses may consider entering into a domestic contract which would preclude a claim for equalization under the FLA. Alternatively, the testator may provide instructions to the executors named in the will that in the event the surviving spouse claims under the FLA, the equalization entitlement be satisfied by way of an asset allocation which would minimize taxes otherwise payable on death.

Finally, the spouses' wills could be changed to match the FLA entitlement of each, or designed with alternative provisions to take effect in the event a spouse elects for an FLA entitlement.

In order to preserve the planning, it may be appropriate for the spouses to enter a limited domestic contract. In this way, the spouses agree that provided the wills (appended to the agreement) are not altered so as to detrimentally vary the gifts to the surviving spouse, each spouse agrees to accept the provisions of the other spouse's will and waives the right to elect any entitlement under the FLA equalization provisions. In order to be effective, it would be necessary that each spouse make full disclosure of all assets and liabilities and obtain independent legal advice in connection with the execution of the domestic contract which must be signed by both parties and witnessed.

¶606

## ¶608

## Equalization Using a Trust

In some circumstances, the equalization entitlement under the FLA may be satisfied by causing certain assets to be held in trust for the surviving spouse. Since the trust is not created by the taxpayer's will but as a result of a determination under the FLA, the trust would not be a qualifying spouse trust for income tax purposes. Consequently, the deceased would be deemed to have disposed of all property immediately prior to death and realize any inherent gains or losses. However, it appears that if the property were to be transferred outright to the surviving spouse, the transfer or distribution would qualify for a tax deferred rollover under subsection 70(6) in that the property would be transferred or distributed on or after the death, and as a consequence of the death, to a spouse of the deceased. In order for the rollover rules to apply, it would be necessary to satisfy the requirement that the property vested indefeasibly in the surviving spouse within a period ending 36 months after the date of death.

## ¶610

## Tax as FLA Debt or Liability

Of concern in determining the value of net family property is the value of debts and liabilities at the time of determination. Under the FLA, the appropriate date for the determination is the day immediately prior to the date of death (subsection 4(1)). Since property is deemed to be disposed of for income tax purposes immediately prior to death, on the day before death it is arguable that there is no debt or liability which should be deducted from the value of net family property.[32] For the purposes of determining net family property, it may be necessary to take the *Mastronardi* (77 DTC 5217) approach to the question of whether taxes on death are a debt or liability by determining whether death was imminent. That is, if the deceased suffered from a lengthy illness or a steadily deteriorating state of health, it may be justifiable to deduct taxes payable at death as a foreseeable liability when such valuation is made on the date immediately before the date of death.

In addition, in order to quantify the taxes owing on death, it is necessary to know whether the surviving spouse has elected under the FLA and how such property is going to be distributed on equalization. Accordingly, the determination of debts and liabilities is dependent upon the election being made and whether the election is made is generally dependent on the

---

[32] In the case of an equalization in circumstances other than on death, in valuing a RRSP or RRIF, a discount is applied to take into account the inherent tax liablility associated with such asset.

relative values of net family property. It will be necessary, therefore, to make careful calculations and determinations of which assets are to be distributed to equalize in order to ultimately determine the debts and liabilities and the relative values. Since the equalization payment is capital in nature, the deceased will not be entitled to a tax deduction for this payment. Where property is ordered transferred to satisfy the equalization payment, or where an equalization payment is ordered, the courts are inclined to consider the tax arising on the disposition or notional disposition of the property (*McPherson v. McPherson* (1988), 63 O.R. (2d) 641; *Heon v. Heon* (1989), 69 O.R. (2d) 758; and *Starkman v. Starkman* (1990), 73 D.L.R. (4th) 746).

## ¶612

## Post Mortem Tax Planning

The FLA may present an opportunity for post mortem tax planning. That is, by making a claim under the FLA the bequest to the surviving spouse is revoked and the balance of the estate passes as a gift over. If, for example, the testator had established a qualifying spouse trust by will with a gift over to children who survived the life-tenant spouse, by electing under the FLA the gift to the surviving children would become payable after satisfaction of the equalization entitlement. In order to minimize tax at death, assets having an inherent capital gain could be distributed directly to the surviving spouse on a rollover basis and the balance of property representing non-appreciated assets could be distributed to the residuary beneficiaries. This would have the added advantage of possibly reducing the amount of income generated in favour of the spouse and present an opportunity for distributing income to other beneficiaries of the estate. However, it should be noted that the surviving spouse would be assuming a deferred tax liability by reason of the rollover.

In order to avoid upsetting the general scheme of the deceased's will, under the will of the surviving spouse the assets received as an equalization payment could be bequeathed to the ultimate beneficiaries of the original spouse trust on similar terms and conditions. In addition, should the surviving spouse remarry, the survivor would require a new will and a domestic contract would be advisable in order to ensure that the survivor's will would not be upset by a claim by the second spouse under the FLA.

An election under the FLA may also serve to reduce taxes where a tainted spouse trust is established under the will, for example, by reason of a power to encroach on capital in favour of children of the deceased. The trust could be untainted by way of a disclaimer by those beneficiaries. However, should they be unwilling or unable to disclaim their interest, an election could be made by the spouse under the FLA. Properties having an inherent capital gain could be transferred to the spouse in satisfaction of the equalization entitlement, and a full or partial rollover for tax purposes could be achieved.

## ¶614

## Clearance Certificates

A personal representative of the deceased who distributes the property of the estate without first receiving clearance certificates from the Canada Revenue Agency acknowledging that no further tax is payable either in respect of the deceased or the estate, may be personally liable for taxes owing. The personal representative's liability is limited such that it cannot exceed the value of the property distributed without a clearance certificate. Accordingly, where an equalization claim is made under the FLA, the personal representative may be reluctant to distribute assets pursuant to the court order if a clearance certificate has not yet been received or if, as a result of the equalization payment, insufficient assets, and in particular insufficient liquid assets, remain in the estate to satisfy the income tax liability. Furthermore, in determining the net family property, it may not be possible for an accurate assessment of debts and liabilities to be determined until such time as a clearance certificate is received from the Canada Revenue Agency. That is, it may be difficult to quantify the amount of tax owing until a determination is made as to the amount of equalization payment to the spouse and the manner in which the equalization is to be satisfied. In those circumstances, the legal representative may wish to delay making a distribution to the spouse until a clearance certificate is received. Alternatively, the personal representative may wish to obtain a ruling from the Canada Revenue Agency that a distribution pursuant to a court order in accordance with the FLA would not be considered a transfer of property in the possession and control of the personal representative as contemplated in subsection 159(1) of the *Income Tax Act.*

## ¶616

## Registered Retirement Savings Plans

Where the surviving spouse who claims equalization under the FLA is the beneficiary under a pension plan or similar plan which provides a payment on the death of a deceased spouse, the beneficiary spouse is deemed to have disclaimed the right to receive payment under a pension plan or similar plan unless the deceased has made a written designation which expressly provides that such payment is in addition to any entitlement under an equalization claim. It is not specific in the FLA whether a payment under an RRSP would also be deemed to be disclaimed, and the legal representative may be forced to seek guidance of the court prior to making or withholding a distribution of same.

In some circumstances the equalization entitlement of the surviving spouse may be satisfied with funds in the deceased's RRSP. The *Income Tax Act* allows a spouse or common-law partner beneficiary of such a plan to transfer a refund of premiums to an RRSP of the surviving spouse or common-law partner and thereby defer any tax otherwise payable on death. The Act defines a refund of premiums as an amount paid to a spouse or common-law partner of the annuitant as a consequence of the annuitant's death. A significant tax burden could result if the Canada Revenue Agency were to deny the rollover and take the position that the payment of the RRSP proceeds as equalization to the spouse was not as a consequence of death but as a result of an election being made under the FLA.[33]

---

[33] Paragraph 146(16)(*b*) of the *Income Tax Act* permits a rollover from a taxpayer's RRSP to an RRSP or RRIF of his or her spouse, common-law partner or former spouse or common-law partner pursuant to a court order or written separation agreement on a breakdown of a marriage or common-law partnership.

# 7

# The Taxation of Partnerships*

## ¶700

## Income and Loss of the Deceased Partner from the Partnership Up to Date of Death

When determining the tax implications of owning an interest in a partnership at death, it is necessary to consider the effects on the deceased partner, on the partner's beneficiaries, on the partnership and on the surviving partners. A number of factors will be relevant in determining these taxation consequences. The factors to be considered include:

- the extent to which the deceased partner is entitled to income in respect of the stub period (i.e., from the last year end of the partnership up to the date of death);

- the disposition of the partnership interest itself . . . to whom and at what value;

---

* Effective in 1993, subsection 252(4) provided that words referring to a spouse of a taxpayer include the person of the opposite sex who cohabits at that time with the taxpayer in a conjugal relationship and

- has cohabited with the taxpayer throughout a 12-month period, or
- would be a parent of a child of whom the taxpayer would be a parent.

Subsection 252(4) was repealed effective for 2001 and later years as a result of the definition of common-law partner being added in subsection 248(1). The definition of common-law partner is similar to the extended definition of spouse contained in subsection 252(4) but has been extended to cover same-sex partners.

Throughout this chapter a reference to spouse and spouse trust should be construed as meaning a spouse or common-law partner and spouse trust or common-law partner trust for 2001 and subsequent years.

- whether the partnership was a Canadian partnership as defined in section 102; and

- whether the partnership terminates and dissolves on death.

## ¶702   Income and Loss Allocated to a Partner in the Year of Death

Partnerships will ordinarily allocate a share of income or loss to a partner who died during the fiscal year of the partnership.

The partnership agreement should, however, be quite specific. It should clearly distinguish:

(a) amounts to be paid to the deceased in respect of earnings for the stub year; and

(b) amounts to be paid from the partnership as consideration for the partnership interest.

Frequently, the latter amount will be computed with reference to items that have the appearance of ordinary income (such as unbilled work in progress). The partnership agreement should clearly distinguish what is intended as terminal stub period ordinary income and what is intended as a payment for a capital interest in a partnership (regardless of how it is calculated).

When the deceased's income or loss for the stub period is determined, the tax treatment will depend on:

(a) whether the death caused a year end of the partnership; and

(b) whether this is the second fiscal period ending in the calendar year.

The issue of whether the stub period income is in the second fiscal period will only arise where the members of the partnership have filed an election under subsection 249.1(4) to use an off-calendar fiscal year end for 1995 and subsequent years. The election under subsection 249.1(4) can only be made by a member of the partnership where:

(a) each member of the partnership is an individual; and

(b) the partnership is not a member of another partnership.

It should also be noted that the treatment accorded stub period losses differs slightly from that of stub period income. First, consider the treatment of stub period income.

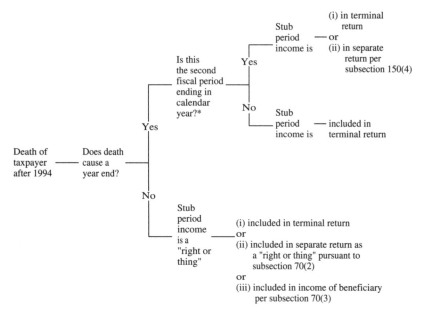

* Subsection 249.1(4) election filed.

## ¶704  Death Does Not Cause a Year End

If there is *no* actual or deemed fiscal year end of the partnership when the partner dies, the deceased partner's right to share in profits from the end of the last fiscal period to the date of death is a "right or thing", the value of which is to be included in income pursuant to subsection 70(2). There are special provisions of the Act dealing with rights or things (see Interpretation Bulletin IT-212R3).

Rights or things of the deceased at the date of death may be treated in three ways:

(1) included in the ordinary return of the deceased, subject to appropriate adjusted cost base adjustments made pursuant to section 53;

(2) elected upon and included in a separate return of the deceased taxpayer as if the deceased had been another person (subsection 70(2)); or

(3) included in the income of the beneficiary if the right or thing is transferred to the beneficiary within the prescribed time.

In the separate return for rights or things, full personal tax credits may be claimed as if the taxpayer were another person. If more beneficial, tax credits in respect of charitable donations and medical expenses paid by the deceased taxpayer may be claimed on the separate return rather than the ordinary return of the deceased.

If a separate return under subsection 70(2) is filed, it must include the total value of all rights or things other than those transferred to beneficiaries pursuant to subsection 70(3).

To be valid, an election to file a separate return under subsection 70(2) must have been made within one year from the date of death of the taxpayer or within 90 days after the mailing of any notice of assessment in respect of the return of the taxpayer for the year of death, whichever is later.

Subparagraph 53(1)(e)(v) increases the adjusted cost base of the deceased partner's partnership interest by the amount included in income pursuant to subsection 70(2).

It should be noted that any tax payable on the subsection 70(2) return is due on the same day as any taxes due on the terminal period return (see ¶206).

The additional tax payable by virtue of subsection 70(2) may be paid in up to ten equal consecutive annual instalments when the conditions in subsection 159(5) are met, including the provision of acceptable security.

Alternatively, subsection 70(3) provides that the tax liability for the right or thing will be transferred to beneficiaries of the estate if the transfer or distribution of the right or thing takes place within one year from the date of death, or within 90 days from the date of a notice of assessment in respect of the year of death (whichever is later). The recipients of the right or thing are deemed by virtue of subsection 69(1.1) not to have acquired such an asset at fair market value, but to have acquired it at a cost equal to such part of the cost to the deceased that was not deducted in computing income for any taxation year, plus any expenditures the recipient made or incurred to acquire the asset.

If subsection 70(3) applies, the amount received by the beneficiary is included in computing income for the taxation year in which the beneficiary received it, and is excluded completely from the income of the deceased.

Subparagraph 53(1)(e)(v) also increases the adjusted cost base of the deceased partner's partnership interest by any amount excluded from the terminal return of the deceased, but that is included in income of a beneficiary pursuant to subsection 70(3) (see Interpretation Bulletin IT-278R2, paragraph 3).

¶704

## ¶706 Death Does Cause a Year End

If the death of the partner causes a fiscal period of the partnership to end, the deceased partner's share of the partnership income for that short fiscal period is included in a regular return of income for the year of death by virtue of paragraphs 12(1)(*l*) and 96(1)(*f*). This amount increases the adjusted cost base of the partnership interest by the amount included in income (subparagraph 53(1)(*e*)(i)) and is taken into account in computing the fair market value of the deceased partner's partnership interest.

If the death of the partner causes the fiscal period of the partnership to end, and if the partnership had a previous fiscal year end in the calendar year in which the death occurred, a separate return of this stub period income may be filed (subsection 150(4), Interpretation Bulletin IT-278R2).

See ¶220 for a discussion of the additional income inclusion under section 34.1 on death where a separate return is filed under subsection 150(4).

## ¶708 Losses Allocated to a Partner in the Year of Death

When a share of a partnership loss arising prior to death is allocated to a deceased partner, Interpretation Bulletin IT-278R2 provides that:

(a) If the partnership has a fiscal year end when the partner dies, the deceased partner's share of the partnership loss is included in computing income in the regular return of income for the year of death pursuant to paragraphs 12(1)(*l*) and 96(1)(*g*). Subparagraph 53(2)(*c*)(i) reduces the adjusted cost base of the partnership interest by the amount of the deceased's share of the loss; and

(b) If there is no actual or deemed fiscal year end of the partnership when the partner dies, the deceased partner's share of the partnership loss from the end of the last fiscal period to the date of death may be included in computing income in the deceased partner's regular return of income for the year, provided that the adjusted cost base of the partnership interest is reduced by the same amount. Otherwise, the loss is not deductible in computing the deceased partner's income, and does not reduce the adjusted cost base of the partnership interest.

## ¶710 When a Partner Dies with an Untaxed Reserve re 1971 Receivables

A deduction in respect of 1971 accounts receivable may not be claimed in the year a partner (or a retired partner with a residual interest) dies (ITAR 23(4)(a)). Therefore, the full amount of the previous year's deduction must be included in income for that year. The additional tax due to this amount being included in income may be paid in ten equal annual instalments, plus interest, if the conditions of subsections 159(5) and (5.1) are met. Any amount included in income in respect of 1971 accounts receivable cannot be included in a separate return permitted to be filed on behalf of a deceased partner by virtue of subsection 150(4) since the income included by virtue of ITAR 23(3)(c) is not contemplated by subsection 150(4). In addition, the amount of the reserve which is included in income is not considered to be a right or thing and consequently cannot be reported on a separate return filed pursuant to subsection 70(2) (Interpretation Bulletin IT-278R2, paragraph 18).

## ¶712 December 31, 1995 Income Reserve and the Alternative Method

See ¶220 for a discussion of the treatment of the December 31, 1995 income reserve and the additional income inclusion (where the members of the partnership elected to use an off-calendar fiscal year end) where the deceased was a partner at the time of death.

## ¶714

## Disposition of Partnership Interest on Death

## ¶716 Partnership Interests that may be Owned on Death

There are four types of partnership interests, each of which is accorded different tax treatment upon death. These are:

❏ A continuing partnership interest (see also ¶720);

❏ A residual capital interest in a partnership (see also ¶722);

❏ A right to receive partnership property (this interest arises only on death) (see also ¶724); and

❏ An income interest in a partnership (see also ¶726).

*Continuing Partnership Interest — Defined*

When, on the death of a former partner, the estate, trust or beneficiary becomes an ongoing member of the partnership, the deceased will have transferred an interest in a partnership that is referred to as a continuing partnership interest.

A continuing partnership interest is ordinarily a capital property which is dealt with in section 96 and elsewhere in subdivision j.

*Residual Capital Interest — Defined*

When a former partner ceases to be an active partner or ceases to be a partner (legally), provided the former partner has not drawn all of the capital to which he or she is ultimately entitled from the partnership, the former partner has a residual capital interest in the partnership. On death, this interest becomes a right to receive partnership property to the recipient.

A residual capital interest in a partnership is usually a capital property which is dealt with in section 98.1.

*Right to Receive Partnership Property — Defined*

This partnership interest arises only on the death of a partner. For example:

(a) When an active partner dies owning a partnership interest and the estate, trust or beneficiary are expressly precluded from becoming active partners in the ongoing partnership (e.g., spouse of a deceased doctor would be precluded from becoming a partner in an ongoing medical partnership), then the deceased will have transferred a partnership interest that is converted from an active partnership interest into a right to receive partnership property.

(b) When a retired partner who has retained a residual capital interest in a partnership dies and transfers the right to capital to the partner's estate, trust or beneficiary, the death of the taxpayer converts this residual capital interest into a right to receive partnership property.

A right to receive partnership property is ordinarily a capital property which is referred to in section 98.2.

*Income Interest in a Partnership — Defined*

When a partner has ceased to be a member of a partnership that carried on business in Canada, and the members of the partnership have agreed to continue to allocate a share of income or loss to the former partner, the former partner has an income interest in the partnership.

¶716

An income interest in a partnership is not a capital property. The tax treatment is described in subsection 96(1.1). An income interest which is transferred to an estate, trust or beneficiaries, is an income interest in a partnership to the recipient.

## ¶718   Deemed Disposition on Death — General

Subsection 70(5) of the Act provides that a person is deemed to dispose of all capital properties immediately before death for consideration equal to fair market value. A partnership interest is normally a capital property,[34] and, as such, would be subject to this rule. This rule also applies to a continuing partnership interest, a residual capital interest in a partnership and a right to receive partnership property. The disposition is deemed to take place immediately before the death and any resulting capital gain or loss is taxed in the taxation year ending with the taxpayer's death. If a capital gains exemption election was filed in respect of an accrued capital gain in respect of the partnership interest at February 22, 1994, any remaining exempt capital gains balance could be used to offset any capital gain arising on the death of the taxpayer for deaths occurring before 2005. Any remaining exempt capital gains balance after 2004 is added to the adjusted cost base of the interest (see paragraph 53(1)(*p*)).

Where the property passes to a spouse or spouse trust, subsection 70(6) deems the proceeds of disposition to be equal to the adjusted cost base of the property, resulting in no gain or loss being realized on the transfer. For deaths occurring after January 15, 1987, the transfer will not cause the recognition of a capital gain where the adjusted cost base to the deceased is a negative amount (paragraph 70(6)(*d*.1)). For transfers prior to that date, however, a capital gain would have resulted to the extent of the negative adjusted cost base.

## ¶720   Continuing Partnership Interest

A continuing partnership interest is the ordinary partnership interest of a continuing partner and is a capital property. As with other capital property, a taxable gain or allowable loss may result from the disposition of such an interest. The rules, which ensure that there is neither double taxation of

---

[34] Where, for example, the partnership owns real estate, the sale of a partnership interest may be treated as an adventure or concern in the nature of trade. See, for example, the cases dealing with the sale of shares in real estate companies such as *Fraser v. M.N.R.* 64 DTC 5224 (S.C.C.) and *Burgess et al. v. M.N.R.,* 73 DTC 5040 (F.C.T.D.). Alternatively, the Canada Revenue Agency may challenge the existence of the partnership as an attempt to treat a transaction as a sale of the property rather than a sale of a partnership interest. See, for example, *M.N.R. v. Strauss,* 60 DTC 1060 (Ex. Ct.) in which the taxpayer's position that he sold a partnership interest rather than an interest in land was upheld.

partnership profits nor double deduction of partnership losses, are very complex. For example, contributions of property to a partnership by a partner or the allocation to the partner of taxable and non-taxable partnership income are events which increase the adjusted cost base of that person's partnership interest. Conversely, a withdrawal of property by a partner, or the allocation of deductible or non-deductible losses to that partner, results in a decrease in the adjusted cost base of the partnership interest. Consequently, a partner will not recognize a taxable capital gain if there are undistributed profits accumulated in a partnership when a partnership interest is sold. These earnings will cause an increase in the adjusted cost base of the partnership interest as well as an increase in its fair market value.

Unlike other capital properties, a negative adjusted cost base in a continuing partnership interest does not result in an immediate capital gain. However, subsection 40(3.1) provides that this exception does not apply to a limited partner or a specified member of a partnership, applicable after February 21, 1994, subject to transitional rules where the partnership interest was acquired before 1995.

There are special transitional rules for determining the adjusted cost base of a continuing partnership interest owned on December 31, 1971. The tax-free zone method must be used in determining the taxable gain or allowable loss on such property, and the Valuation Day value is computed in accordance with the provisions of the Act.

If the taxpayer was a member of a partnership on December 31, 1971, the taxpayer is required to use ITAR 26 in determining the cost of a partnership interest owned on December 31, 1971. ITAR 26 is not elective. It establishes V-Day value of a partnership interest even for those taxpayers who otherwise elect to value all their 1971 capital properties as at fair market value (as permitted by ITAR 26(7)). ITAR 26(9) provides for a tax-free zone concept in respect of partnership interests.

Since ITAR 26(5) does not apply to a partnership interest, it is not necessary to look beyond a non-arm's-length acquisition of a partnership interest in order to establish an adjusted cost base.

By operation of law, or pursuant to the terms of a partnership agreement, a partnership may dissolve automatically upon the death of a partner. In general, a partnership transferring property to a partner is deemed to receive proceeds of disposition equal to the fair market value of that property and a taxable gain may result. The deemed fair market value becomes the cost of the property to the partner.

In the absence of a rollover, the termination of a partnership would normally result in the deemed realization of all the partnership properties.

¶720

The termination would result in a distribution of property to the partners, whether as an outright distribution or as a transfer of their property interests to a new partnership. Subsection 98(6) prevents this deemed realization from arising in the case of a Canadian partnership, that is, a partnership the members of which are only Canadian residents. If the deceased was a member of a non-Canadian partnership, death may trigger the dissolution of that non-Canadian partnership and the deemed realization of its assets for Canadian tax purposes.

Under the general rules of subsection 70(5), a partnership interest is deemed to be disposed of for proceeds equal to fair market value. The estate, trust or beneficiary (the recipient) acquires

(a) a partnership interest, if the recipient is a member of the partnership or becomes a member of the partnership by reason of the acquisition, or

(b) a right to receive partnership property, if the recipient does not become a member of the partnership (subsection 100(3))

at a cost equal to such deemed proceeds.

Where a partnership interest is transferred to a spouse or spouse trust as described in subsection 70(6), paragraph 70(6)(*d*.1) will apply. The deceased partner is deemed not to have disposed of the partnership interest. The spouse or spouse trust is deemed to have acquired the partnership interest for an amount equal to its cost to the deceased partner, adjusted by the same amounts as were required to be added or deducted under subsection 53(1) or (2) in determining the deceased partner's adjusted cost base of the interest.

Where a right to receive partnership property is acquired by a spouse or spouse trust as described in subsection 70(6), the proceeds of disposition to the deceased partner and the cost to the spouse or spouse trust are deemed under paragraph 70(6)(*d*) to be an amount equal to the adjusted cost base of the partnership interest to the deceased immediately before death. If the adjusted cost base of the partnership interest is negative at the time of transfer, the deceased partner will have a deemed capital gain equal to the negative adjusted cost base by virtue of subsection 100(2).

*Valuation of a Continuing Partnership Interest*

Where the estate sells the partnership interest of the deceased shortly after death, the actual proceeds of disposition will normally be accepted as being the fair market value of that partnership interest immediately before the death of the partner.

¶720

If the partnership interest is retained by the estate or the beneficiaries and there is no actual disposition at the time of death, the estate must estimate the fair market value of the partnership interest. For example, this would be necessary when a child inherits a parent's interest in a business which is carried on through a partnership.

Fair market value has been defined as the price which a willing and knowledgeable buyer would pay to a willing and knowledgeable seller dealing at arm's length in the open market.

If the partnership interest of another partner has been transferred in an arm's-length transaction close to the time of the taxpayer's death, the price paid on the transfer should provide some indication of the value of the deceased's interest. Other factors which should be considered are the earning power of the partnership, the amount of effort which was required by the deceased partner to produce that income, the liquidation value of the partnership assets and the economic climate at the date of valuation. If the partnership conducts a business which is normally valued by a rule-of-thumb method, that rule of thumb should be considered, even though it may be unscientific.

Partnership earnings cannot be used as a basis for estimating the value of a partnership unless those earnings are reduced by the equivalent of a salary for the efforts devoted by the partners. Otherwise, personal earning power will be mistaken for partnership goodwill. If partnership goodwill is dependent on an individual, goodwill should be discounted proportionately unless it is covered by life insurance and a contractual lock-in.

Finally, if the deceased had sold the partnership interest while living, and had withdrawn from the partnership, the event might have impaired partnership value. In that case, the fair market value which that person could receive for the interest would be reduced by the notional withdrawal. In the case of the death of a partner, the value immediately before a partner's death might be determined by taking into consideration the knowledge of imminent death. (See below.)

*Partnership Agreements and their Effects on Value including the Question of Vesting Indefeasibly*

For the rollover provisions in subsections 70(5.2), (6), (9), and (9.2) of the Act, and ITAR 26(18) to apply, the property must vest indefeasibly in the transferee within 36 months after the death of the taxpayer.

The Act does not define the meaning of vested indefeasibly. Accordingly, the meaning of this term must be construed within the context of the provisions where it is used. In the foregoing context, vested indefeasibly

¶720

refers to particular property that, in consequence of the death of the previous owner, has been transferred or distributed either to a spouse, common-law partner, a trust for the benefit of the spouse or common-law partner or a child of the taxpayer. In the Department's view, a property vests indefeasibly in a spouse, common-law partner or child of the testator when that person obtains a right to absolute ownership of the property in a manner that the right cannot be defeated by any future event (Interpretation Bulletin (archived) IT-449R, paragraph 1).

For the purposes of subsections 70(5.2), (6), (9) and (9.2), it must be established within 36 months after the death of the taxpayer (or upon written application to the Minister of National Revenue, within such longer period as the Minister considers reasonable in the circumstances) that the property vested indefeasibly.

It is the opinion of the Canada Revenue Agency that if the partnership interest is subject to a buy-sell agreement, the vesting of the property in the beneficiary would depend on the terms of the buy-sell agreement (Interpretation Bulletin (archived) IT-449R). Where the terms of the agreement provide that it is compulsory for the executor to sell and for the other party to buy, the property subject to the buy-sell agreement will *not* be considered to vest indefeasibly in the beneficiary. Similarly, property that the will directs to be sold by the executor before settling the estate will not be considered to vest indefeasibly in the beneficiary. On the other hand, property subject to a buy-sell agreement will vest indefeasibly in the beneficiary where the executor transfers the property to the beneficiary before the option is exercised and the buy-sell agreement is merely an option that may or may not be exercised.

The effect of agreements among partners on the value of a partnership interest should also be considered. If a partner must offer the partnership interest to the other partners at a price determined by a formula before the partner is able to sell the partnership interest to an outsider, that formula price could set a ceiling on the value of the partnership interest. The partnership interest could only be acquired subject to the agreement and consequently the agreement would govern the liquidation value.

Where the partnership agreement provides a valuation formula that takes effect only on the death of a partner, or where the partnership has insured the life of the partner, further problems might arise. As noted earlier, the deceased is deemed to have disposed of capital property immediately before death in order to ensure that the resulting gain is taxed in the taxation year ending with the death. This raises the question as to whether the fair market value immediately before death would be the same in the knowledge of the partner's imminent demise. Tax cases under the former *Estate*

*Tax Act* and provincial succession duty Acts provide little assistance in the area since those statutes taxed the value of property transmitted at death, not its value immediately before death. Clearly, the value of a property transferred at death may not be the same as its value when held by an owner who appeared to be in good health. Thus, the question arises as to whether partnership buy-outs operating on death, and the proceeds of insurance policies payable to the partnership on the death of a partner, can be considered in determining the fair market value of a partnership interest immediately before death.

The one case that dealt with such matters is *Mary Mastronardi et al. v. The Queen* (76 DTC 6306, F.C.T.D.; 77 DTC 5217, F.C.A.). This case dealt with the value of shares of a private corporation which held a term insurance policy on the life of the shareholders. The shareholder died suddenly and the shares had to be valued for the purpose of the deemed disposition provisions. It was agreed that the shares were worth $323.58 each excluding the value of the insurance policy, and $778.59 each when the value of the policy was included. The Court held that the shares were worth $323.58 because the words "immediately before death" did not import a necessity of valuing capital property by taking into account the imminence of death. The judgment was upheld by the Federal Court of Appeal.

The Canada Revenue Agency, in Interpretation Bulletin IT-416R3, "Valuation of Shares of a Corporation Receiving Life Insurance Proceeds on Death of a Shareholder", provides that most corporate-owned insurance policies will be valued at their cash surrender value for purposes of determining the fair market value of the shares of the company immediately prior to the death of a shareholder (see the discussion in Chapter 3 under "Shareholdings and Death"). For dispositions prior to October 2, 1996, subsection 70(5.3), dealing with valuation issues where insurance is corporate owned, did not apply to insurance owned by a partnership in valuing a partnership interest on the death of a partner. For dispositions after October 1, 1996, subsection 70(5.3) is amended to apply to dispositions of any property deemed to have been disposed of under subsection 70(5). Therefore the value of insurance owned by the partnership on the deceased partner's life will be valued at its cash surrender value in valuing the deceased's partnership interest.

The Canada Revenue Agency takes the position that, where the deceased and the surviving party to the buy-sell agreement did not deal at arm's length, it is a question of fact whether the fair market value for purposes of subsection 70(5) will be determined with reference to the buy-sell agreement (Interpretation Bulletin IT-140R3).

¶720

A taxpayer may be deemed to have disposed of a partnership interest for a high value immediately before death. However, on a subsequent actual disposition, the estate might realize a much lower value, resulting in a capital loss.

Subsection 164(6) allows the net capital losses realized in the first taxation year of an estate to be applied as if realized by the deceased in the year of death. Therefore, if the buy-out value is less than the deemed proceeds of disposition on death, any capital loss recognized can, by way of election, be deemed to be losses of the deceased in the terminal period return of the deceased. This has the same effect as using the buy-out value as an estimate of the fair market value of the partnership interest immediately before death. If the estate disposes of the interest after the first taxation year of the estate, or if the interest is paid out by the partnership over several years, a taxable capital gain may be recognized on the deceased's terminal period return. However, it may not be possible to use losses subsequently realized in the estate.

*The Canada Revenue Agency Roundtable — Treatment of Life Insurance Receipts*

*Question:*

Subparagraph 53(1)(*e*)(iii) of the Act provides for an increase in the adjusted cost base of a partnership interest by the taxpayer's share of life insurance proceeds (net of the adjusted cost basis of the policy). It is unclear as to whether and to what extent the net insurance proceeds increase the adjusted cost base of the partnership interest if they arise when net life insurance proceeds are allocable solely to the deceased partner and are used to pay the estate of the deceased for the partnership interest. Would the total net insurance proceeds increase the adjusted cost base of the partnership interest of the deceased partner? Alternatively, would the adjusted cost base be increased on a proportionate basis?

*Department's Position:*

In our opinion, the provisions of subparagraph 53(1)(*e*)(iii) apply only to the surviving partners, as that subparagraph refers to the taxpayer's share of any proceeds of a life insurance policy *received* by a partnership in consequence of the death of any person insured under the policy. As the adjustment can only take place once the proceeds are received by the partnership, and as the deceased partner is deemed to have disposed of the interest immediately before death and is no longer a partner at the time the proceeds are received, no adjustment is possible with respect to the deceased's former interest in the partnership. Although the proceeds received by the partnership may be earmarked for use by the partnership to fund a payment to the

¶720

deceased's estate, the estate does not have a right to any direct share in the actual life insurance proceeds.

Where the estate does not become a member of the partnership, it is deemed, pursuant to subsection 100(3) of the Act, to have acquired a right to receive partnership property at a cost equal to the proceeds determined under subsection 70(5), which deems the deceased partner to have disposed of a partnership interest immediately before death for proceeds equal to the fair market value of the interest at the time. In this case, the payment made by the partnership to the estate will be considered to be in satisfaction of the estate's right to receive partnership property, and the amount received by the estate must be compared with the cost of the right to the estate in order to determine any capital gain or loss.

## ¶722 Residual Capital Interest in a Partnership [Section 98.1]

A residual capital interest in a partnership consists of property which may be withdrawn from the partnership by a former partner.

Until a retired partner's rights to partnership property are satisfied, that person is deemed to have a residual interest in the partnership (section 98.1). This is separate from any income interest that the partner may have. Any retired partner may have both a residual capital interest and an income interest from the same partnership. Any amount received in full or partial satisfaction of such rights is a deduction in computing the adjusted cost base of a partnership interest pursuant to subparagraph 53(2)(c)(v). Therefore, a capital gain arises when the adjusted cost base becomes negative at the end of a fiscal period of the partnership (paragraph 98.1(1)(c)).

A residual interest is a capital property. Therefore, on the death of the retired partner a deemed disposition occurs for proceeds equal to fair market value. If the interest is transferred to a spouse, common-law partner or a trust for the benefit of a spouse or common-law partner pursuant to subsection 70(6), the deemed proceeds of disposition are equal to the adjusted cost base of the residual interest. For purposes of subsection 70(5), the fair market value of the residual interest does not include any amount in respect of income arising after death which is subject to an arrangement pursuant to subsection 96(1.1). Pursuant to section 98.2, the recipient of the retired partner's residual interest is deemed to have acquired a right to receive partnership property rather than an interest in a partnership. The deemed cost is equal to the deemed proceeds of disposition to the deceased (subsections 70(5) or (6)). By virtue of paragraph 53(2)(o), any amount received by a taxpayer in full or partial satisfaction of a right to receive partnership property reduces the adjusted cost base of the right. Where at any time the adjusted cost base becomes negative, the amount by which it is negative is deemed to be a capital gain (subsection 40(3)) and the adjusted cost base is adjusted to zero by virtue of paragraph 53(1)(a). Section 43, dealing with partial disposition of a capital property, does not apply.

The valuation of a residual capital interest in a partnership should present few problems. Generally, the amount and time of the payout can be precisely determined. The method of valuation consists of selecting the appropriate discount rate to compensate for the deferred nature of the payout.

## ¶724 Right to Receive Partnership Property [Section 98.2, Subsection 100(3)]

The third type of partnership interest is a right to receive partnership property. When a continuing partnership interest passes on death to a beneficiary who is not and does not become a partner, the interest constitutes a right to receive partnership property.

Section 98.2 provides that where a beneficiary inherits a residual capital interest in a partnership, the beneficiary shall be deemed to have received a right to receive partnership property and not to have received a residual capital interest. Subsection 100(3) provides that where a taxpayer has acquired a property that was an interest (other than a residual capital interest) in a partnership immediately before the death of the individual, and the taxpayer is not a member of the partnership and does not become a member of the partnership by reason of the acquisition, the taxpayer is deemed to have acquired a right to receive partnership property and not to have an interest in the partnership.

In either case, the right to receive partnership property is a capital property with a cost equal to the deemed proceeds of disposition to the deceased. If the property was inherited from a spouse or common-law partner, the deemed cost to the spouse or common-law partner would be the deceased's adjusted cost base of the partnership interest. In all other cases, the adjusted cost base would be the fair market value of the deceased's partnership interest immediately before death.

Paragraph 53(2)(o) requires that amounts received pursuant to a right to receive partnership property be deducted from the adjusted cost base of that right. Since the right is not a partnership interest, the amount of any negative adjusted cost base which may arise is taxed as a capital gain. The adjusted cost base of the property would become zero. Paragraphs 98.2(c) and 100(3)(c) provide that section 43 does not apply to rights to receive partnership property. Section 43 requires the computation of a capital gain or loss upon the partial disposition of a capital property. Since section 43 is not applicable in this case, it would appear that no capital gain is required to be recognized on the settlement of a right to receive partnership property until a negative adjusted cost base arises, and that no capital loss can be recognized until the final settlement of the right.

## ¶726 Income Interest in a Partnership [Subsection 96(1.1)]

The fourth type of partnership interest is a right to share in profits of the partnership after withdrawal from the partnership. This is referred to as an *income* interest in a partnership. Any income allocated to the former partner, spouse, common-law partner, or an estate is taxed to the former partner or other recipient beneficiaries. This interest is not a capital property. Any proceeds of sale are taxed in full as income and the purchaser of the interest includes in income only those amounts received from the partnership in excess of the cost of the interest.

This provision allows a partnership to provide pensions to its former partners, their spouses, their common-law partners or other beneficiaries. As well, it allows the partnership to compensate the partner for the partner's share of the partnership goodwill in existence at the time of the partner's withdrawal. Since goodwill is the capitalized value of future profits, one effective way to compensate a retiring partner for a share of the goodwill is to pay a portion of future profits.

Even though the payments may be received on a periodic basis (e.g., monthly) they retain their character as partnership income and are includable in income only at the end of each fiscal period of the partnership.

Partnership agreements which provide for periodic distributions to former partners are frequently ambiguous as to whether those payments are on account of an income interest of a retired partner, or are delayed realization of the former continuing partnership interest. Partnership agreements should state explicitly the intent in order to avoid disputes between a retired partner and former associates, and disputes with the Canada Revenue Agency.

Subsection 96(1.1), which applies to income interests, provides that this type of payment is to be regarded as a distribution of partnership profit for the subsection 96(1) calculations. Subsection 96(1.1) applies only if:

(1) the principal activity of the partnership is carrying on a business in Canada;

(2) the members of the partnership have entered into an agreement to allocate a share of the income or loss of a partnership to a former member, a spouse, a common-law partner, an estate or beneficiaries; and

(3) in the case of a predecessor partnership, the present partners have agreed to such allocations of income. There is no requirement for the partnership to continue to exist for the agreement to be effective. The agreement is effective if made among members of a new partnership which includes any member of the former partnership.

The person to whom the income or loss is allocated is deemed to be a member of the partnership for the limited purpose of the flow-through of income under subsection 96(1), as well as for the purposes of sections 34.1, 34.2, 101, 103 and 249.1.

Subsection 96(1.4) deems an income interest in a partnership *not* to be a capital property. Consequently, a retired partner who owns only an income interest in a partnership is not deemed to have disposed of it at death by virtue of subsection 70(5). Instead, subsection 96(1.5) would result in the value of the interest at death to be taxed in full. This subsection provides that when a person owning an income interest in a partnership interest dies, the provisions of subsections 70(2) to (4) apply. The effect of these subsections is to include in the deceased's income the value of rights or things which would have been included in income if realized. Rights or things can be reported in one of three ways:

1. their value can be included in the deceased's terminal period tax return;

2. they can be reported on a separate tax return, together with other rights or things; or

3. if the right or thing has been distributed to the beneficiaries, the value will be taxed as received or realized by the beneficiaries. In this case the deceased's unamortized cost of the income interest becomes the beneficiaries' cost of the interest (subsection 69(1.1)).

The Canada Revenue Agency, in Interpretation Bulletin IT-278R2, applies these provisions only to payments accrued to the death of the taxpayer and not to future income entitlements.

*Example I*

> A retired partner, who was entitled to $1,000 per month (payable in a lump sum of $12,000 on March 31st each year, which is the end of the partnership's fiscal period) as her share of the partnership income under an agreement described in subsection 96(1.1), dies on August 1, 1992. On her death, the $12,000 per year becomes payable to her spouse. On March 31, 1993, $12,000 is paid to her spouse by the partnership, which is included in the spouse's income for the 1993 taxation year

($4,000 is included under subsections 96(1.5) and 70(3) and $8000 under subsections 96(1.1) and (1.3)).

## Example II

The same as Example I except that $1,000 is paid to the retired partner at the end of each month prior to her death, and the $4,000 she receives in the fiscal period before her death is allocated to the estate by the partnership for purposes of subsection 96(1.1). The partnership allocates and pays the remaining $8,000 to the spouse. In this example, $4,000 is included in the deceased partner's income by virtue of subsections 96(1.5) and 70(2). No amount is included in the estate's income since the $4,000 that is required to be included by subsection 96(1.1) is considered to be reduced by a cost of $4,000. Pursuant to subsection 96(1.1), $8,000 is included in the spouse's income.

## When an Income Interest is Created Only by the Premature Death of a Partner

In many professional partnerships, the premature death of an active partner will entitle the spouse, common-law partner or the estate of the deceased partner to a stream of payments, usually for a fixed term. These payments will ordinarily be in addition to

- stub period income earned in the terminal period, and

- a return of the partner's capital account.

When a share of the income or loss of the partnership arising after death is to be allocated to the spouse, common-law partner, estate or beneficiaries, and the other conditions of subsection 96(1.1) are met, that subsection applies. Where the right comes into effect only on the death of the partner in respect of income or loss arising after death, subsection 96(1.5) does not apply to include any amount in respect of the right into the deceased partner's income. Further, the fair market value of the partnership interest, for purposes of subsection 70(5), does not include any value for the right.

## Income Interest Held by Non-residents

Subsection 96(1.6) provides that when a partnership carries on a business in Canada in a taxation year, each taxpayer who is deemed by subsection 96(1.1) to be a member of the partnership, shall, for the purposes of subsection 2(3), be deemed to carry on that business in Canada in that year.

It is unclear whether a person not resident in Canada who dies owning only an income interest in a Canadian partnership is subject to Canadian tax because of this interest. Section 115 is silent on this point. However, it is likely that pursuant to subsection 96(1.6) and subsection 2(3), Canada would assert its right to tax the deceased partner and/or the non-resident beneficiary. A tax treaty may apply and present a conflict with the deeming provision in subsection 96(1.6).

¶726

*Valuation of an Income Interest in a Partnership*

When a former partner dies owning an income interest in a partnership, that interest is a right or thing, the value of which is included in the income of the deceased unless the interest is distributed to beneficiaries within a prescribed time.

If the income interest ceases on the death of the partner, it has no value at death other than any income allocation which the partnership has yet to make for the year of death. The deceased partner's estate is taxed on the value of the interest at the time of death and not on its value immediately before death since it is a right or thing and not a capital property.

If the income interest continues despite the partner's death, its valuation is more difficult. Valuation problems might be avoided by ensuring that the residual income interest is transferred to the beneficiaries of the estate before the later of the following dates:

(a)  12 months after the death of the former partner; or

(b)  90 days after the issuance of the assessment notice for the deceased's income for the year of death.

In such circumstances, subsection 70(3) provides that the value of the residual income interest is not required to be included in the income of the deceased. Instead, the beneficiaries are liable for tax only when income is allocated to them by the partnership. This approach would avoid a valuation problem, defer the tax until the payments from the partnership are made, and possibly reduce the total tax liability by spreading the recognition of income over a number of years. In this case, subsection 69(1.1) carries over the deceased's unamortized cost of the income interest as the cost of that interest to the beneficiaries.

It may not always be possible to transfer the residual income interest within the prescribed time limits and the rollover might not be automatic. In that case an estimate of value must be made.

If the payments from the partnership are of a level amount over a defined period of time, the valuation problem is a matter of selecting an appropriate discount rate to compute the present value of the payments. Consideration should also be given to any effect the prospective taxes on the future annual payments may have on the value of the interest.

If the payments pursuant to a residual income interest in a partnership are contingent upon the life of another person, such as the surviving spouse of a partner, their life expectancy would be factored into the valuation as would any reduction in the income allocation upon the death of the partner

¶726

or of the surviving spouse or common-law partner. The valuation process would be similar to those for joint and survivor annuities.

If the payments fluctuate with partnership profits, the valuation is as difficult as in the case of a continuing partnership interest and the same factors will have to be considered.

If a person owning a residual income interest dies and the value of the interest is included in the deceased's income as a right or thing, the income cannot be offset with any unapplied cost of that residual income interest. The cost of an income interest in a partnership can be offset only against income from its disposition, or against income allocated by the partnership under it by subsections 96(1.1) or (1.2). Amounts included in income as the value of a right or thing do not qualify as such because they are included in income by subsection 70(2) and are not considered to be proceeds of disposition.

If a taxpayer fails to recover the full cost of the income interest and receives no more income from the interest, he or she is unable to deduct the cost from income. This arises even though the person from whom the taxpayer purchased the interest paid tax on the full purchase price.

Subsection 96(1.1) provides that, where a taxpayer has an income interest in a partnership which ceases to exist, that income interest can be transferred to another partnership if the other partnership is deemed to be a continuation of the original partnership by subsection 98(1), or if at least one of the members of the new partnership was a member of the original partnership. The members of the new partnership must agree to make the necessary allocation of income.

This provision allows a new partnership formed by the merger of two or more partnerships to honour the residual income interests of the predecessor partnerships.

# ¶730

## Other Issues

### ¶732 Payments to the Partnership from the Estate of the Deceased Partner

If a partner has overdrawn a capital account so that at the time of death the partner owes capital to the partnership (and presumably has a negative adjusted cost base for tax purposes), Interpretation Bulletin IT-278R2 offers guidance as to the administrative treatment.

Where a deceased partner's estate or beneficiaries who do not acquire a partnership interest are required to make a payment to the partnership of which the deceased was a member, and the amount, if it had been paid by the partner while alive, would have increased the adjusted cost base of the partnership interest pursuant to subparagraph 53(1)(e)(iv), the adjusted cost base of the deceased partner's partnership interest immediately prior to death may be increased by the amount paid (Interpretation Bulletin IT-278R2, paragraph 13).

## ¶734   Work In Progress at Death

Pursuant to section 34, a taxpayer having income from a business that is a designated profession may choose not to treat work in progress as an asset when computing taxable income. That is, the partnership may elect to expense all the unbilled time of its employees rather than set up an inventory of work in progress.

Where a partnership has elected to write off its work in progress for tax purposes, it may still compensate a partner or the estate for the partner's share of the work in progress at the time of death. This allocation of value may be taxed in one of three ways, depending on the circumstances (Interpretation Bulletin IT-278R2). The amount may be treated as

(a) income of the recipient,

(b) income of the deceased, or

(c) capital.

Treatment (a) applies if the estate of the deceased partner has an income interest in the partnership. In that case, the value of the work in progress at the partner's death could be allocated to the estate as a payment of the income interest.

Treatment (b) applies if all of the partners enter into an agreement to that effect prior to the death of a particular partner, or if the surviving partners and the deceased's executor and any beneficiaries agree. In that case, pursuant to subsection 96(3), the deceased's share of the work in progress at the time of death may be allocated as part of the partner's share of partnership profits for the stub period. In these circumstances the partnership would not set up any work in progress as an asset. Instead, the survivors' share of the partnership income for that year would be reduced accordingly. That share will later be increased by an offsetting amount when the work in progress is realized.

*Example (per Interpretation Bulletin IT-278R2)*

> Three professionals enter into a partnership agreement which provides that, for accounting purposes, partnership profits and losses calculated on the full accrual basis will be allocated equally among the three partners. A valid election under section 34 is made pursuant to subsection 96(3). One of the partners dies during the second fiscal period of the partnership. Partnership income for tax purposes from the end of the preceding fiscal period to the date of death is $120,000 and partnership work in progress at the date of the partner's death is $30,000. In this situation, the Department will accept an allocation of $50,000 (¹/₃ of $120,000 plus ¹/₃ of $30,000) to the deceased partner as the share of income for purposes of paragraph 96(1)(*f*) or subsection 70(2), and the allocation of the remaining $70,000 ($120,000 - $50,000) equally between the two remaining partners provided that there is unanimous agreement to this treatment, as noted above. If there is no provision for the fiscal period to end when a partner dies, the above allocation would be made at the end of the second fiscal period, and the amount shown as being allocated to the two remaining partners ($70,000) would be increased (or decreased) by partnership income (or loss) arising after the partner's death and before the fiscal year end.

If treatment (a) and (b) above do not apply, any amount allocated to the deceased partner which is based on the value of the partnership's work in progress at death:

(i) reduces the adjusted cost base of the recipient's right to receive partnership property (which was the deceased partner's partnership interest) when the amount is received from the partnership where the recipient is deemed under subsection 100(3) to have acquired a right to receive partnership property (paragraph 53(2)(*o*)); or

(ii) reduces the adjusted cost base of the recipient's partnership interest where the recipient acquires a partnership interest and is or becomes a member of the partnership (subparagraph 53(2)(*c*)(v)).

The amount allocated to the deceased partner cannot be deducted from the partnership profits required to be allocated for tax purposes.

The accounts receivable of a cash-basis partnership, such as a farming partnership, entail the same problems.

## ¶736  Death Benefit — Is it Available to the Spouse or Common-Law Partner of a Deceased Partner?

A death benefit is defined in section 248. To the extent that an amount qualifies as a death benefit it will be deductible to the payer and may be tax-free (up to $10,000) to the recipient.

Is a partnership able to allocate income to a partner's estate as a death benefit where the partner formerly had been an employee of the firm? The definition of a death benefit in subsection 248(1) requires the payments to be in recognition of the deceased's service in an *office* or *employment.* If a partner died after admission to the partnership and after long service as an employee, would a death benefit paid to the surviving spouse qualify under section 248? Although the definition refers to amounts received after the death of an employee, thereby rendering it unlikely that an amount paid to a deceased partner's beneficiaries qualify, it is not a certainty.

## ¶738 Continuation of a Canadian Partnership Upon the Death of a Partner [Subsection 98(6)]

By operation of law or by reason of the partnership agreement, the death of a partner may automatically trigger a termination of a partnership. A premature termination of the partnership could result in an additional year end, allocation of additional income and a disposition at fair market value of the assets of the partnership.

If the partnership is a Canadian partnership (as defined in section 102), subsection 98(6) provides for a rollover when a Canadian partnership ceases to exist if all the property of the old partnership has been transferred to another Canadian partnership consisting only of members of the old partnership.

This provision would apply where a partnership is dissolved upon the death of a partner and a new partnership is immediately constituted by the survivors and all the property of the old partnership becomes the property of the new partnership.

- The rollover is automatic but it applies only to partnerships. There are no forms to be completed.

- Since each partner's interest in the new partnership is deemed a continuation of the old partnership, there is no stub fiscal period, no allocation of income, no deemed disposition of partnership assets and no disposition of the partnership interest.

- Not all former partners need become partners of the new partnership, but all of the partners of the new partnership must have been members of the old partnership.

- Since the new partnership may not immediately thereafter have any members who were not members of the old partnership, any new partners should be admitted *after* the new partnership has been formed and after the tests in subsection 98(6) have been satisfied.

- Interpretation Bulletin (archived) IT-338R2 offers the interpretation that even though subsection 98(6) provides that *all* of the property of the old partnership must become property of the new partnership, this requirement will be satisfied if all of the property of the old partnership (net of satisfying the retiring partner's partnership interest) is transferred to the new partnership.

## ¶740  Death of One of Two Partners and the Creation of a Sole Proprietorship

In many two-person partnerships, the deceased partner will be precluded from transferring a continuing partnership interest to a beneficiary either because of:

(a) a partnership agreement which triggers a sale to the surviving partner (precluding the indefeasible vesting in the beneficiary), or

(b) rules of professional partnerships which preclude the non-professional beneficiary from being a partner in a partnership carrying on a profession such as medicine, law or accounting.

Subsection 98(5) provides a rollover but only in respect of a Canadian partnership. Subsection 98(5) is not elective but operates automatically when all of its conditions are met. It applies when:

(a) a Canadian partnership has ceased to exist;

(b) within three months thereafter, one (but not more than one) of the partners at the time the partnership ceased (referred to as the proprietor) carries on alone the business of the partnership; and

(c) the surviving partner continues to use *any* property in the course of the business that was, immediately before cessation, partnership property that was received by the proprietor as proceeds of disposition of that person's interest in the partnership.

The following rules apply:

1. When all other persons who were members of the partnership before its cessation dispose of their interests in the partnership to the proprietor, the proprietor is deemed to have acquired partnership interests from the former partner and not to have acquired any property that was partnership property.

This resulting capital disposition will allow the deceased to use the unused lifetime capital gains exemption (for deaths prior to February 23, 1994) or the deceased's unused exempt capital gains balance if an election is filed to recognize any of the accrued capital gain as of February 22, 1994 on the partnership interest (after 2004, any unused exempt capital gains balance would be added to the adjusted cost balance of the interest under paragraph 53(1)(*p*)). However, it will not give the acquiring proprietor a step up in the cost for tax purposes of the underlying partnership assets.

2. The partnership is deemed to dispose of all of its assets at cost amount immediately before its cessation.

3. The proprietor will have a deemed disposition of the partnership interest for proceeds of disposition equal to the *greater* of:

   (a) the adjusted cost base of the proprietor's partnership interest immediately before cessation, plus the cost of any partnership interests purchased from the former partners; and

   (b) the cost amount of partnership property received by the proprietor, plus any other proceeds of disposition of the proprietor's interest in the partnership received.

Although subsection 98(5) is generally considered to be a rollover provision, a capital gain could result to the proprietor if the adjusted cost base is less than the cost amount of the proprietor's share of the partnership assets (or if the former partners are bought out for a price less than the *pro rata* underlying cost amount).

4. Conversely, as in subsection 98(3), if the proprietor's total adjusted cost base (i.e., the adjusted cost base of the old partnership plus the price paid to the former partners for their partnership interests) exceeds the cost amount of the underlying assets of the partnership, the excess may be applied to bump up the carrying value of any non-depreciable capital assets, but subject to the following rules:

   (a) Both subsections 98(3) and (5) fail to deal with the liabilities of the partnership. Administratively, the Canada Revenue Agency agrees that net cost amount (i.e., net of partnership liabilities assumed) is used to determine the amount of the bump.

   (b) Non-depreciable capital property may be bumped up only to fair market value, and any unabsorbed excess will not be applied. It does not produce a capital loss.

   (c) For any depreciable property acquired pursuant to subsection 98(5), the proprietor will be deemed to have a capital cost in the property equal to that of the old partnership and will be liable for all of its recapture on disposition.

*Comment 1*

For transactions prior to December 5, 1985, the proprietor was able to apply the bump to all property acquired and not just to non-depreciable capital property. These old rules *may* continue to apply when the property is received in satisfaction of an interest in the partnership acquired after

¶740

December 4, 1985 pursuant to an agreement in writing entered into on or before that date. It is arguable that the old bump is available when a proprietor acquires the partnership interest of a deceased partner after the relevant date pursuant to a buy-sell or partnership agreement in writing prior to December 5, 1985.

*Comment 2*

When subsection 98(5) applies, it is not clear who is taxable on income of the partnership up to the time it becomes a proprietorship. This is especially uncertain when the proprietor buys out other living partners before the usual year end of the partnership. If the proprietorship emerges on death when the surviving partner buys out the deceased partner, the issue remains uncertain.

*Comment 3*

If the surviving partner and the beneficiary are not compelled by a buy-sell agreement to deal with each other, and if the partnership ceases and the beneficiary sells to the surviving partner within three months, subsection 98(5) automatically applies. If the sale takes place more than three months after cessation, subsection 98(5) cannot apply.

*Comment 4*

When on the death of a partner the partnership ceases and the beneficiary is not bound to sell to the surviving partner, or if the deceased was a partner in a non-Canadian partnership, the beneficiary should be in a position to choose to be dealing in either:

(a) a capital property,

(b) a right to partnership property, or

(c) an undivided interest in each and every asset of the partnership (subsections 98(1) and (3)).

# 8

# Farmers and Farm Property*

## ¶800

## Introduction

There are specific provisions in the Act which allow for special tax treatment of farmers. In part, this is due to the special difficulties inherent in starting up and maintaining a farming business. However, it is also due to the particular configuration of assets involved in a farming business.

In effect, the preferential taxation reflects the importance traditionally ascribed to the role of the farmer in Canadian business and society.

## ¶802   What is Farming?

The first issue that must be addressed is whether an operation constitutes farming. Farming, as defined in the Act (subsection 248(1)), includes tillage of the soil, livestock raising or exhibiting, maintaining of horses for racing, raising of poultry, fur farming, dairy farming, fruit growing and the keeping of bees, but does not include an office or employment under a person engaged in the business of farming.

---

* Effective in 1993, subsection 252(4) provided that words referring to a spouse of a taxpayer include the person of the opposite sex who cohabits at that time with the taxpayer in a conjugal relationship and

  • has cohabited with the taxpayer throughout a 12-month period, or

  • would be a parent of a child of whom the taxpayer would be a parent.

Subsection 252(4) was repealed effective for 2001 and later years as a result of the definition of common-law partner being added in subsection 248(1). The definition of common-law partner is similar to the extended definition of spouse contained in subsection 252(4) but has been extended to cover same-sex partners.

The word "includes" implies that the list of meanings may be extended from time to time (*Oeming Investments v. M.N.R.*, 72 DTC 1057 (T.C.C.)). Interpretation Bulletin IT-433R sets out additional activities which, while not listed in subsection 248(1), have been considered farming activities. The activities include tree-farming, the operation of a wild game reserve, raising fish, market gardening, the operation of nurseries and greenhouses and the operation of a chick hatchery.

Farming, and the business of farming, are not necessarily synonymous. As noted later in the section on hobby farmers, in order to be carrying on a business of farming, the taxpayer must have a profit or a reasonable expectation of profit (*Moldowan v. The Queen*, 77 DTC 5213 (S.C.C.)). This expectation need not relate to the immediate future (*The Queen v. Matthews*, 74 DTC 6193 (F.C.T.D.)).

However, reasonable expectation of profit has been held not to be a criterion for farming *per se* (*Matthews v. M.N.R.*, 72 DTC 1526 (T.C.C.); *The Queen v. Graham*, 85 DTC 5256 (F.C.A.)). That is, farming, as defined, may be carried on at various levels of activity, and depending on the level of activity and the expectation of profit, all, a portion of, or none of the expenses incurred in the course of farming may be deductible.

If there is no expectation of profit, the activity of farming is considered to be personal and recreational. Therefore, expenses are not deductible (paragraphs 18(1)(*a*) and 18(1)(*h*)).

If there is expectation of profit, but farming is carried on as a sideline business where the farmer does not look to farming or to farming and some subordinate source of income for the taxpayer's livelihood, deductions or losses related to this operation are restricted (section 31).

Again, some guidelines are available from Interpretation Bulletin IT-322R. Paragraph 4 provides that in determining whether a farming operation is a business, some of the following criteria must be considered:

❑ *The extent of activity in relation to that of businesses of a comparable nature and size in the same locality.* The main test is the size of the property used for farming. If it is much too small to give any hope of profit, the presumption is that the property is being held for personal use or enjoyment of the taxpayer. On the other hand, where the land is large enough to be profitable, it may also be non-business, but in limited circumstances. Where, for example, the taxpayer has made no attempt at farming or developing the land and has no viable plans to do so, it is presumed the land is held for personal use or enjoyment or for capital gain, and expenses (net of incidental income) should be disallowed. This is particularly so where the taxpayer has a more or less regular job and devotes little time to the farm. This, of course, assumes that the taxpayer has not employed other persons to carry on a farming operation. The farm may also be non-business where the taxpayer, over a number of years, has demonstrated that there was no intention of utilizing more than a fraction of the land (e.g., the taxpayer who buys a farm but uses only one field as a paddock for one or two horses).

❑ *Time spent on the farming operation in comparison to that spent in employment or other income-earning capacity.* If the taxpayer spends most of his or her time during the crop season attending to the farm, there is a strong presumption that the taxpayer is carrying on a farming business. This is particularly so where the taxpayer has farming background or experience.

❑ *The development of the farming operation and commitments for future expansion according to the taxpayer's available resources.* This test is based on the capital investment of the taxpayer in the operation over a number of years and on the acquisitions of buildings, machinery, equipment and inventory by the taxpayer.

❑ *Qualification of the taxpayer for some type of provincial farming assistance.* The particular assistance program may be useful to determine whether the granting authority requires or presumes the recipient to be in the business of farming.

Where it is determined that the farming income represents the taxpayer's chief source of income, the full amount of the loss will be deductible against other sources of income. In determining if the farming activity is the taxpayer's chief source of income, the Canada Revenue Agency considers whether the farming operation would reasonably be expected to provide the bulk of the income, or be the centre of the work routine, and is the taxpayer's major preoccupation (Interpretation Bulletin IT-322R, paragraph 1(a)). Current jurisprudence (*The Queen v. Graham*, 85 DTC 5256 (F.C.A.)) indicates that in determining whether the farming operation is the taxpayer's chief source of income, it is not necessary that it yield a current profit. In the 1985 Canada Revenue Agency Round Table discussion, the Canada Revenue Agency indicated that the decision reached in the above case was based upon unique circumstances where it has always been the taxpayer's intention to become a farmer. In this regard, they indicated that decision does not change the general application of section 31, and outline some general principles which are considered in addition and complementary to those outlined above. The factors are:

• the taxpayer's knowledge of and background in farming,

¶802

- substantial commitment of time and capital to farming,

- stated intention to farm for a livelihood, and

- implementation of plans to such an extent that farming generated a gross profit capable of providing a livelihood.

In addition, the Canada Revenue Agency indicated that a comparative and quantitative analysis of income should not be given undue weight in making any determination as to the taxpayer's chief source of income.

## ¶804

## Farm Property Rollovers

### ¶806   Rollovers Available

The spouse and spouse trust rollovers are available to any taxpayer, including farmers (see Chapter 5). However, the Act goes further in the case of specified farm property to allow a rollover to the farmer's child, either directly or through a spouse trust. The Act also provides for the rollover of interests in family farm partnerships and shares in family farm corporations.

### ¶808   Enhanced Capital Gains Exemption

The capital gains exemption is $500,000 (of capital gains) with respect to the disposition of qualified farm property (see Chapter 2). The definition of a qualified farm property of an individual (including a personal trust) is outlined in subsection 110.6(1) and in general terms is defined to be:

(a) real property that was used by

  (i) the individual or a beneficiary of a personal trust in respect of whom a designation has been made under paragraph 104(21.2)(*b*) with respect to taxable capital gains realized by the trust,

  (ii) a spouse, common-law partner, child or parent of the individual or beneficiary,

  (iii) a corporation, a share of which represents a share of stock of a family farm corporation owned by the individual referred to in (i) or (ii) above, or

  (iv) a partnership, an interest in which represents an interest in a family farm partnership of an individual referred to in (i) or (ii),

in the course of carrying on the business of farming in Canada;

(b) a share of capital stock of a family farm corporation of the individual or the individual's spouse or common-law partner;

(c) an interest in a family farm partnership of the individual or the individual's spouse or common-law partner; or

(d) eligible capital property (for 1988 and subsequent taxation years) used by those listed in (a)(i) to (iv) above or by a personal trust from which the individual acquired the property in the course of carrying on the business of farming in Canada.

Additional restrictions exist with respect to determining whether the property is used in the course of carrying on the business of farming in Canada. In general, if the property (including eligible capital property) was acquired by an individual or partnership prior to June 18, 1987, and was used in the business of farming by any of those persons or partnerships listed in (a)(i) to (iv) above in the year of disposition, or in at least five years during which the property was owned, then the property should qualify for the enhanced capital gains exemption. Where the property (including eligible capital property) is acquired by the individual or partnership after June 17, 1987 (unless an agreement in writing existed with respect to the transfer prior to that date), the tests are as follows:

(1) the property (or properties substituted therefor) must have been owned for a period not less than 24 months; and

(2) in at least two years while the property was owned, the gross revenue of the taxpayer or the taxpayer's spouse, common-law partner, child or parent (i.e., the individual who uses the property in the course of carrying on the farming business and who is actively engaged in the farming business on a regular and continuous basis) from the farming business carried on in Canada, must exceed the individual's income from all other sources in the year; or

(3) where the entity who uses the property in the farming business is a corporation or a partnership, the property must be used principally in the course of carrying on the farming business in Canada throughout a period of at least 24 months during which time an individual referred to in (a)(i) or (ii) above was actively engaged on a regular and continuous basis in the particular farming business.

Whether a person is "actively engaged on a regular and continuous basis" is a question of fact. However, it is considered that the requirement is met when the person is "actively engaged" in the management and/or day-to-day activities of the farming business. Ordinarily the person would be expected to contribute time, labour and attention to the business to a

¶808

sufficient extent that such contributions would be determinant in the successful operation of the business. Whether an activity is engaged on a "regular and continuous basis" is also a question of fact, but an activity that is infrequent or activities that are frequent but undertaken at irregular intervals would not meet the requirements (Interpretation Bulletin IT-349R3, paragraph 16).

A share in the capital stock of a family farm corporation is defined for purposes of the capital gains exemption in subsection 110.6(1). An interest in a family farm partnership is also defined in that subsection. The definition outlines that a share in the capital stock of a family farm corporation is a share of capital stock of the corporation at a particular time owned by the taxpayer. Furthermore, at that time, all or substantially all of the fair market value of the assets owned by the corporation was attributable to property used principally in the course of carrying on the business of farming in Canada by the corporation, the taxpayer or the taxpayer's spouse, common-law partner, child, parent or a family farm partnership. In addition, the property must be used primarily throughout a period of at least 24 months before the particular time in the course of carrying on a farming business in Canada in which the taxpayer or the taxpayer's spouse, common-law partner, child or parent is actively engaged on a regular and continuous basis. Holding corporations will also qualify if their assets consist of shares and debt of family farm corporations. A similar definition is provided for family farm partnerships.

## ¶810 Extended Definition of Child

The Act defines "child" to include child, grandchild, and great-grandchild (subsection 70(10)). This definition is extended by subsection 252(1) to include:

(a) a person of whom the taxpayer is the natural parent, whether born within or outside marriage;

(b) a person who is wholly dependent on the taxpayer for support, and of whom the taxpayer has, or immediately before such person attained the age of 19 years, did have, in law or in fact, the custody and control;

(c) a spouse or common-law partner of a child of the taxpayer;

(d) a child of the taxpayer's spouse and an adopted child of the taxpayer.

## ¶812 Rollover to a Child

Pursuant to subsection 70(9), if a taxpayer's land in Canada that is capital property or depreciable property of a prescribed class in Canada and

(a) is transferred or distributed on or after the taxpayer's death and as a consequence of the taxpayer's death, to a child of the taxpayer, and

(b) can be established within 36 months of death, or where the taxpayer's legal representative has made written application to the Minister within the 36-month period, such longer period as is determined reasonable in the circumstances, to have vested indefeasibly in the child,

and if

(c) the property was, before the taxpayer's death, used principally in a farming business in which the taxpayer, the taxpayer's spouse or common-law partner, or any of the taxpayer's children, was actually engaged on a regular and continuous basis or for deaths occurring after December 10, 2001, in the case of property used in the operation of a woodlot, was engaged to the extent required by a prescribed forest management plan in respect of that woodlot, and

(d) the child was resident in Canada immediately before the death of the taxpayer,

the property is deemed to have been disposed of by the taxpayer and acquired by the child at its adjusted cost base, in the case of land that is capital property, or the lesser of the capital cost and cost amount in the case of depreciable property to the taxpayer immediately before death.

The legal representative of the deceased may elect to dispose of land and depreciable property at an amount between the deceased's tax cost and fair market value immediately before death. This will enable the deceased's representative to take full advantage of any tax preference items, such as the capital gains exemption. Since the use of the property is tested only immediately before the taxpayer's death, it is not necessary that the property be used in the farming business after that time to take advantage of this rollover provision.

## ¶814 Recapture and Tax-free Zone Preserved

Where the *deemed cost* to the child (subparagraph 70(9)(*b*)(i)) of depreciable property transferred pursuant to the rollover is less than the capital cost thereof to the taxpayer, the capital cost of the property to the child is deemed to be that of the parent. The difference between these two amounts

¶814

is deemed to have been allowed to the child as capital cost allowance and may be subject to recapture on a subsequent disposition by the child (paragraph 70(9)(c)).

Where the legal representative of the taxpayer has made an election under subsection 70(9), subsection 13(21.1) may redetermine the elected amounts for dispositions occurring after 1992. Where, as a result of the election, a terminal loss is triggered on a building while the land has a capital gain, subsection 13(21.1) will increase the elected amount for the building to restrict the potential terminal loss, while decreasing the elected amount for the land by a corresponding amount. Subsection 13(21.1) will also apply to an election made by a spousal trust under subsection 70(9.1).

Where subsection 70(9) applies to a transfer of land which was owned by the taxpayer on December 31, 1971 (or which was owned on June 18, 1971 by a person who did not deal at arm's length with the taxpayer and no arm's length owners intervened to the date of such transfer), the tax-free zone is preserved in the hands of the transferee in the usual manner (ITAR 26(3), (5)).

The tax-free zone may also be preserved in respect of depreciable property of a prescribed class, transferred pursuant to subsection 70(9) (ITAR 20(1.1)). If depreciable farm property is transferred to a child pursuant to subsection 70(9), ITAR 20(1.1) provides that the normal rules of ITAR 20(1) do not apply to the bequest. However, ITAR 20(1.1) provides that on a subsequent disposition the child is treated as if the taxpayer was the owner of the property on December 31, 1971, thereby making ITAR 20(1) potentially applicable on a subsequent disposition by the child. The effect is to permit the child to recover the pre-1972 gain of the deceased taxpayer as a tax-free receipt (Interpretation Bulletin IT-349R3, paragraphs 27 to 30).

## ¶816   Leased Assets

Interpretation Bulletin IT-349R3 provides as follows:

> A lessor of farm property is not considered to be using the property in the business of farming. Thus, the property which immediately before the lessor's death was leased to another person (including a sharecropper) is not eligible for transfer or distribution under subsection 70(9), unless it was used principally in the business of farming by a lessee who is the spouse or child of the lessor and that person was actively engaged in the business on a regular and continuous basis.

> The term "sharecropper" means a farmer who is a tenant and gives a share of the crop to the landlord in lieu of rent. There may be other types of sharing arrangements, for example, where an individual is actually an employee of the farm owner and not a tenant and receives a share of the crop as remuneration for services rendered. Under such an arrangement the farm property may be eligible for transfer or distribution under subsection 70(9).

Reference should also be made to Technical Interpretation 2004-0068501E5, dated September 10, 2004, for the Canada Revenue Agency's comments on custom working arrangements and sharecropping arrangements.

## ¶818 Shares of Family Farm Corporations and Interests in Family Farm Partnerships

The Act allows a total deferral of tax where shares of a farming corporation or an interest in a family farm partnership are transferred to the taxpayer's children on the death of the taxpayer (subsection 70(9.2)). The requirements are similar to those in subsection 70(9) for the transfer of farm land and depreciables.

Subsection 70(9.2) provides for the rollover treatment on the transfer of an interest in a family farm partnership and shares of the capital stock of a family farm corporation from a parent to a child upon the death of the parent.

A share of the capital stock of a family farm corporation of a person at a particular time is defined in subsection 70(10) for 1992 and subsequent years to mean a share of the capital stock of a corporation where, at that time, all or substantially all of the fair market value of the property owned by the corporation was attributable to:

(a) property that has been used by the corporation, that person, a spouse, common-law partner, a child, the person's parent or a partnership (an interest in which was an interest in a family farm partnership of the person, spouse, common-law partner, child or the person's parent) principally in the course of carrying on the business of farming in Canada in which that person or the spouse, common-law partner, child or parent was actually engaged on a regular and continuous basis (or for transfers, after December 10, 2001, in the case of the operation of a woodlot, was engaged to the extent required by a prescribed forest management plan in respect of that woodlot); or

(b) a share of a capital stock or indebtedness of a holding corporation where all or substantially all of the fair market value of the holding corporation's property is shares or debt obligations of the farm corporation involving the same family, or property that has been used by the holding corporation in carrying on the business of farming in which the family is actively engaged on a regular and continuous basis.

A similar definition is contained in subsection 70(10) for an interest in a family farm partnership.

The definition of share of a family farm corporation and interest in a family farm partnership for purposes of subsection 70(9.2) (and subsection 70(9.3) as discussed in ¶822) differs from the definitions as outlined in subsection 110.6(1). In particular, there is no 24-month period test.

In order to qualify for the rollover, the child must be a resident of Canada immediately before the taxpayer's death, and the interest must be transferred or distributed to the child on or after the death of the parent (and as a consequence thereof). The property must vest indefeasibly in the child within 36 months of the parent's death. However, a reasonable period longer than 36 months may be allowed by the Minister of National Revenue if a written application is made within the 36-month period.

Similar to the provisions in subsection 70(9), the legal representative may elect in the deceased's terminal return, pursuant to subsection 70(9.2), to deem the interest to be disposed of immediately before death at an amount which is between the fair market value and the adjusted cost base. The deemed proceeds of disposition to the deceased are deemed to be the cost to the child. These provisions will enable the legal representative to take advantage of the enhanced capital gains exemption if the shares are considered qualified farm property or losses are available to the deceased.

## ¶822   Spouse Trust Rollover [Subsections 70(9.1) and (9.3)]

Where property which would otherwise qualify for the farm property rollovers to a child has passed to a spouse trust on death (or it has passed to the spouse trust by virtue of an *inter vivos* transfer pursuant to subsection 73(1) for transfers before 2000 and pursuant to subparagraph 73(1.01)(c)(i) after 1999), the available rollovers may be preserved. Subsections 70(9.1) and (9.3) provide for a rollover of the property from the spouse trust to a child of the taxpayer in whom it vests indefeasibly, provided the property is transferred on the death of the beneficiary spouse or common-law partner and as a consequence thereof. Subsection 70(9.1) also extends the application of the rollover provisions to farm property of a trust that is a replacement property in respect of which the trust has made an election under subsections 13(4) and 44(1). The effect is the same as if the property were left directly to the child.

Farm land and depreciable property situated in Canada, which belonged to the settlor of a spouse trust, is deemed to have been disposed of by the spouse trust and acquired by the child at its adjusted cost base or undepreciated capital cost, as the case may be, to the trust if immediately before the death of the surviving spouse or common-law partner.

(a) the particular property was used in the business of farming; and

(b) the child was resident in Canada.

For shares of a family farm corporation or an interest in a family farm partnership which belonged to the settlor of a spouse or common-law partner, the same rollover provisions apply if:

(a) immediately before the death of the spouse or common-law partner, all or substantially all of the fair market value of the property of the corporation was used principally in the course of carrying on a farming business in Canada, or an interest in a partnership that carried on the business of farming in Canada in which it used all or substantially all of its property; and

(b) the child was resident in Canada.

Accordingly, the property passes to the successor child as though the trust had never been interposed between farmer and child. The capital cost and tax-free zone provisions discussed above also apply in these circumstances. The deceased's legal representative may elect that the deceased disposed of these assets at any amount between the adjusted cost base and fair market value. As discussed in ¶818, the definition of shares of a family farm corporation and interest in a family farm partnership which are relevant for subsection 70(9.3) are not identical to those used for purposes of the capital gains exemption (subsection 110.6), and care should be taken to review all details of the specific situation.

## ¶826 Cash Method of Computing Income

Most farmers are in the business of farming. As businessmen, farmers must generally calculate their profits in accordance with recognized accounting principles and other statutory requirements as provided in the Act. Consequently, income is calculated on an accrual basis. Prior to 1989, farmers had the option of using the cash method so that income was recognized when received, rather than when it was earned, and expenses were recognized when paid, rather than when incurred. For taxation years commencing after 1988, farmers are required to use a modified cash method (subsection 28(1)). Changes to the treatment of livestock and other farm inventory have revised the method to be used by farmers in computing the income or loss from the farming business in a particular taxation year. In general terms, the changes result from two inventory adjustments — one optional (paragraph 28(1)(*b*)) and one mandatory (paragraph 28(1)(*c*)).

## ¶828   Election to Use the Cash Method

Section 28 provides that a taxpayer may elect to compute income from a farming business on a cash basis. This election may be made by merely filing on a cash basis (Interpretation Bulletin IT-433R). Once the cash method has been chosen, ministerial concurrence is required in order to convert to the accrual method (subsection 28(3)), but it appears that it would be possible to convert from the accrual method to the cash method at any time without ministerial concurrence. If two or more people carry on a farming business jointly, all persons involved must agree to use the cash method. Otherwise, the accrual method must be used (subsection 28(2)).

## ¶830   Cash-Basis Inventories and Receivables

Accrual-basis inventories and receivables are included in the computation of the deceased's taxable income for the terminal year. Cash-basis inventories and receivables may be reported in any one of three ways. Because they are considered to be rights or things, they may be:

(1) included in the taxpayer's terminal return (subsection 70(1)),

(2) included in a separate return (subsection 70(2)), or

(3) transferred to beneficiaries and taxed in their hands (subsection 70(3)).

## ¶832   Cash-Basis Payables and Accruals

There are no specific provisions governing the taxation of cash-basis payables and accruals when a taxpayer dies. Presumably as a matter of administrative practice, the Canada Revenue Agency will allow these amounts as deductions in the farmer's terminal year (*Lount v. M.N.R.*, 62 DTC 486).

## ¶833   Mandatory Inventory Add-Back

Paragraph 28(1)(*c*) requires a cash-basis taxpayer to include an amount in the taxpayer's income where the cash method of computing income has otherwise created a loss in the particular taxation year. The mandatory income inclusion is computed to be the lesser of:

(a) the taxpayer's loss from the business of farming computed without reference to paragraph 28(1)(*b*) and the optional inventory adjustment (¶834),

and

(b) the value of inventory of the farming business which was *purchased* by the taxpayer and that was owned at the end of the taxation year.

Inventory for this purpose includes property which would normally be included as inventory of a business if the income of the business were computed on an accrual rather than cash method, but does not, however, include animals included in the taxpayer's basic herd (Interpretation Bulletin IT-427R, paragraph 2). Valuation for purposes of paragraph 28(1)(*c*) is defined in subsection 28(1.2) generally to be the lower of cost or fair market value at the end of the taxation year. Special valuation principles were introduced for inventories of "specified animals" (generally horses and certain bovine animals).

The adjustment pursuant to paragraph 28(1)(*c*) was subject to transitional rules for taxation years commencing after 1988 and before 1995 in respect of a farming business that was carried on by the taxpayer before 1989. The transitional provisions outlined two alternative methods of calculating relief to reduce the effect of the mandatory adjustment where the taxpayer had inventory, which was purchased before 1989, on hand at the end of the taxation year.

The amount included in income pursuant to paragraph 28(1)(*c*) in a particular taxation year is deducted in the following year as outlined in paragraph 28(1)(*f*). The treatment of this reserve will be the same as that of the reserve created by the optional inventory add-back outlined in ¶834 below.

Interpretation Bulletin IT-526 discusses in detail the mandatory inventory and optional inventory add-backs.

## ¶834   Optional Inventory Add-Back

Paragraph 28(1)(*b*) allows a cash-basis taxpayer to include any amount of farm inventory, other than animals in the basic herd, as long as such amount does not exceed the amount, if any, by which the fair market value of the inventory at the end of the year exceeds the amount, if any, computed pursuant to the mandatory inventory adjustment as discussed above. Prior to 1989, the cash-basis taxpayer was entitled to include any amount of the taxpayer's livestock inventory (excluding basic herd) up to the fair market value of the livestock inventory at the end of the taxation year. The intention was to allow cash-basis taxpayers, especially those commencing a farming business who incur large losses in the process of starting up, to regulate income and to extend the period of loss carryforward to more profitable times.

The amount included in one year must be deducted in the next year (paragraph 28(1)(*f*)). Hence, the provision operates to establish a reserve.

On the death of a taxpayer, the amount deducted in respect of the preceding year's add-back would normally be offset by the inclusion of the inventory in the deceased's income as a right or thing, and the creation of a potentially unusable loss will be prevented.

However, if the inventory is transferred to a beneficiary under subsection 70(3), the following problems may arise:

(1) the deduction in respect of the preceding year will not be offset by the inclusion of the right or thing inventory in the deceased's terminal year return and may create a loss which cannot be used; or

(2) despite any losses caused as outlined above, and notwithstanding the fact that a certain portion of livestock inventory has previously been included in income, the full value of the inventory will be taxed in the hands of the beneficiary.

In these circumstances, consideration should be given to not using the add-back if death is anticipated in the near future. In any event, no amount should be added back in the terminal return.

## ¶836   Cash-Basis Partnerships

If all partners are in agreement, they may elect to compute income on the cash basis.

On death, the partner is deemed to have disposed of the partnership interest at its fair value. Presumably, this fair value includes the value of the cash-basis inventories and receivables. As a result, any capital gain on the transaction would include these amounts since they would not have increased the adjusted cost base of the partnership interest as not having been recognized as income. However, the value of the interest would have increased. When the partnership later realizes on those assets, their value would be taxed again as business income and double taxation may result.

This problem can be avoided by having the partnership allocate to the deceased the value of the partner's share of inventories and receivables net of payables as an addition to the partner's share of cash income for the year of death. The survivors' shares of income would be reduced accordingly in that year, but would increase by an offsetting amount when the inventories and receivables are later realized. Since the allocation of income is a right or thing covered by subsection 70(2), subparagraph 53(1)(*e*)(v) increases the deceased's adjusted cost base in the partnership by the amount of the allocation. As a result, the capital gains impact of the receivables and inventories is eliminated.

## ¶838

## Basic Herds

The pre-1972 Act recognized that it was not appropriate to tax the farmer on the proceeds of sale of livestock which was acquired in some manner not involving a deduction from income. Such acquisitions would include purchases out of capital funds, gifts, inheritances and, in certain circumstances, natural increase. The Canada Revenue Agency established a method for determining the number of this basic herd, the disposition of which would be treated as a capital and not an income transaction.

With tax reform in 1971 and the introduction of the taxation of capital gains, the need to distinguish the basic herd was considered less important. As a result, the basic herd is now being phased out. The amended legislation provides that no basic herds may be established, and no additions to existing herds are allowed in respect of acquisitions made after 1971. Rules for reducing the herd on a systematic basis were also introduced with tax reform. IT-427R provides for a concise statement of the present position:

> 6. Where a farmer who determines income using the cash method dies and has an inventory of livestock, the value of the livestock is a right or thing for purposes of subsections 70(2) and 70(3). Subsection 70(2) requires the legal representative of such a deceased farmer to include the value of livestock at death in the deceased farmer's income tax return for the year of death or elect to file a separate return to include the value of all the decedent's rights or things (including livestock) and pay tax thereon for the taxation year in which the farmer died as if the farmer were another person. Subsection 70(2) will not apply by virtue of subsection 70(3) in respect of livestock that is transferred or distributed to the beneficiaries before the time for making an election under subsection 70(2) has expired. Subsection 70(3) also provides that on the subsequent realization or disposition of the livestock by the beneficiaries, the proceeds will be income to them. The legal representative may, in computing income for the deceased and the beneficiaries, include an amount for the value of part of the herd of livestock in the return of income of the deceased for the year of death under subsection 70(2) and to transfer or distribute the remainder to the beneficiaries so that subsection 70(3) applies.

> 7. An example of a situation where the apportionment referred to in 6 above may be advantageous is as follows:

> (a) The deceased's income for the part year prior to death — $10,000 loss;

> (b) Fair market value of livestock at the date of death — $50,000;

> (c) The deceased's legal representative wishes to transfer the livestock to the beneficiaries under subsection 70(3), but also wishes to utilize the $10,000 loss the deceased has incurred in the part year prior to death and the deceased's non-refundable personal tax credits.

*Solution:*

The value of livestock equal to $10,000 plus an amount sufficient to utilize the personal tax credits of the deceased is included as a right or thing under subsection 70(2). The livestock not included in the value under subsection 70(2) is transferred to the beneficiaries under subsection 70(3) and on the subsequent realization or disposition of the livestock, the proceeds will be income to them.

8. Where under subsection 70(2) the inventory of livestock, including a basic herd, is a right or thing on the death of a farmer, the valuation day value of the basic herd that remains on hand at the time of death may be deducted from the value of livestock included as a right or thing. In such cases, paragraph 69(1)(c) is applicable to deem the beneficiaries to acquire the herd at fair market value at the time of acquisition. The fair market value is normally the value used in computing the income of the deceased under subsection 70(2). The beneficiaries are not, however, permitted a basic herd deduction under section 29 for the inherited livestock.

9. If subsection 70(3) is applicable to the transfer of livestock from a deceased taxpayer, the deceased will not be subject to tax in respect of the livestock. The amount received by one of the beneficiaries or other persons beneficially interested in the estate or trust upon realization or disposition of the herd or part of the herd will be included in computing income for the taxation year in which it was received. The cost to the beneficiary of the herd for the purpose of subsection 70(3) will be as described in subsection 69(1.1) as an amount equal to the deceased's cost that has not been deducted by the deceased in computing income plus any expenditures made or incurred by the beneficiary to acquire the herd. Since the cost of livestock of a farmer using the cash method would, except the basic herd, have been deducted by the deceased in some year, the cost of the livestock to the beneficiary would normally be nil.[35] In the case of the basic herd, the cost of the beneficiary will be considered to be an amount equal to the fair market value at December 31, 1971 of the basic herd minus the amounts previously deducted by the deceased pursuant to section 29.

10. The optional inventory adjustment and the mandatory inventory adjustment mentioned in 3 above do not apply in a year in which a farmer died.

# ¶840

# Net Income Stabilization Account (NISA)

NISA was a voluntary program designed to help a farmer achieve improved long-term income stability. The farmer deposited money annually into an individual account with after-tax dollars and the government matched the farmer's contribution (the farmer's funds were held in NISA Fund No. 1, whereas the government's funds and all interest earned on both funds were held in NISA Fund No. 2). Both the farmer's deposits and the government contributions earned interest on a tax-sheltered basis. When the farmer withdrew funds in the future, funds derived from NISA Fund No. 2 would have been taxable to the farmer in the year of receipt.

---

[35] This would not necessarily be the case where the deceased had made the optional or mandatory inventory adjustments as described in paragraphs 28(1)(b) and (c).

Subsection 70(5.4) provided that if, at the time of death, the farmer has a NISA, all amounts held for or on behalf of the farmer in the farmer's NISA Fund No. 2 would have been deemed to be have been paid out of that fund to the farmer immediately before the farmer's death, and as such, would have been taxable to the farmer in his or her terminal tax return. The income arising under subsection 70(5.4) was deferred under subsection 70(6.1) if, on or after the death and as a consequence thereof, the farmer's NISA was transferred or distributed to his or her spouse or to a qualifying spousal trust. If the farmer had losses that could have been used up in the year of death, the deceased farmer's legal representative may have elected under subsection 70(6.2) to have subsection 70(5.4), rather than subsection 70(6.1), apply to the deceased's NISA Fund No. 2 (Interpretation Bulletin IT-305R4, paragraphs 30 to 32).

The NISA program was replaced by the Canadian Agricultural Income Stabilization (CAIS) program beginning in 2003. Commencing March 31, 2004, a farmer has five years to wind down his/her NISA Fund No. 1 and No. 2 account to zero. Each year a minimum amount must be withdrawn.

# ¶842
## Hobby Farmers

The Act provides a rollover of capital assets from a parent to a child on the parent's death, and from a spouse trust to a child on the death of the surviving spouse or common-law partner for whom the trust was established (subsections 70(9) and (9.1)).

Whether these rollovers are available to hobby farmers is determined by a close examination of the provisions of these sections. In both cases, the property must have been used in the business of farming immediately before the death of the transferor parent.

Although farming is defined in the Act, the term "business of farming" is not (subsection 248(1)). The Supreme Court has held that, in order to be carrying on a business of farming, the taxpayer must have a profit or a reasonable expectation of profit (*Moldowan v. The Queen*, 77 DTC 5213).

Even though a farmer's *chief* source of income may not be farming, or a combination of farming and some other subordinate source for the purpose of determining allowable deductions, the farmer should nonetheless be carrying on business immediately before death for the purposes of the tax-free rollover provisions (subsection 31(1)). (See *Moldowan v. The Queen*, 77 DTC 5213.) The hobby farmer who carries on a farm business, but only as a sideline, would qualify for the tax-free rollover.

## ¶844

## Miscellaneous Items

### ¶846  Farm Crops

A taxpayer who farms land that is owned or rented, or who rents owned land to a sharecropper, may have an interest in a crop that is sown but not harvested. Where a taxpayer dies having such an interest, the Department does not insist that any amount representing the value of the unharvested crop be included in computing the terminal period income. However, the value may be included if the personal representative desires (subsection 70(2)).

In the event that the deceased's representative wishes to include the value of the unharvested crop in the income of the deceased, the following rules apply:

(a) in the case of a deceased taxpayer who farmed land that was owned or rented, the value of the deceased's interest in the crop at the time of death is included in the deceased's income as a right or thing under subsection 70(2); and

(b) in this case of a deceased taxpayer who rented land to a share-cropper, the value of the deceased's interest in the crop at the time of death is included in income as a periodic or accrued amount under subsection 70(1). If the deceased's personal representative wishes to take advantage of the elective provisions, the Department considers that the value may be reported as a right or thing.

Any amount included in income pursuant to these provisions reduces the amount to be included in the income of the estate or beneficiaries when they actually receive proceeds of disposition of the crop. If this election is not made, the estate or beneficiaries will pay tax on the full amount of the ultimate proceeds from the sale of the crops.

Farm land formerly owned by the deceased taxpayer may be sold after death but before the crop is harvested. In that event, no amount in respect of the growing crop is included in the income of the deceased, the estate or the beneficiaries, unless the agreement of sale or other instrument specifies the crop's selling price. Where land rented by the deceased is not retained under lease by the estate or beneficiaries until the crop is harvested, no amount for the crop is included in income of the group unless a payment in respect of the crop is received upon or after relinquishment of the lease (Interpretation Bulletin IT-234).

## ¶848   Grain Sales

When grain is sold to a licensed public elevator, the farmer receives as payment either a cash purchase ticket or a deferred cash purchase ticket (subsection 76(4)). Farmers using accrual accounting would recognize income on a cash purchase ticket when they receive it. Deferred cash purchase tickets are payable at some future date and income is recognized at that time (subsection 76(4)). Cash-basis farmers would recognize income when the cash is received.

Therefore, with the exception of non-deferred tickets held by an accrual basis farmer, tickets which are uncashed at the time of death would be treated as rights or things (subsection 70(2), Interpretation Bulletin IT-212R3).

## ¶850   Government Rights and Quotas

Costs incurred prior to 1972 for various "nothings", such as agricultural product quotas, were not recognized for tax purposes. Subsequent to 1971, a portion of such costs were considered to be eligible capital expenditures. In addition, after 1971 a portion of the proceeds of sale of these nothings is required to be included in income (section 14).

In order to prevent a farmer from selling a right or a quota at a real loss while it continues to be taxable on the proceeds, a series of special transitional rules were instituted for government rights and original rights. The effect is to ensure that the value of rights in existence at December 31, 1971 will not be subject to tax on their disposition (section 14, ITAR 21).

On the death of a taxpayer, any eligible capital property which is transferred to a beneficiary is deemed to have been disposed of for an amount equal to four-thirds of the cumulative eligible capital, and the cumulative eligible capital account becomes nil. The net result is that there will be no tax effect (subsections 70(5.1), 24(2)).

## ¶852   Principal Residence Exemption

When the taxpayer's principal residence is situated on land used in a farming business, the taxpayer may calculate the gain on disposition of such property by either of two prescribed methods (paragraph 40(2)(c)).

*Methods of Calculation*

(1) Under the first method, the property must be divided into two portions. One would include the principal residence, plus adjoining land which may reasonably be regarded as contributing to the taxpayer's use and enjoyment of the residence. Interpretation Bulletin IT-120R6 provides that if

the adjoining land exceeds one acre (one-half hectare), it must be established that the excess is necessary to the use and enjoyment of the residence.

However, on April 9, 1987 the Canada Revenue Agency announced a change in policy dealing with the definition of principal residence for income tax purposes. As a result of a Federal Court of Appeal decision, (*The Queen v. Date*, 86 DTC 6296) the Minister instructed the Canada Revenue Agency to consider the minimum lot sizes imposed by municipal authorities in the determination of the principal residence status. This means that the minimum residential lot size under a zoning by-law in force at the time of purchase will qualify as part of the principal residence.

In addition, calculation of the value of land, in excess of that included as part of the principal residence, will involve consideration of the severability of the excess in view of the zoning by-laws in force at the time of disposition.

The revised position is applied to the 1982 and subsequent taxation years. This position is outlined in paragraphs 15 and 16 of Interpretation Bulletin IT-120R6.

The other portion would include the remainder of the land, part or all of which is used in the business of farming.

Proceeds of disposition must be allocated between the two portions. Any capital gain relating to the first portion would qualify for the principal residence capital gain exemption. Any capital gain relating to the second portion would be subject to tax in the usual manner and may be eligible for the capital gains exemption available for qualified farm property.

(2) Under the second method, no allocation is necessary. Rather, the overall capital gain on both portions is calculated. It may then be reduced by the total of $1,000 plus $1,000 for every taxation year after 1971 for which the taxpayer was resident in Canada, and for which the property was the taxpayer's principal residence.

Any gain on the business-use portion of the residence and any recapture of capital cost allowance cannot be reduced by the $1,000 exemption (Interpretation Bulletin IT-120R6, paragraph 23).

Should the farmer or the personal representative wish to compute tax in accordance with this second method, it is necessary to file the requisite elections pursuant to regulation 2300.

Farm buildings, such as barns, sheds and silos, do not qualify as housing units, and therefore cannot qualify for the principal residence exemption.

If a farmer's principal residence is owned by a corporation or a partnership, the principal residence exemption is unavailable since the exemption is only available to individuals. While the corporation will not be deemed to have disposed of the principal residence when the farmer dies, when the corporation does actually dispose of the residence, it will be taxable on any gain which may be realized. Accordingly, for income tax purposes it may not be advisable to own a principal residence through a farm corporation or partnership.

The rules relating to the principal residence exemption for a principal residence in section 54 of the Act provide that, with respect to capital gains which accrue after 1981, a family unit may treat only one residence as its principal residence for a taxation year. Subsection 40(6) of the Act provides transitional rules where more than one principal residence was owned by members of a family unit at the end of 1981. This subsection provides that the capital gain realized after 1981 on the disposition of a principal residence cannot exceed the amount of the gain calculated as if it were determined in two parts — that part of the gain calculated to the end of 1981, and that part calculated on the basis of the new rules. Thus, if the residence of a taxpayer qualified as a principal residence at the end of 1981 but did not qualify after that date, only the portion of the gain that accrued before 1982 may qualify for the principal residence exemption. This may occur where, for example, the taxpayer and the taxpayer's spouse or common-law partner each owned a residence before 1982, each of which qualified as a principal residence in a taxation year. After 1981, only one property may qualify as a principal residence for a family unit in a taxation year.

¶852

# Appendix 1*

## ¶900

## Canadian Taxation and the Non-Resident

### ¶901 Residency

The Canadian tax system is generally based on the concept of residency. Canadian residents are taxed on their world income for the period that they are resident (section 2) and non-residents are taxed only on certain Canadian-source income (section 115). An individual may be taxed as a resident for part of a taxation year, that is, up to or subsequent to the period when the resident or non-resident status ceases, and as a non-resident for the balance.

The Act does not define the meaning of the term resident. The definition has, however, developed through a series of court decisions. Residency is a question of fact and many issues are reviewed in determining this status, including the taxpayer's intention and the manner in which the taxpayer conducts personal affairs. In determining whether an individual is a resident

---

* Effective in 1993, subsection 252(4) provided that words referring to a spouse of a taxpayer include the person of the opposite sex who cohabits at that time with the taxpayer in a conjugal relationship and

- has cohabited with the taxpayer throughout a 12-month period, or
- would be a parent of a child of whom the taxpayer would be a parent.

Subsection 252(4) was repealed effective for 2001 and later years as a result of the definition of common-law partner being added in subsection 248(1). The definition of common-law partner is similar to the extended definition of spouse contained in subsection 252(4) but has been extended to cover same-sex partners.

of Canada some of the factors that will be considered by the Canada Revenue Agency are:

- number of days an individual is physically present in Canada,
- the individual's underlying intention with respect to their presence in and/or absence from Canada,
- the individual's heritage,
- the individual's routine with respect to their daily affairs, and
- the individual's connections or ties with Canada.

An individual may also be deemed to be a resident of Canada for the purposes of the Act (subsections 250(1) and (2)). These provisions deem the following individuals to be residents of Canada for the entire taxation year (Interpretation Bulletin IT-221R3):

(1) individuals who sojourn (i.e., are temporarily present) in Canada for a total of 183 days or more in any calendar year. The individual must be a resident of another country during the 183 (or more) days in question. As a result, the individual may be considered a resident of more than one country;

(2) persons who were members of the Canadian Forces at any time in the year;

(3) officers or servants of Canada or a province who were resident in Canada or deemed to be resident in Canada (e.g., members of the Canadian Forces who have been serving abroad) immediately prior to their appointment or employment by Canada or the province;

(4) individuals who perform services outside Canada under an international development assistance program of the Canadian International Development Agency described in Part 3400 of the Regulations to the *Income Tax Act*, provided they were resident in Canada at any time in the three-month period prior to the day the services commenced;

(5) persons who were, at any time in the year, members of the overseas Canadian Forces school staff who have filed their returns for the year on the basis that they were resident in Canada throughout the period during which they were such members; and

(6) the spouse or common-law partner of a person described in (2) to (5) above if living with that person during the year and if a resident of Canada in a previous year, and any children of that person who were dependent on that person for support and whose income for the year did not exceed the amount used in paragraph 118(1)(*c*).

¶901

A person referred to in (2) to (6) above is deemed to be resident in Canada regardless of where that person lives or performs services, even if the individual would not be a resident under the normal rules. If, at a date in the year, that person ceases to be a person so described, he or she will be deemed to be resident in Canada only to that date.

Whether a taxpayer has ceased to be a resident of Canada is generally a question of fact. An individual who was taxed as a resident of Canada and subsequently leaves to perform duties of employment in another country, may or may not give up residence upon departure, depending on the facts. The courts have indicated there is no particular length of stay abroad that necessarily results in an individual becoming a non-resident. Generally, if there is evidence that an individual's return to Canada was foreseen at the time of his or her departure, the Canada Revenue Agency will attach more significance to the individual's remaining residential ties with Canada in determining whether the individual continued to be a factual resident of Canada subsequent to his or her departure (Interpretation Bulletin IT-221R3). Some points of note with respect to the requirements for non-resident status are outlined below.

## ¶902   Residential Ties Within Canada

An individual who leaves Canada but maintains a dwelling place in Canada will generally be considered a resident if the dwelling is kept suitable for year-round occupancy by that individual or the individual's family. This would include leaving the dwelling vacant, leasing it to a non-arm's-length person or leasing it at arm's length with the right to terminate the lease on short notice (less than three months).

Where an individual leaves a spouse or common-law partner in Canada, the individual will be considered to remain a resident unless the individual was living separate and apart from.[36]

The individual should not retain any residential ties in the form of personal property (e.g., furniture, clothing, automobile, bank accounts, credit cards, etc.). In addition, social ties such as club memberships should be ceased. Where such ties are retained with Canada, the Department may take the position that the individual has not ceased to be a resident.

Other ties which should be terminated include provincial hospitalization, medical insurance coverage, seasonal residences, professional or other

---

[36] his or her spouse or common-law partner by reason of a breakdown in marriage or common-law partnership. Similarly, where an individual leaves dependants in Canada, the individual will be considered to remain a resident.

memberships in Canada (on a resident basis), and Child Tax Benefits for 1993 and subsequent years.

## ¶904   Residential Ties Elsewhere

Where a resident of Canada goes abroad but does not establish a permanent residence elsewhere, that person is presumed to remain a resident of Canada. This is based on various court decisions which have held that an individual must be resident somewhere.

## ¶906   Regularity and Length of Visits to Canada

An individual who leaves Canada to become a non-resident will generally not be considered resident if occasional business and pleasure trips are made to Canada. However, where visits are frequent, the Department will consider this factor along with those noted above in determining the individual's residence status.

By way of illustration, an individual was held to be a resident of Canada even though he had been employed in Ireland for more than three years (*Leon Roy v. MNR*, 83 DTC 576). Based on the facts in that case, the taxpayer had not broken his residential ties with Canada and had not established residence in Ireland. The individual had rented a housing unit, maintained bank accounts, purchased an automobile and furniture. However, he did not attempt to establish Irish residence. The taxpayer had maintained an interest in a house in Canada, worked under a Canadian passport and therefore as a Canadian citizen, did not acquire Irish citizenship when made available and did not pay income taxes in Ireland.

These factors in and of themselves are not conclusive. However, the courts reviewed these along with other details, and assessed the factors as a whole. Therefore, when a taxpayer claims to have ceased to be resident, the taxpayer must review factors connected with the situation to ensure they are consistent with the non-resident status.

In a 1984 case (*Bergelt v. MNR*, 84 DTC 1042), the Tax Court of Canada held that the taxpayer ceased to be a resident of Canada despite the fact that his absence was for a period of less than two years. The taxpayer was transferred to the United States to take what was considered to be a *permanent* job. He moved to the U.S. while his family remained in Canada until the house was sold. The taxpayer did attempt to break social ties. Prior to his family moving, the employer advised him that he would be transferred back to Canada when he had completed the project. The main issue in the case points to the fact that the taxpayer's intention was to leave Canada and become resident in the U.S. It was circumstances he could not control which resulted in his return. He had, in many respects, broken residential and social ties with Canada. The fact that some ties remained did not prejudice his case to claim non-residency for the period while outside Canada. Therefore the *intention* of the taxpayer is an important issue. The relevant facts must support that intention.

The Canada Revenue Agency's position is that the date on which a Canadian resident becomes a non-resident for tax purposes is generally the latest of the dates on which:

(a) the taxpayer departs Canada,

(b) the taxpayer's spouse or common-law partner and/or dependants depart Canada (if applicable), or

(c) the taxpayer becomes a resident of the country to which he or she is immigrating.

Where an individual is considered to be a resident of Canada and therefore subject to Canadian tax on worldwide income, the same taxpayer may be subject to tax in another country, either by residency or citizenship. In calculating the Canadian tax liability, the taxpayer will be allowed foreign tax credits to reduce the incidence of double taxation (section 126). The foreign country may have similar foreign tax credit provisions. In situations where there exists an Income Tax Convention between Canada and the foreign country, the incidence of double taxation is often reduced or completely eliminated.

## ¶908  Taxation of Part-Year Residents

A part-year resident is taxed as a resident for the part of the year during which the individual is resident in Canada (or was employed or carried on business in Canada while not resident), and as a non-resident for the part of the year during which the individual is a non-resident of Canada and is neither employed nor carrying on business in Canada.

For 1992 and subsequent years, section 114 applies to determine the taxable income of an individual who was resident in Canada during part of the year only and who, during any other part of the year, was not resident.

For years prior to 1992, section 114 applied to determine the taxable income of an individual who was resident in Canada during part of the year only and who, during any other part of the year was not resident, not employed and not carrying on business in Canada. Section 114 did not apply where an individual was resident in Canada part of the year, non-resident the other part of the year, and during the entire period of non-residence was either employed in Canada or carried on business in Canada. In that case the provisions of subsection 2(1) taxed the individual on world income for the entire year (Interpretation Bulletin IT-193 [Special Release]).

For purposes of section 114 for 1991 and prior years, the period of residency was deemed to include the period during which the taxpayer was employed in Canada or carrying on business in Canada even while a non-resident. Therefore, if the individual was employed in Canada or carrying on business in Canada after the date determined to commence the non-residency period, this time period was *deemed* to be included in (and taxed as) the period of residency.

For years prior to 1998 and subsequent to 1991, both resident and non-resident taxation periods are reported in aggregate on the taxpayer's Canadian T1 personal income tax return in the dual-status year, though the taxable income is calculated separately for each period. Therefore, losses generated in one period may not be used to offset any gains accruing in the other period, even if the maximum deduction has not been taken in one of the periods (Interpretation Bulletin IT-262R2).

For 1998 and subsequent years, a part-year resident's taxable income is the individual's income for the entire year using only those amounts of income and losses for the non-resident period that are included in calculating taxable income earned in Canada under section 115. This allows the taxpayer to now offset losses generated in one period against gains generated in the other period.

For years subsequent to 2002, an individual who ceases to be, and later becomes resident in Canada in the same taxation year is subject to proposed new paragraph 94.2(5)(*c*) relating to a participating interest in a foreign investment entity in respect of which the mark-to-market regime applies.

All deductions that are available to residents of Canada are available with respect to the period of residence. However, personal tax credits must be prorated by the ratio of the period of residence to the full taxation year. For the period of non-residence, credits for certain charitable donations, tuition fees for the individual, disability amount for the individual and *Canada Pension Plan* and Employment Insurance contributions may be claimed to the extent they relate to that period. Credits for all other personal amounts may be claimed only if all or substantially all of the non-resident's world income for the year is included in computing the individual's taxable income earned in Canada for the year (section 118.94).

## ¶910   Taxation of Non-Residents

Where an individual is a non-resident of Canada for the entire taxation year, taxation may arise under subsection 2(3) or section 212. Certain types of income are subject to the regular income tax provisions as described above and are reported on a T1 (subsection 2(3) as calculated under section 115), and other types are subject to special provisions to be taxed at a flat rate (section 212), subject to withholding at source by the payor or agent.

Pursuant to section 115, earnings from employment in Canada, income or losses from businesses carried on in Canada and net taxable capital gains arising on the disposition of taxable Canadian property, as defined, will be included in income and taxed at the progressive rates at which residents are taxed, but subject to more limited deductions (see previous section). For 1998 and subsequent years, a non-resident must also include income from employment outside of Canada if the person was resident in Canada when the duties were performed. In addition, if an individual became a non-resident after 1992 and before October 2, 1996, an election can be made to have this new rule apply to such income received after becoming a non-resident.

A non-resident of Canada must report income received from any duties of office or employment performed in Canada or performed outside Canada while the individual was resident in Canada, regardless of whether the services were performed in the current year or in a preceding year. Therefore, where an individual makes various employment-related trips to Canada, Canadian tax will be exigible unless exempted by the provisions of the applicable Income Tax Convention. For example, if the taxpayer is a resident of the United States and a non-resident of Canada, employment income earned from a Canadian source will not be subject to Canadian taxation if:

(a) the compensation does not exceed C$10,000, or

(b) the employee's compensation is not borne by an employer that is either a resident of Canada or who has a permanent establishment in Canada, and the taxpayer has not been present in Canada for a period exceeding 183 days.

This rule is effective for taxation years beginning on or after January 1, 1985, unless the provisions of the prior Convention provided greater relief to the taxpayer. Under the prior Convention, the U.S. resident would not be subject to tax in Canada if the employment income was less than $5,000 and the individual was not present in Canada for more than 183 days. If the income was greater than $5,000, the employee would still be exempt from Canadian tax provided the services were performed for and paid by a U.S. resident employer.

Where income is earned from self-employment, the *Canada–U.S. Income Tax Convention, 1980* will subject the income to tax in Canada only if the U.S. resident has a fixed base or permanent establishment readily available in Canada. Similarly, income from a business will be subject to tax in Canada only if such income is attributable to a permanent establishment in Canada.

A non-resident must also report net taxable capital gains from the disposition of taxable Canadian property other than treaty-protected properties. The definition of taxable Canadian property has been modified over the years. Effective October 1, 1996, taxable Canadian property as defined in subsection 248(1) means:

1. real property situated in Canada;

2. property used in, eligible capital property in respect of, or property described in an inventory of a business carried on in Canada;

3. a share in the capital stock of a corporation (other than a mutual fund corporation) resident in Canada that is not listed on a prescribed stock exchange;[37]

4. a share in the capital stock of a non-resident corporation that is not listed on a prescribed stock exchange where at any time in the 60-month period preceding the disposition more than 50% of the fair market value of all of the properties of the corporation is in the form of taxable Canadian property, Canadian resource property, a timber resource property, an income interest in a trust resident in Canada or an interest in or option in respect of these types of property (other than taxable Canadian property), and more than 50% of the fair market value of the share is derived from real property situated in Canada, Canadian resource properties and timber resource properties;

5. substantial shareholdings (at least 25%) at any time in the 60-month period preceding the disposition in a corporation otherwise described in (3) or (4) that is listed on a prescribed stock exchange or a mutual fund corporation;

6. an interest in a partnership where at any time in the 60-month period preceding the disposition more than 50% of the fair market value of all of the properties of the partnership is in the form of taxable Canadian property, Canadian resource property, a timber resource property, an income interest in a trust resident in Canada or an interest or option in respect of these types of property (other than taxable Canadian property);

---

[37] Proposed new subsection 55(6) treats a taxpayer's unlisted shares of a public corporation that were issued to the taxpayer after April 26, 1995 and redeemed in the course of a tax-deferred reorganization spin-off by the public corporation, to be listed on a prescribed stock exchange under certain conditions. As a result, such shares will be considered excluded property for the purposes of the clearance certificate rules in section 116.

¶910

7. a capital interest in a trust (other than a unit trust) resident in Canada;

8. a unit of a unit trust (other than a mutual fund trust) resident in Canada;

9. substantial unitholdings (at least 25%) in a mutual fund trust at any time in the 60-month period preceding the disposition; and

10. an interest in a non-resident trust with holdings similar to that of a non-resident corporation described in (4).

Treaty-protected property is defined in subsection 248(1) to mean property any income or gain from the disposition of which by the taxpayer would, because of a tax treaty with another country, be exempt from Part I tax.

In addition to the above, section 115 specifically includes the following items in the non-resident's calculation of taxable income earned in Canada (Interpretation Bulletin IT-420R3):

(a) a negative amount of cumulative Canadian development expense as described in subsection 66.2(1), if not already included as income from a business carried on in Canada (subparagraph 115(1)(a)(iii.1));

(b) a negative balance in the undepreciated capital cost of depreciable properties including a timber resource property (Class 33), if not already included as income from a business carried on in Canada (subparagraph 115(1)(a)(iii.2));

(c) the amount in respect of a reserve claimed for debt forgiveness in a prior year under section 61.4 and required to be included in income under section 56.3 (subparagraph 115(1)(a)(iii.21));

(d) the excess of the proceeds from the disposition of an income interest in a trust resident in Canada as required to be included in income under subsection 106(2) over the amount that would be deductible under subsection 106(1) in respect of the disposition had the taxpayer been resident in Canada throughout the year (subparagraph 115(1)(a)(iv));

(e) proceeds from the disposition of a right described in subsection 96(1.1) to share in the income or loss of a partnership whose principal activity is carrying on a business in Canada, subject to a deduction for any cost of acquisition that has not previously been claimed (subparagraph 115(1)(a)(iv.1)); and

(f) any gain arising from the disposition, after November 12, 1981, of certain life insurance policies in Canada (as defined in subsection 138(12)), provided the policy or annuity was issued or effected upon

¶910

the life of a person who was resident in Canada at the time the policy was issued or effected (subparagraph 115(1)(a)(vi)).

The non-resident will pay tax on these sources of income at progressive Canadian tax rates. Where, for example, the individual is also subject to tax on the same source of income in the United States (either by residency or citizenship) the *Canada–U.S. Income Tax Convention, 1980* may exempt the income source from tax in the United States or Canada. The *Canada–U.S. Income Tax Convention, 1980* limits Canada's right to tax the gain on taxable Canadian property to the following types of property:

(a) property which is currently associated with a fixed base or permanent establishment in Canada or has been within the 12 months preceding the sale,

(b) real property situated in Canada,

(c) the shares of a corporation that is a resident of Canada where the principal value (greater than 50%) of the corporation arises from real property situated in Canada, and

(d) an interest in a partnership, trust or estate where the principal value arises from real property situated in Canada.

Where the taxpayer has previously elected to treat certain assets as taxable Canadian property (see departure tax section) and thereby defer the Canadian tax, as a U.S. resident the taxpayer will be subject to tax on the gain if the gain arises from the disposition of real property situated in Canada or the disposition of shares of a corporation, or an interest in a partnership trust or estate whose principal value is derived from real property situated in Canada.

Where the taxpayer was resident in Canada at any time during the 10 years preceding the disposition, and if during the 20-year period preceding the disposition the taxpayer was resident for at least 120 months (not necessarily consecutive), the gains from the disposition of any property classified as taxable Canadian property or elected to be taxable Canadian property by the taxpayer will be subject to Canadian tax.

Under section 212, passive income from sources within Canada such as interest, income from a trust, gross rents from property in Canada, royalties from the use of property in Canada, pension benefits (other than Old Age Security or *Canada Pension Plan* benefits paid before 1996), retiring allowances, payments out of a deferred profit sharing plan, payments out of an income-averaging annuity contract, payments out of a registered savings plan or registered retirement income fund and taxable dividends, will be taxed at a withholding tax rate of 25% on the gross amount (unless otherwise reduced by an income tax convention).

Under subsection 212(5.1), amounts paid, credited, or provided as a benefit after 2000 to a non-resident person or a related corporation in respect of film and video acting services provided by the non-resident person in Canada will be taxed at a withholding tax rate of 23% of the gross amount.

Under the provisions of the *Canada–U.S. Income Tax Convention, 1980*, the following rates of withholding taxes apply:

- interest income — 10% [38]

- dividends — 15%

- estate or trust income — 15%

- gross rental income from immovable property — 25%

- gross rental income from movable property (payments for the use of, or right to use industrial, commercial, or scientific equipment) — 10%

- royalties for the use of or right to use any copyright of scientific work, any patent, trademark, design or model, plan, secret formula or process and information concerning industrial, commercial or scientific experience — 0%[39]

- royalties for copyright on the production or reproduction of any literary, dramatic, musical or artistic work other than a motion picture film or a videotape for use in connection with television — 0%

- periodic pension benefits — 15%

- periodic annuity benefits (other than income annuity contracts) — 15%

- payments out of an income-averaging annuity contract — 25%

- lump-sum pension or annuity benefits — 25%

- Old Age Security and *Canada Pension Plan* benefits — 0%.

Certain sources of interest income are exempt from withholding tax, such as interest paid on Canadian government bonds and securities, interest

---

[38] The third Protocol amending the *Canada–U.S. Income Tax Convention* reduced the withholding tax on interest income to 10%, effective for amounts paid or credited on or after January 1, 1996.

[39] The third Protocol amending the *Canada–U.S. Income Tax Convention* eliminated the withholding tax on payments for the use of a right to use any patent or any information concerning industrial, commercial or scientific experience. The effective date of this amendment was January 1, 1996.

¶910

paid on real property mortgages where the property is located outside Canada and such interest has not been deducted from the income of the payor, interest payable on a deposit with a Canadian Chartered Bank (if the deposit is in a currency other than Canadian dollars), and interest payable on certain medium-term securities of Canadian resident corporations (obligations issued after June 23, 1975 in an arm's-length situation where not more than 25% of the principal amount of the obligation is due to be repaid within five years of issuance).

*Special Elections to Reduce Withholding Tax*

*Section 216* — Subsection 212(1) (Part XIII) of the Act taxes non-residents when a Canadian resident pays or credits an amount which includes rents from a real property located in Canada. The tax liability would be 25% of gross rents paid (or credited) to the non-resident.

Section 216 of the Act provides that a non-resident may file a separate Canadian T1 personal income tax return in respect of real property rentals under Part I of the Act in lieu of paying non-resident withholding tax filing under Part XIII. This permits the individual to pay tax at personal marginal rates applicable to a Canadian resident individual on net rental income (or loss) after deducting all expenses, rather than 25% of gross rentals. Generally this results in a significant decrease in Canadian tax payable. This special return must be filed within two years after the end of the taxation year in which the rentals were paid or credited. The payor is required to remit withholding tax on the gross rental amount unless the non-resident has applied for a reduction in non-resident withholding tax in prescribed form (NR6). If the non-resident has filed the prescribed form, the special return must be filed within six months (rather than two years) after the end of the taxation year.

*Section 216.1* — Section 216.1 of the Act allows a non-resident person who receives income from the provision of acting services to elect to be taxed under section 115. This will result in the individual paying tax on this income at personal marginal rates rather than at the 23% rate under subsection 212(5.1). Section 216.1 is effective for 2001 and subsequent taxation years.

*Section 217* — The rules under section 217 of the *Income Tax Act* were amended effective for 1997 and subsequent taxation years. A non-resident may elect to have "Canadian benefits" taxed under Part I of the Act rather than under section 212. Canadian benefits are defined under subsection 217(1) to include pension benefits, retiring allowances, registered retirement savings plans, deferred profit sharing plans and registered retirement income funds. By electing under section 217, the non-resident will pay tax

¶910

on the Canadian benefits at the personal marginal rates rather than pay non-resident withholding tax. In this manner, the taxpayer may be able to reduce the taxation on such receipts. In determining the marginal tax rate that applies to the Canadian benefits, the non-resident's total income including foreign income is taken into consideration. The Part I tax is calculated based on total income including foreign income, but a special credit is allowed whereby the tax related to foreign-source income is deducted from the Part I tax owing. For example, if a non-resident has Canadian benefits of $15,000 and foreign-source income of $65,000, the Part I tax is calculated based on total income of $80,000. Part I tax is reduced by an amount equal to the proportion of Part I tax that foreign-source income is of total income. The effect of this rule is that the Part I tax on the $15,000 of Canadian benefits is applied at the highest marginal tax rate. Where the non-resident's Canadian benefits, together with the other Canadian-source income gains described in paragraphs 115(1)(*a*) and (*b*) make up all or substantially all of the person's income (90% or more), the tax credits found in sections 118 to 118.91 and 118.94 will apply in determining the tax payable under Part I. Where the non-resident's Canadian benefits, together with the other Canadian-source income gains, do not make up all or substantially all of the non-resident's income, the non-resident may still be allowed certain tax credits, but these credits will be limited to a maximum of 16% of the Canadian benefits for 2001 and subsequent years (17% for 1988 to 2000).

Prior to 1997, the marginal tax rate used to calculate the Part I tax on income eligible for the section 217 election did not consider total income of the non-resident and tax credits would only be available where more than one-half of the non-resident's total income was taxable income earned in Canada.

New section 218.3 applies a 15% income tax, as a tax on gains, where a non-resident investor receives a distribution from a Canadian property mutual fund investment and the distribution is not otherwise subject to tax under Part I or Part XIII of the Act. Further, where a non-resident investor realizes a loss on a Canadian property mutual fund investment, the loss may in certain circumstances be applied against a gain on similar investments. The loss can be carried back three years and forward indefinitely.

## ¶912 Entering Canada — Deemed Acquisition Rules

When a taxpayer becomes a resident of Canada during the year, there is a deemed acquisition at that time of certain capital property, at a cost equal to its fair market value (paragraph 128.1(1)(*b*)). The fair market value, as determined, will be the cost used for the computation of capital gains and losses for Canadian tax purposes when the property is disposed of.

¶912

Effective after October 1, 1996, a taxpayer is deemed to have disposed of and reacquired all property other than:

- property that is taxable Canadian property (defined in subsection 248(1));

- property that is described in the inventory of a business carried on by the taxpayer in Canada at the time of disposition;

- eligible capital property in respect of a business carried on by the taxpayer in Canada at the time of disposition; and

- an excluded right or interest of the taxpayer (other than an interest in a non-resident testamentary trust that was never acquired for consideration).

Subsection 128.1(10) defines an excluded right or interest of an individual to mean:

- a right of the individual under, or an interest in a trust governed by, an RRSP, RRIF, RESP, DPSP, EPSP, employee benefit plan, a plan under which the individual has a right to receive in a year remuneration in respect of services rendered by the individual in the year or a prior year, a superannuation or pension fund, a retirement compensation arrangement, a foreign retirement compensation arrangement, or a registered supplementary unemployment benefit plan;

- a right of the individual to a benefit under a certain employee benefit plan;

- a right of the individual under an employee stock option arrangement;

- a right of the individual to a retiring allowance;

- a right of the individual in a trust that is an employee trust, amateur athlete trust, cemetery care trust, or trust governed by an eligible funeral arrangement;

- a right of the individual to receive a payment under an annuity contract or income-averaging annuity contract;

- a right of the individual to a benefit under the *Canada Pension Plan, Old Age Security Act* or a plan instituted by the social security legislation of a country other than Canada;

- a right of the individual to a benefit described in any of subparagraphs 56(1)(a)(iii) to (vi);

- a right of the individual to a payment out of a NISA Fund No. 2;

¶912

- an interest of the individual in a personal trust resident in Canada if the interest was never acquired for consideration;

- an interest of the individual in a non-resident testamentary trust if the interest was never acquired for consideration; or

- an interest of the individual in a life insurance policy in Canada, except for that part of the policy in respect of which the individual is deemed by paragraph 138.1(1)(e) to have an interest in a related segregated fund trust.

## ¶914  Leaving Canada — Deemed Disposition Rules

A taxpayer is deemed to dispose of certain assets at their respective fair market value when the taxpayer ceases to be a resident of Canada (paragraph 128.1(4)(b)). The disposition is deemed to occur immediately before the taxpayer ceases to be a resident of Canada. The deemed disposition of assets may create a significant income tax liability in the taxpayer's final year return.

The taxpayer may elect under subsection 220(4.5) to defer payment of any tax owing under Parts I and I.1 as a result of the deemed disposition of a particular property, provided acceptable security is provided to the Minister. Interest does not start to accrue until such time as the amount becomes unsecured. In addition, relief is provided from any penalty to the extent it is computed with reference to the unpaid tax with respect to the amount secured. An individual will not be required to provide security for an amount at least equal to the taxes payable on their first $100,000 of capital gains resulting from the deemed disposition.

Effective after October 1, 1996, the taxpayer is deemed to have disposed of and reacquired all capital assets other than:

- real property situated in Canada, Canadian resource properties and timber resource properties (subparagraph 128.1(4)(b)(i));

- property of a business carried on through a permanent establishment in Canada including capital property, eligible capital property and inventory (subparagraph 128.1(4)(b)(ii));

- property that is an excluded right or interest of the individual as defined in ¶912 above (subparagraph 128.1(4)(b)(iii));

- where an individual has been resident in Canada for 60 months or less in the 10 years prior to emigration, property the individual owned on becoming resident in Canada or inherited while resident (subparagraph 128.1(4)(b)(iv)); and

- certain property of a short-term non-resident (see below) (subparagraph 128.1(4)(*b*)(v)).

Paragraph 128.1(4)(*d*) also permits the taxpayer to elect and be deemed to dispose of property described in subparagraphs 128.1(4)(*b*)(i) and (ii). This election (Form T2061A) must be filed on or before the taxpayer is required to file an income tax return in the year of departure. These assets will be deemed to be disposed of immediately before departure and will therefore be eligible for the enhanced capital gains exemption where the assets are qualified farm property, provided the taxpayer was a resident of Canada throughout the immediately preceding year. This would provide the taxpayer some flexibility to ensure the entitlement to the enhanced capital gains exemption is not lost. Since capital gains and losses incurred by a taxpayer during the period of non-residency do not affect the taxpayer's entitlement to the capital gains exemption, the taxpayer may wish to maximize capital gains to take advantage of the available capital gains exemption. See ¶258 for a discussion of the changes to the capital gains exemption provisions for 1994 and subsequent years.

Where an individual emigrates from Canada holding shares acquired before February 28, 2000 under an employee stock option granted by a Canadian-controlled private corporation, they are deemed to dispose of the share for capital gains purposes but there is no corresponding disposition with respect to the stock option rules. In this situation, paragraph 128.1(4)(*d*.1) provides for a decrease in the deemed proceeds of disposition equal to the amount of the stock option benefit that would have been added to the adjusted cost base of the shares had the stock option rules applied.

Special rules are provided in subsection 128.1(6) for individuals who cease to be resident in Canada at any time after October 1, 1996, and re-establish Canadian residence at any particular time after that time. These rules provide on a retrospective basis that when such an individual returns to Canada, they are no longer treated as having realized accrued gains when they departed. Individuals who plan to return to Canada can defer payment of any tax arising when they leave Canada by using the security provisions under subsection 220(4.5) as outlined above.

Similar rules are available where an individual trust beneficiary leaves Canada after October 1, 1996, receives trust distributions while non-resident and subsequently returns to Canada. Generally, upon returning to Canada, the beneficiary and the trust may jointly elect to unwind the tax consequences to the trust that occurred when it distributed the property to the non-resident beneficiary (subsection 128.1(7)).

¶914

Where an individual ceased residence in Canada after October 1, 1996, and subsequently disposes of a taxable Canadian property for proceeds less than the deemed proceeds that arose upon leaving Canada, subsection 128.1(8) allows the individual to elect to reduce the deemed proceeds by the least of:

1. an amount specified by the individual,

2. the amount of the gain otherwise determined on the deemed disposition,

3. the amount of the loss from the actual disposition.

Where a Canadian resident taxpayer expatriates to the United States of America, the deemed disposition rules may cause a double incidence of tax. The tax paid to Canada with respect to a deemed disposition may not be available for full credit in the United States.[40] In addition, the United States will recognize a gain or loss on the property to be based upon its original cost and not the fair value as at the date of deemed disposition. The *Canada–U.S. Income Tax Convention, 1980* provided some relief (Article XIII, paragraph 7) for U.S. citizens by enabling them to elect to have the same assets deemed to be disposed of for U.S. tax purposes. But no relief is available for those taxpayers who are not U.S. citizens.[41]

Where the taxpayer elects to defer the disposition of certain assets, Canadian tax will be paid on the actual disposition of the asset. A foreign tax credit is provided under Canadian law (subsection 126(2.2)) to reduce the Canadian tax cost subject to limitations by the tax paid to other countries. As a result, the double taxation effect is reduced.

## ¶920 Death of a Non-Resident Taxpayer

In the year of death, the non-resident taxpayer would be subject to all of the rules to which a resident taxpayer would be subject unless the computation were adjusted under Division D of the Act (section 115). Therefore the taxpayer would be deemed to dispose of all capital property (subsections 70(5), (5.1) and (5.2)) to the extent the property was taxable Canadian property as defined in subsection 248(1). The tax liability would be calculated at

---

[40] For its citizens, Canadian departure tax may be creditable against subsequent U.S. tax (unless creditable against other foreign-source income during the intervening period) and the subsequent gains would have to be foreign-source income under U.S. tax concepts. In some cases, this relief may also be available for a "dual resident". For most non-U.S. citizens, the Canadian departure tax will not be creditable but may be available as an addition to the cost base of the property for U.S. tax purposes.

[41] Under amendments proposed on September 18, 2000 to the *Canada–U.S. Income Tax Convention, 1980*, where one country treats an individual as having disposed of a property at the time of departure, the individual may choose to be treated in the other country as having disposed of and reacquired the property, thereby reducing or eliminating any double taxation.

marginal rates based upon the accrued gain or loss, measured as the difference between the fair market value of the asset immediately before death, and one of the following balances:

(1) the fair market value at the date the individual ceased to be a resident of Canada where the property was subject to the deemed disposition rules in paragraph 128.1(4)(b), or was the subject of an election under paragraph 128.1(4)(d); or

(2) the cost amount of the property where the individual was never a resident of Canada or where the property was not subject to the deemed disposition rules in paragraph 128.1(4)(b).

Subsection 70(6) relating to a rollover to a spouse or common-law partner requires that the deceased be a resident of Canada immediately before death. As a result, there is no deferral of tax for assets which become vested indefeasibly in the deceased's spouse or common-law partner, or a trust for the benefit of the spouse or common-law partner. However, pursuant to paragraph 5 of Article XXIXB of the *Canada–U.S. Tax Convention* (1980), where an individual was a resident of the U.S. immediately before the individual's death, for purposes of subsection 70(6), both the individual and the individual's spouse or common-law partner are deemed to have been resident in Canada immediately before the individual's death. If certain conditions described in paragraph 5 of Article XXIXB are met, a trust for that spouse or common-law partner will be treated as being resident in Canada (Interpretation Bulletin IT-305R4, paragraph 33).

In general, when a non-resident disposes of taxable Canadian property, section 116 provides procedures for making payments on account of tax relating to the disposition. In Interpretation Bulletin IT-150R2, the Department indicates that section 116 does not have application to property that is transferred or distributed on or after death and as a consequence thereof. This position does not relieve the non-resident deceased from tax on such disposition or deemed disposition by virtue of section 115, but merely does not require the taxpayer to request a certificate under section 116 of the Act.

In addition to the accrued gains above, the non-resident taxpayer must report income from the following sources in the year of death:

(a) earnings from employment in Canada up to the date of death (subsection 70(1)), and

(b) income from a business carried on in Canada accrued up to the date of death (subsection 70(1)).

Where the non-resident taxpayer was previously a resident of Canada and had acquired shares of a Canadian-controlled private corporation to which subsection 7(1.1) applied, on the taxpayer's death, the stock option benefit would be included in employment income. On departure from Canada, the shares of the corporation would have been subject to the deemed disposition rules under subsection 128.1(4). However, for 1993 and subsequent years, subsection 7(1.6) deems such shares not to have been disposed of for purposes of section 7 and paragraph 110(1)(d.1).

These two sources of income, together with the deemed capital gains arising from taxable Canadian property, will be reported in the non-resident's terminal T1 personal income tax return. Filing requirements parallel those outlined in ¶200 relating to Canadian resident taxpayers. Special elective returns for rights and things (¶210) and income from a business (¶220) may be filed. However, the taxpayer will be subject to limited tax credits and deductions such as personal tax credits, if all or substantially all of the deceased's income in the year of death is not from sources within Canada. The benefit of separate returns will therefore be restricted to the lower marginal rates.

Where the deceased was the annuitant of certain deferred income plans, deemed or actual dispositions may occur at the date of death. For example, where the deceased is the annuitant of an unmatured RRSP, in general the value of the plan is deemed to be received by the annuitant immediately before death (paragraphs 214(3)(c), 212(1)(l), and subsections 146(8) and (8.8)). These deemed proceeds would therefore be subject to withholding tax (paragraph 212(1)(l)) at a rate of 25% unless otherwise reduced by an applicable income tax convention. The provisions of paragraph 214(3)(c) deem the amount to be received by the annuitant immediately before death. Therefore, the legal representatives may file an election under section 217 if beneficial.

If the proceeds were paid to the deceased's spouse or certain dependants (resident or non-resident), that portion which is a refund of premiums (¶236) would be deducted from the income of the deceased (subsection 146(8.9)) and included in the income of the beneficiary (subsection 146(8)). Where the recipient is a resident of Canada, the amount will be included in the recipient's personal T1 income tax return and be subject to Canadian tax at normal marginal rates. Where the recipient is a non-resident of Canada, Part XIII tax will be withheld at source at the rate of 25% unless otherwise reduced by an applicable income tax convention. This tax may be refunded if the recipient files the appropriate election under section 217, subject to the relevant restrictions. The amounts that are a refund of premiums which are contributed to the recipient's own registered retirement savings plan, registered retirement income fund or are used to purchase a qualifying annuity

¶920

will be eligible for a tax deferred rollover (paragraphs 214(3)(*c*), 212(1)(*l*), and 60(*l*), and subsection 146(8.9)).

Where the annuitant dies after the maturity of the plan, the deceased will be deemed to have received, immediately before death, amounts not received by the surviving spouse or common-law partner as a consequence of the death (paragraph 214(3)(*c*), subsection 146(8.8)). An election may be made to deem the spouse to be the annuitant and to have received payments out of the plan (paragraph 214(3)(*c*) and subsection 146(8.91)).

Where an amount is deemed by virtue of subsection 146(8.1) to be received by a non-resident spouse or common-law partner as a refund of premiums or in a case where, by virtue of subsection 146(8.91), the spouse or common-law partner is deemed to be the annuitant under the plan and to have received benefits under the plan, the amounts are subject to non-resident tax under paragraph 212(1)(*l*) by virtue of paragraph 214(3)(*c*). The non-resident tax liability would be calculated with reference to the amount deemed to be included in the taxpayer's income for the particular taxation year. These deemed receipts are not subject to the rollover provisions of paragraph 212(1)(*l*) since, in the case of a subsection 146(8.1) designation, a plan-to-plan transfer cannot be made by reason of the payment made to the annuitant's legal representative. In the case of the subsection 146(8.91) designation, the amount does not qualify as a refund of premiums having come out of a matured plan.

Where the non-resident taxpayer dies and is the annuitant under a registered retirement income fund (RRIF), the payment will be subject to non-resident tax at the rate of 25% (paragraph 212(1)(*q*)) unless otherwise reduced by an applicable income tax convention. The amount subject to tax is that amount that would be required to be included in income by section 146.3 had the taxpayer been a resident of Canada throughout the year. Paragraph 214(3)(*i*) deems amounts to be included in a taxpayer's income notwithstanding that the amounts have not been received. Therefore, the deceased is deemed to have received an amount from the RRIF immediately before death (subsection 146.3(6)) except to the extent that amounts are received by the spouse or common-law partner (subsection 146.3(5)). Where the taxpayer dies after 1998, similar exclusions from the deceased's income can be made where amounts are paid to or are elected to be paid to a child or grandchild, provided such person was financially dependent upon the deceased, as defined, at the time of death, even if there is a surviving spouse or common-law partner (see ¶246 for a discussion of the rules prior to 1999).

As the annuitant under an employee profit sharing plan (EPSP), a deceased taxpayer would be subject to tax on the allocation made by the trustee to the deceased in the year of death.

¶920

In computing the taxable income of the deceased from an office or employment performed by the deceased in Canada during a taxation year, amounts allocated to the deceased by an EPSP trust, except for allocated capital gains and capital losses, must be included in income (subparagraph 115(1)(a)(i), paragraph 6(1)(d), and subsections 144(3) and (4)).

The non-resident who is a beneficiary under an EPSP is required to include all capital gains allocated by the EPSP trust during the taxation year to the extent that such capital gains arise as a result of the disposition or deemed disposition by the EPSP trust of a taxable Canadian property (subparagraph 115(1)(a)(iii), paragraph 115(1)(b), and subsections 144(4), (4.1) and (4.2)).

Payments out of a deferred profit sharing plan (DPSP) are subject to withholding tax under paragraph 212(1)(m) to the extent that the amount would be included in the income of a resident beneficiary under section 147 of the Act.

Where the beneficiary was a resident of Canada and received a lump-sum distribution of property from a DPSP, an election to exclude from income certain amounts is available (subsection 147(10.1)). This election is not available to non-residents and therefore the entire fair market value of the property received would be subject to non-resident withholding tax (paragraph 212(1)(m)).

¶920

# Appendix 2

## United States Estate Tax

*Carol A. Fitzsimmons*
*Edward C. Northwood* [42]

In accordance with Internal Revenue Service Circular 230, we advise you that any discussion of a federal tax issue in this communication is not intended or written to be used, and it cannot be used, by any recipient, for the purpose of avoiding penalties that may be imposed on the recipient under the United States federal tax laws.

## ¶1001 Introduction

Taxation at death becomes even more complicated when a Canadian resident dies owning U.S. property. The estate of a deceased Canadian could be subject to federal U.S. estate tax on the full value of the deceased's taxable estate located in the United States. There may also be a separate estate, death or inheritance tax imposed at the state level[43]. Planning for the interaction of Canadian and U.S. tax taxes on the decedent (or his or her estate) has not

---

[42] Both of Hodgson Russ, LLP, Attorneys at Law with offices in Toronto, Ontario (practice restricted to U.S. law); Buffalo, New York City, and Albany, New York; and Boca Raton, Florida. (enorthwo@hodgsonruss.com; cfitzsim@hodgsonruss.com).

[43] In addition to the federal U.S. transfer tax system, many states, but not all, impose a tax on death. A full discussion of state death taxes is beyond the scope of this appendix, but it should be noted that: (i) some states impose estate taxes on the basis of residency; (ii) virtually all states which impose estate taxes do so with respect to real property and tangible personal property owned by the decedent and situated in such state; and (iii) some states also impose estate tax with respect to companies that are incorporated in such state and whose stock was owned by the decedent at death.

necessarily become easier, in spite of changes in 1995 to the tax treaty between the two countries[44] that attempted to better co-ordinate cross-border taxation.

In addition, there is continued political debate over the future of the U.S. transfer tax system (gift, estate and generation skipping taxes). On June 7, 2001, the U.S enacted a substantial tax cut bill, phasing in changes over nine years. This 2001 Tax Act provides, in part, for a phase-out and repeal (albeit temporary) of the U.S. estate and generation-skipping transfer taxes. It does not, however, repeal the U.S. gift tax. The table below summarizes the effects of that law on the basic exemption from estate taxes and the reduction in maximum rates during the nine-year period. Although this table refers to the exemption for a U.S. citizen or resident alien, the amount of this exemption also affects the estate taxes that may be imposed on a Canadian resident, as is discussed in ¶1004. Remarkably, the 2001 Tax Act includes a "sunset" provision that, if left unchanged, has the effect of re-imposing on January 1, 2011 the exact transfer tax system that was in place prior to its enactment (as it would have applied in 2006 under the prior law, which is to say the exemption would return to $1,000,000, for example). Thus, by its terms, the total repeal of the estate tax is effective only for 2010. The U.S. political controversies over the transfer tax system have not been reduced by the 2001 Act, as U.S. lawmakers continue wrestling with a number of issues, including whether repeal may become permanent, a certain level of estate tax exemption may become permanent, rates may be lowered, and the like. As of press time, there is no certainty concerning the future of the U.S. transfer tax system.

| Calendar Year | Estate and Generation-Skipping Transfer Tax Exemption (for U.S. Citizens and Resident Aliens)[1] | Highest Estate and Gift Tax Rates |
|---|---|---|
| 2002 | $1,000,000[2] | 50% |
| 2003 | $1,000,000 | 49% |
| 2004 | $1,500,000 (gift tax exemption remaining at $1,000,000 in 2004 and after) | 48% |
| 2005 | $1,500,000 | 47% |
| 2006 | $2,000,000 | 46% |
| 2007 | $2,000,000 | 45% |
| 2008 | $2,000,000 | 45% |
| 2009 | $3,500,000 | 45% |
| 2010 | N/A (Taxes Repeated) | Top individual rate under the bill (gift tax only) |
| 2011 | $1,000,000 | 55% |

[1] The estate tax exemption results is from application of the "unified credit" under the U.S. Internal Revenue Code.

[2] All amounts are in U.S. dollars.

[44] Convention Between the United States of America and Canada with respect to Taxes on Income and on Capital signed at Washington on September 26, 1980 (the "Treaty"), as amended by subsequent protocols.

¶1001

In contrast to the U.S. transfer tax system, Canadian estate tax was repealed with the introduction of the tax on capital gains in 1972 whereby at death, a taxpayer is deemed to realize all accrued gains and losses on capital property owned immediately before death, unless such property is transferred on death to a surviving spouse, or to a qualifying spousal trust. Due to the different nature of each country's tax system at death, for persons owning property in both jurisdictions it is possible that some double taxation may arise because each jurisdiction imposes a different tax without necessarily giving full credit for the imposition of tax by the other. Although the issue of double taxation is addressed in a revised Protocol, signed on March 17, 1995 and fully ratified November 9, 1995 (the "Protocol") that amended the Treaty, the Protocol does not eliminate all possibility of double taxation.[45]

The following discussion is restricted to federal U.S. estate tax rules with respect to the property held at death by a non-resident alien of the United States. Substantially different U.S. tax rules apply to non-U.S. citizens who die as U.S. residents, to U.S. citizens, and to non-residents who formerly were U.S. citizens ("expatriates").

# ¶1002 Transfer Taxation of Non-Resident Aliens

Unless eliminated by deductions or credits, estate tax is imposed upon those assets, situated within the United States, of a deceased person who is a non-resident and non-citizen of the United States (a "non-resident alien" under U.S. tax law). The tax is applied on the value of the property at death, without reduction for its original cost. Of course, ownership of U.S. property may also pose U.S. income tax issues, and implicate other types of transfer taxes such as gift or generation-skipping transfer tax. Generally speaking, the U.S. can only tax U.S. "source" or U.S. "situs" property of non-resident aliens. Part of the complexity of the U.S. tax system relates to the fact that there are three different sets of source or situs rules for income, estate and gift taxation. The situs rules are discussed in ¶1003. The chart at the end of the Appendix summarizes the U.S. taxes that may apply to non-resident aliens with property located in the United States.

If the deceased is a U.S. resident (or U.S. citizen), transfer tax applies to worldwide assets. For that reason, generally speaking a Canadian with worldwide assets in excess of the U.S. exemption amounts would prefer that he or she does not become a U.S. resident for U.S. transfer tax purposes. This residency test differs from the residency tests for U.S. income tax purposes. For U.S. transfer tax purposes, a resident of the United States is a person who is domiciled in the United States, meaning someone who is physically present in the United States, however briefly, with the intention of permanently remaining there or with no present intention to leave. On the other hand, domicile is not the basis on which a non-citizen may be deemed a resident for U.S. income tax purposes, which generally is based on being physically

---

[45] The U.S. estate tax provisions of the Protocol are generally effective for estates of decedents dying after November 8, 1995.

present in the United States for a specified number of days or becoming a "permanent resident" ("green card" holder) under U.S. immigration laws. Thus, the mere fact of U.S. resident status for income tax purposes may not be sufficient to establish residency for U.S. transfer tax purposes; conversely, a person who is not a U.S. resident for income tax purposes still may be deemed a U.S. resident for transfer tax purposes if the person is domiciled in the United States.

The residency tests and situs rules for subjecting an individual's estate to taxation during life or at death for state-law purposes may vary from the U.S. federal law rules since each state, within federal constitutional restraints and without following the Treaty, may enact its own rules.

## ¶1003   Assets within the United States for U.S. Tax Purposes

Only assets of a non-resident that are "situated" in the United States are subject to U.S. estate tax. (The gift tax situs rule is a subset of the estate tax rule, as discussed in ¶1005). The U.S. tax rules take an expansive view of what constitutes an asset "situated" in the U.S., and in some cases both U.S. and non-U.S. entities owning property located in the U.S. may be "looked through" and with the result that some or all of the entities assets are considered U.S. situs assets. The following discussion briefly describes the most important U.S. estate tax situs rules for non-resident alien decedents.

*Real and tangible personal property*

Real and tangible personal property located within the United States is treated as situated in the United States. An exception is provided for works of art that are on exhibition in the United States.

Certain types of intangible property may be deemed situated in the United States for estate tax purposes. For example, stock of a U.S. corporation is deemed to be property situated within the United States, regardless of where the stock certificate is located or whether it is held in "street name" at a non-U.S. brokerage or financial institution. Debt instruments issued by U.S. persons, including governmental bodies, generally are treated as property located in the United States. However, monies on deposit with certain U.S. financial institutions are not part of the U.S. taxable estate if the interest on those deposits is not subject to U.S. income tax (i.e., if the deposit is not associated with carrying on a trade or business in the United States). Moreover, debt obligations of a U.S. person that are in "registered form" and issued after July 19, 1984 also generally are excluded as U.S. situs property.

*Partnership interests*

Under present U.S. estate tax rules, the status of the taxation of partnership interests as U.S. situs property is unclear. It seems likely the IRS would take the position that if the partnership assets are themselves situated in the United States or the partnership is engaged in a trade or business in the

United States, the partnership interest will be deemed situated in the United States for U.S. transfer tax purposes.

Limited liability companies ("LLCs") are now commonly used in lieu of partnerships as the preferred vehicle for U.S. citizens or residents to hold investment or business property. It is generally believed that an LLC will be considered a partnership for U.S. transfer tax purposes, provided that the LLC qualifies as a partnership for U.S. income tax purposes. If the LLC "checks the box" to be treated as a corporation for U.S. tax purposes, and that corporate characterization applies for transfer tax purposes, as seems likely, ownership of the LLC interest by a non-resident alien would be a U.S. situs asset.

Similar look through rules may be applied to non-U.S. business entities. Thus, for example, a Canadian partnership may not insulate its NRA partner from U.S. estate taxation if it holds U.S. situs assets. As with the U.S. LLC, however, the non-U.S. entity may elect to be treated as a corporation for U.S. purposes. In that event, because it would then be a non-U.S. corporation, the look through rule would be avoided.

*Life insurance*

Life insurance on the non-resident alien decedent's life is excluded from the U.S. taxable estate, even if the life insurance policy is issued by a U.S. company. However, if the deceased non-resident alien owned a life insurance policy on the life of another person, the value of that policy (if any) is includable in the U.S. estate if issued by a U.S. insurance company.

*Trusts*

The United States has complicated provisions that apply to determine whether assets held by trusts created by a non-resident alien, and/or in which a non-resident alien has an interest, will be subject to U.S. estate tax at the time of the non-resident alien's death. The general rule is that a trust's assets will be considered part of the estate for U.S. estate tax purposes if:

(a) the deceased resident alien made a transfer of property to the trust during life and retained certain powers or interests in the trust, either as a beneficiary or a trustee (or in some other quasi-fiduciary capacity); or

(b) in the case of a trust created by someone else for the decedent, the decedent possessed the unrestricted power to distribute trust assets to himself or herself (or for his or her benefit).

If a trust is considered part of the worldwide estate of a deceased non-resident alien, then the U.S. situs assets in such trust at the date of death are subject to U.S. estate tax. Moreover, under a particularly strange rule, a proportionate value of the trust is subject to U.S. estate tax if the decedent had contributed U.S. situs assets to such trust. This is true even if such assets were sold by the trust during the decedent's lifetime.

¶1003

Examples of retained powers or interests in trusts that would cause U.S. estate taxation include retention of a right to income or to use property held in the trust; the unrestricted discretionary power as a trustee (or otherwise) or pursuant to a power of appointment, to determine who benefits from the trust either during its term or upon termination, if the person holding the power can receive trust property; or a retained power in the grantor[46] to alter, amend, revoke or terminate the trust.

*Options and pension assets*

The IRS takes the position that an option to acquire ownership of U.S. stock is itself a U.S. situs asset. Pension obligations, such as a 401(k) plan, of a U.S. company generally are deemed U.S. situs assets because they are considered debts of U.S. pensions.

*Special considerations*

Special rules apply to U.S. property which the deceased non-resident alien held jointly with rights of survivorship. For jointly-held property, 100% of its value is included in the taxable estate except where the surviving joint tenant is a spouse who is a U.S. citizen or there is evidence that the surviving tenant contributed to the property's cost of acquisition. This issue is further discussed in ¶1007.

Note that for U.S. estate tax purposes, a decedent's worldwide estate will include the value of many assets not generally considered part of the decedent's estate under Canadian law. Retirement assets, a principal residence, life insurance proceeds, and many types of interests in trusts all may be considered part of decedent's gross estate. This is important because even if these assets are not U.S. situs, if certain deductions or credits are claimed, the value of the worldwide estate determines the portion of deduction or credits available to a non-resident alien. And, if certain deductions or credits are claimed, the ownership of all of these assets must be reported to the United States.

## ¶1004 Deductions and Credits for U.S. Estate Tax Purposes — The Effect of the Protocol

As noted above, double taxation could result from the imposition of Canadian income tax and U.S. estate tax. The Protocol is intended to ameliorate, if not altogether eliminate, such double taxation, primarily by exempting certain transfers or assets from tax in one or the other country, by allowing deductions from the gross estate, or by providing credits against tax.

---

[46] The grantor is the person who contributes property, directly or indirectly, to the trust without adequate and full consideration. A settlor who contributes a nominal amount to create the trust generally is not considered the grantor for U.S. tax purposes. The IRS applies these rules very expansively, so what may not be viewed as a contribution, or what is viewed as full and adequate consideration, under Canadian law may be viewed quite differently under U.S. law.

*Deduction for estate expenses and liabilities of the decedent*

Prior to applying the graduated U.S. estate tax rates, a deduction (not a credit) from the gross U.S. estate is allowed for certain expenses of the estate, indebtedness of the deceased, and other similar items. The actual deduction available is based upon the ratio of the deceased's gross U.S. estate to the deceased's worldwide estate. In order to be eligible for this deduction, full disclosure of the deceased's worldwide assets must be made.

*Charitable deduction*

A deduction generally is also allowed for charitable bequests to qualifying charities located in the United States, provided the amounts are applied to qualifying uses in the United States. In contrast to the previously mentioned prorated deduction discussed above (for indebtedness, expenses and the like), the charitable deduction is available without reduction for Canadians. Importantly, under the Protocol, the category of charities is expanded to include all Canadian registered charities, with respect to transfers resulting from a non-resident's death. According to the IRS and case law, the decedent's will must provide that the U.S. situs assets are to be used to satisfy such charitable bequest or the U.S. situs assets are actually so used.

*Marital deduction*

Under certain circumstances, a deduction will be allowed in the estate of a deceased non-resident for assets passing to a spouse. If the surviving spouse is a U.S. citizen, the usual U.S. tax rules on allowance of the marital deduction apply. This generally requires that the property pass either outright to the surviving spouse or in a trust that provides certain terms and conditions for the benefit of the surviving spouse (virtually identical to the Canadian qualifying spousal trust terms). If the surviving spouse is not a U.S. citizen, the marital deduction is available only if the property passes to a qualified domestic trust ("QDOT"). There are stringent requirements imposed for a trust to qualify as a QDOT, including the condition that at least one trustee be a U.S. person.

Regardless of whether the spouse is a U.S. citizen or not, passing the property to the surviving spouse in a form that qualifies for the marital deduction will not eliminate U.S. taxation of the assets in the surviving spouse's estate upon his or her later death, or upon distribution (in the case of the QDOT) of principal during the life of the surviving spouse[47]. For this reason, use of the special marital credit under the Protocol, discussed below, may provide a greater U.S. estate tax advantage.

*Unified credit (exemption equivalent)*

U.S. estate tax on a deceased non-resident alien's U.S. situs estate (reduced by the deductions described above) is imposed on a graduated rate scale, beginning at 18% and rising to 47% (in 2005) for taxable estates over

---

[47] Under the Protocol, a QDOT which is not a Canadian resident trust may qualify for the spousal rollover provisions of the Income Tax Act if a "competent authority" request is made to the Canada Customs and Revenue Agency.

$2,500,000. Unless a treaty provides otherwise, estates of non-resident aliens receive an estate tax credit of $13,000 (the "unified credit"), which has the effect of exempting the first $60,000 of a taxable estate from U.S. estate tax. This is contrasted with the "exemption equivalent" available to U.S. citizens and residents, as shown on the prior table.

The Protocol allows estates of non-resident aliens to qualify for some or all of the exemption equivalent credit accorded to U.S. citizens and residents. For example, under the Protocol, the estate of a deceased non-resident who dies in 2005 would be eligible for an exemption equivalent determined by multiplying $1,500,000 by a fraction, where the numerator is the value of the U.S. situs assets and the denominator is the value of the worldwide assets.[48] This has the effect of completely eliminating U.S. estate tax on the estate of a Canadian whose worldwide estate is less than $1,500,000 (or the applicable exemption equivalent in the year of death). However, for Canadians whose worldwide estates exceed $1,500,000 (or the applicable exemption equivalent), allowance of an expanded unified credit under the Protocol may not eliminate the U.S. estate tax on U.S. situs property in the estate.

*Marital credit*

The Protocol also permits an additional marital credit on transfers at death to a surviving spouse equal to the unified credit allowable under either U.S. domestic law (which results in a $60,000 exemption) or the Protocol, whichever is greater, where, at the time of death:

- the deceased was a citizen of the United States or a resident of either Canada or the United States;

- the surviving spouse was a resident of either Canada or the United States; and

- if both were U.S. residents, at least one was a Canadian citizen.

For example, assume that two married people are both Canadian citizens and residents, and one dies owning U.S. real property. The estate would be eligible to elect to take the Protocol marital credit (essentially resulting in a doubling of the unified credit), if the estate passes to the surviving spouse in a way that would qualify for the marital deduction if the surviving spouse were a U.S. citizen (for example, by outright transfers or, generally, to a Canadian spousal trust). If the Protocol marital credit is elected, the marital deduction under U.S. domestic estate tax law is not available, so both alternatives need to be considered in determining which results in greater tax and practical advantages.

*Credit for U.S. estate tax against Canadian tax*

A non-resident alien of the United States who was a resident of Canada immediately before death may be able to take, as a deduction against the

---

[48] The actual calculation involves the credit, no the exemption amount. Therefore, because there are increasing marginal estate tax rates, the actual amount that may pass fee of U.S. estate tax will differ from multiplying the ratio by the exemption equivalent.

¶1004

Canadian tax payable in the year of death, certain U.S. (including state) estate and death taxes paid, to the extent such U.S. taxes were imposed on the total of:

(a) income, profits or gains of the deceased arising in the United States in the year of death, and income and profits earned by the deceased in the year of death that the United States may tax; and

(b) if the value of the deceased's worldwide gross estate exceeds $1,200,000, any income, profits or gains of the deceased in the year of death from property situated in the United States at the time of death.

A deduction for Canadian tax purposes for U.S. estate or death taxes paid by a trust described in subsection 70(6) of the Income Tax Act or that is deemed to be resident in Canada under the Protocol as a result of the death of a surviving spouse also may be allowed with respect to the extent of the income, profits and gains on the U.S. situs property described above. Any U.S. estate tax imposed during the lifetime of the surviving spouse on distributions from a QDOT also may be creditable in Canada if a "competent authority" request is made.

*Small estate exemption*

The Protocol provides a special exemption applicable to the estate of a deceased non-resident alien of the United States with a worldwide gross estate not in excess of $1,200,000. For such an estate, U.S. estate tax will be imposed only on U.S. real property held directly or indirectly by the deceased (including interests in U.S. partnerships, LLCs or corporations that hold real property located in the United States) and personal property that forms part of a permanent establishment or a fixed base of the deceased in the United States. As a practical matter, this exemption is unlikely to be necessary as long as the estate tax exemption equivalent is greater than this amount, as it will be at least until 2011. This is because a Canadian with a worldwide estate not in excess of the exemption equivalent qualifies, due to the operation of the pro-rated unified credit under the Protocol, for exemption from all U.S. estate tax. However, in determining whether an estate is below the $1,200,000 threshold (or the exemption equivalent if that amount is greater), it is important to remember that the United States takes an expansive view of what assets are included in the gross estate.

## ¶1005   U.S. Gift Tax Applicable to Non-Resident Aliens

Generally, the United States imposes a tax on gifts by non-resident aliens of real property and tangible personal property located in the United States. On the other hand, gifts of intangible property, such as stock in a U.S. corporation or debt obligations of a U.S. person, made by a non-resident alien are exempt from U.S. gift tax. This dichotomy between the gift and estate tax rules provides both traps for the unwary and planning opportunities (as discussed in ¶1007). Moreover, the gift tax is not scheduled to be repealed in 2010, even though the estate tax is, and no Treaty relief is available to alleviate the impact of the gift tax to Canadians.

For non-spousal gifts, a $11,000 (in 2005, as indexed for inflation) per donee "annual exclusion" applies to exclude gifts of that or lesser amounts from U.S. gift tax, but only if the gift transferred is deemed to be a "present interest", i.e., passing either outright to the donee or to a trust in which the donee has the right to withdraw that amount. No credit against the gift tax is available to a non-resident alien gifting U.S. situs real or tangible property in excess of (or in a form not qualifying for) the annual exclusion (e.g., there is no "unified credit" or "exemption equivalent" from gift tax for a non-resident alien).

Special gift tax rules apply under U.S. law to transfers made by non-resident aliens to their spouses. Under certain circumstances, annual gifts of up to $117,000 (in 2005, as indexed for inflation) of U.S. real property or tangible personal property may be made free of gift tax to a non-resident alien spouse. If the donee spouse is a U.S. citizen, then the non-resident donor spouse may give unlimited amounts to the spouse without U.S. gift tax. However, it should be kept in mind that a U.S. citizen is subject to U.S. estate tax on worldwide assets, so that any gift made to a U.S. citizen spouse will be subject to U.S. estate tax exposure at the time of that spouse's death (unless the property is removed from the estate prior to death).

## ¶1006　U.S. Generation-Skipping Transfer Tax

Canadians should also be aware that the United States imposes another form of transfer tax along with the estate and gift tax, called the generation-skipping transfer tax ("GSTT"). Some states also impose a similar tax. The GSTT is imposed on transfers that "skip" a generation, e.g. a transfer from a grandmother to her grandson. The GSTT is a tax that generally applies in addition to gift or estate tax (so combined tax rates may be in excess of 70%). Each transferor has an exemption from the GSTT, as noted in the table under ¶1002. For non-resident aliens, the United States imposes the GSTT on transfers of U.S. situs property (applying the same situs rules as noted above with respect to the U.S. estate or gift tax regime, as the case may be) that are subject to U.S. gift or estate tax.

## ¶1007　Planning Property Ownership

Given the high U.S. transfer tax rates and the fact that the transfer tax applies on the value of, not the appreciation in, U.S. situs assets, it has been recommended that non-resident aliens re-assess their holding of U.S. investments and that those considering investments in the U.S. plan well in advance. As well, more recent changes to the various taxing and exempting provisions and the coming-into-force of the Protocol emphasize the need to obtain U.S. tax advice before undertaking any restructuring of existing holdings in anticipation of an investment.

*Joint Ownership Considerations for Spouses*

Jointly-owned U.S. situs property can be very problematic when held by non-resident aliens. For property held as joint tenants with right of survivorship, estate tax can arise on both tenants' deaths.

Under the presumption rule described in ¶1003, 6, 100% of the value of the U.S. property is potentially taxable on the first tenant's death unless it can be shown that the survivor contributed to the purchase of the property. On the death of the surviving joint tenant (assuming there were only two joint tenants), estate tax would again apply to the full value of the property as at that date. A credit is available to the second estate for the estate tax previously paid on the first joint tenant's death, although the available credit declines every two years after the first death and expires after ten years, so double tax is entirely possible.

To avoid this potential double tax problem, it generally is more advantageous for spouses who wish to hold property jointly to do so as "tenants in common", e.g., with no survivorship rights. Transferring U.S. property originally owned jointly with right of survivorship to a tenancy in common needs to be carefully considered, however, if U.S. real or tangible property is implicated, as that may raise U.S. gift tax problems.

*Taking advantage of exemptions/credits*

To minimize U.S. estate taxes at the time of the surviving spouse's death, it often is helpful to provide in each spouse's will that an amount of property that could pass free of U.S. estate tax because of application of the unified credit (e.g., the amount of the exemption equivalent) pass in trust for the benefit of the surviving spouse (a so-called "bypass" or "credit shelter" trust). The terms of this trust would be such that the trust property is not includable in the surviving spouse's estate upon his or her later death. This allows the marital couple to fully utilize each spouse's exemption equivalent.

When spouses are considering how to own U.S. situs property, they should first consider whether the use of available credits (especially the pro-rated unified credit and martial credit under the Protocol) may reduce or eliminate U.S. estate tax exposure. For example, in 2005 where the estate tax exemption equivalent is $1,500,000, if one spouse has a worldwide estate less than that amount, that spouse could hold title to the U.S. property and avoid U.S. estate tax on his or her death, assuming the exemption equivalent stays at least that high and that the value of assets in that spouse's estate do not increase above the exemption equivalent amount. If the property is left to the survivor spouse in a trust with terms[49] that avoid inclusion in the survivor's estate, there would be no estate tax at either spouse's death.

It is important to recognize, however, that planning in this manner is successful in reducing or eliminating U.S. estate tax exposure only if the assumptions remain true. Since there is so much uncertainty in this area,

---

[49] These terms are rather peculiar to U.S. law, so a "typical" discretionary spousal trust generally would not have the right terms for this purpose, without some modifications.

¶1007

particularly concerning how the U.S. estate tax rules may operate in the future, planning to keep the property out of both spouses' estates can be challenging.

## Gifting Property

As discussed in ¶1005, the United States does not impose gift tax on gifts of intangible U.S. situs property by non-resident aliens. Therefore, transfer of such intangible property by gift during the non-resident's life is a planning opportunity, because otherwise ownership of such property at death will be includable in the non-resident alien's gross estate for U.S. estate tax purposes. Of course, the Canadian tax consequences of such gifts need to be considered as well.

Gift transfers of U.S. real property and tangible personal property, although generally subject to the U.S. gift tax rules, may be made free of gift tax if they are within the $11,000-plus annual exclusion limit (for non-spousal transfers), or, if the transfers are to a spouse, within the $117,000-plus limit applicable to non-citizen spouses (and without limitation to a U.S. citizen spouse).

## Qualified Domestic Trusts

A QDOT only provides deferral of U.S. estate tax. The QDOT estate tax is imposed at the rate applicable to the deceased spouse's estate as though no deferral were permitted. It is imposed on capital invasions made for the surviving spouse during life (except for hardship), as well as on the balance remaining in the QDOT at the surviving spouse's death.

The non-resident alien's will may specifically provide for formation of a trust that would qualify as a QDQT. If the will does not do so, it still would be possible for the executor or the surviving spouse to create a QDOT if certain steps are taken within a specific time after death. It may be disadvantageous to rely on that type of post mortem planning to establish a QDOT because of practical and other tax factors, however, so establishing a trust that could qualify as a QDOT under the terms of the will is desirable. If the will has sufficient flexibility, the executor could then decide whether the QDOT election should be made, or whether it would be more beneficial to utilize the marital credit under the Protocol rather than a QDOT. As noted previously, only one of those alternatives may be selected.

## Real Property Mortgages

A deduction from the U.S. gross estate is available for certain outstanding mortgages on U.S. real property.

A nonrecourse mortgage, where the borrower has no personal liability and the lender may only look to the property for satisfaction of the debt, is fully deductible from the gross estate. Nonrecourse mortgages are becoming more popular, especially in areas of the United States where property values have been consistently appreciating. Usually the lender will provide a nonre-

¶1007

course mortgage up to only 50–65% of the property's value, however, so this technique may not completely eliminate estate tax exposure.

A deduction for a recourse mortgage is available, but it is prorated based on the ratio of the deceased's worldwide debt to worldwide assets (as are other debts and expenses, as described in ¶1004, 1). Therefore, use of a recourse mortgage for estate planning purposes is often of limited utility. Moreover, to claim the pro-rated deduction, complete disclosure of the deceased's worldwide assets and liabilities is required.

*Ownership of U.S. Situs Property by a Trust*

Having the U.S. situs property owned by a properly-structured trust from the outset can avoid U.S. estate tax altogether for a non-resident alien and his or her family. This can be a particularly attractive structure for holding U.S. real estate. In the usual situation, the trust is created by one spouse (the grantor) and funded with his or her separate assets. The other spouse is the beneficiary during his or her life (the couple's descendants can also be beneficiaries during the beneficiary spouse's life if desired). The couple's descendants typically would be the remaindermen. The grantor may occupy the property at the "sufferance" of the beneficiary spouse during the beneficiary spouse's life, but if the beneficiary spouse dies first, the grantor cannot use the property unless he or she pays fair market rent to the trust. Special terms need to be drafted into the trust agreement, particularly if the beneficiary spouse is to be a trustee (which is permissible as long as certain limitations are placed on his or her discretion), and to maintain flexibility. The grantor cannot have any reversionary interest in the property or its proceeds of sale.

In addition to the estate tax advantages to use of the trust structure, under current U.S. income tax law, there is an income tax advantage when the property is sold, as contrasted with corporate ownership of that property (discussed immediately below). For example, the preferential long term capital gains rate, a maximum of 15% federally (in 2005), is available if the trust owns the property, whereas the corporate capital gains rate applies generally at 34% rate federally (in 2005).

*Ownership by a Canadian Corporation*

Although previously a favoured approach, use of a Canadian (or non-U.S.) corporation to own U.S. property poses significant disadvantages and estate tax risks particularly if the U.S. property is not owned by the corporation from the outset.

Among the disadvantages are that (i) there are Canadian "shareholder benefit" problems; (ii) the IRS may attempt to impose U.S. estate tax on the U.S. situs assets owned by such corporation (under either a "retained interest" analysis, or a "sham/lack of substance" theory); and (iii) under the present U.S. income tax scheme, corporate capital gains are generally taxed at 34% federally, whereas an individual or trust with capital gains that qualify as

¶1007

long term (e.g., property held greater than one year) may obtain a 15% federal income tax rate.

### Purchase of Life Insurance

Instead of avoiding U.S. estate tax, some non-resident aliens may prefer to purchase life insurance. The amount of insurance may replace the amount of U.S. estate tax payable on death and provide a source of funds for the estate.

### Transfer of Existing Ownership

The transfer of existing ownership of US. property requires careful consideration because any restructuring planned to avoid U.S. estate taxation at death may trigger immediate US. income or gift tax to the existing owner and Canadian tax may also arise.

Transferring U.S. situs property to a non-U.S. corporation owned and controlled by the transferor, although sometimes a recommended approach, is likely to be deemed ineffective by the IRS in removing U.S. situs property from the estate, either on a "retained interest" theory, or a "sham/lack of substance" theory.

Finally, potential cross-border tax mismatching resulting in possible "double tax" may arise under certain planning approaches, so these issues must be carefully considered.

### U.S. Tax Effects for U.S. Holdings of Non-Resident Alien Individuals Not Engaged in Business in U.S.

| Form of U.S. Investment[1] | U.S. Income Tax on Income Generated by U.S. Investment?[2] | U.S. Estate Tax? | U.S. Gift Tax? |
|---|---|---|---|
| A.  *Direct Ownership* | | | |
| 1.  Non-resident alien individual owning: bank accounts; CDs; certain Treasury bills, bonds, notes or portfolio debt obligations (issued post 7-18-84)[3]; life insurance[4] ("Exempt U.S. Situs Assets") | No | No | Transfer of intangibles by non-resident alien individual is not subject to U.S. gift tax, except for cash transferred in the U.S. |
| 2.  Non-resident alien individual owning stock of U.S. corporations; pre 7-19-84 bonds or Treasury obligations; money market funds; real property; tangible personal property ("Non-Exempt U.S. Situs Assets") | Yes, at reduced Treaty rate if available | Yes | No, except for U.S. real property and U.S. tangible personal property |
| B.  *Corporate Ownership* | | | |

¶1007

| Form of U.S. Investment[1] | U.S. Income Tax on Income Generated by U.S. Investment?[2] | U.S. Estate Tax? | U.S. Gift Tax? |
|---|---|---|---|
| 1. Non-resident alien individual owning stock of non-U.S. corporation that owns Exempt U.S. Situs Assets | No | No | No |
| 2. Non-resident alien individual owning stock of a non-U.S. corporation that owns Non-Exempt U.S. Situs Assets | Yes, and corporate rates apply (unless Treaty reduces rates, or it involves capital gains from other than a U.S. real property interest) | Maybe, if IRS asserts a "retained interest" or "lack of substance" theory | Maybe, if real property or tangible property in the U.S. is held by the corporation and the IRS "looks through" the structure |
| *C. Partnership Ownership[5]* | | | |
| 1. Non-resident alien individual owning a partnership interest that owns Exempt U.S. Situs Assets | No | No | No, except for a partnership interest where cash is located in the U.S. |
| 2. Non-resident alien individual owning a partnership interest that owns Non-exempt U.S. Situs Assets | Yes | Probably[6] | Probably |
| *D. Trust Ownership* | | | |
| 1. Trust with no retained interests[7] by grantor (as trustee, beneficiary or otherwise) | No | No | Transfer into trust should not be subject to U.S. gift tax, except for cash transferred in the U.S. |
| 2. Trust with retained interests by grantor (e.g., settor is a trustee, a beneficiary, or holds certain other powers)[8] | Yes, unless Exempt U.S. Situs Assets held in trust | Yes, unless Exempt U.S. Situs Assets held in trust | Yes, if transfer into trust is U.S. real property or tangible personal property located in the U.S. |

1   All assets listed are U.S. source (i.e., physically located in the U.S. or issued by a U.S. person or entity).

2   In general, capital gains of non-residents are not taxed by the U.S. as long as they are not effectively connected with a U.S. business or related to U.S. real property interests.

3   Note that in general obligations of a U.S. person held by a non-resident alien are subject to U.S. income and estate tax. The items listed in #1 are the exception to this rule.

4   Proceeds from a life insurance policy written by a U.S. company on the life of a non-resident alien are not subject to U.S. estate tax.

5   Additional considerations are involved if the partnership engages in a U.S. business and the U.S. tax consequences in that circumstances may differ from those set forth herein

6   The U.S. gift or estate tax consequences of transferring an interest in a partnership that owns Non-Exempt U.S. situs assets that would be subject to U.S. gift or estate tax if owned directly by the individual are uncertain under present law; there is a high risk of such taxation.

7   "Retained interests" that present potential tax problems are described at ¶1003, 4.

8   Under Section 2104 of the Internal Revenue Code of 1986, as amended, if non-exempt U.S. situs property is transferred to such a trust during life without full and adequate consideration, or owned by the trust at death, there is U.S. estate tax exposure, even if the U.S. situs property is disposed of by the trust before death.

¶1007

# Appendix 3

---

## ¶1100

## Checklist of Filing Requirements

❏ File a terminal period return for the period from January 1 of the year of death up to the date of death, including all income accruing up to that time. If the taxpayer died after October 1 in the year before the individual's filing due date for the year, outstanding returns must be filed on or before the later of six months from the date of death and the day when the return would otherwise have been required to be filed (paragraph 150(1)(*b*), ¶200). If the taxpayer dies in the first ten months of the year, the deadline is April 30 of the following year or, in the case of an individual or the spouse or common-law partner of such individual who carried on a business during the year, June 15 of the following year (paragraph 150(1)(*d*)). See ¶200 for a discussion of the deadlines where the deceased or deceased's spouse or common-law partner was carrying on a business in the year of death. Where the provisions of subsection 70(7) have been applied to "untaint" a spouse trust or common-law partner trust, the terminal period return must be filed within 18 months after the date of death (¶504).

❏ File a separate return for rights and things, as necessary. Election to be made by the later of one year from the date of death or 90 days after the notice of assessment of the terminal period return is mailed (subsection 70(2)).

❑ File a separate return for income from the stub year of a proprietorship or partnership whose fiscal year ended prior to the date of death, as applicable. A separate return must be filed by the later of six months after death and the individual's filing due date for the year of death (subsection 150(4), paragraph 150(1)(*b*)).

❑ File a separate return for income from a testamentary trust of which the deceased was a beneficiary, as applicable. A separate return must be filed by the later of six months after death and the individual's filing due date for the year of death (paragraph 104(23)(*d*)).

❑ File returns for years prior to the year of death where those returns have not been filed by the deceased taxpayer during his or her lifetime.

❑ If no election has been made in prior taxation years for Valuation Day value or tax-free zone value with respect to the disposition of capital property acquired by the deceased prior to 1971, that election may be made by the personal representative.

❑ File elections and post security for payments in instalments of tax pertaining to specified items (see ¶286).

❑ If the will contains transfers or distributions to a spouse, common-law partner, spouse trust or common-law partner trust, consider filing an election pursuant to subsection 70(6.2) in the terminal return to not have the rollover provisions of subsection 70(6) apply to property specified in the election.

Rather, subsection 70(5) will deem the deceased to have disposed of capital property for proceeds of disposition which may result in capital gains, capital losses, recapture or a terminal loss.

Utilize to:

(i) offset any losses carried forward by triggering gains or recapture without incurring any tax liability and increasing the cost base in the property to a spouse, common-law partner, spouse trust or common-law partner trust,

(ii) offset any income in the year of death including, for example, a refund of premiums under a registered retirement savings plan where the assets otherwise transferred have accrued losses or a terminal loss, and

(iii) trigger capital gains in year of death to take advantage of any capital gains exemption of the deceased then remaining.

¶1100

- [ ] If the will contains a spouse trust or common-law partner trust which is charged or tainted, file an election pursuant to subsection 70(7) to untaint the trust by designating certain assets deemed to be realized at fair market value immediately before death. This election makes it possible for the remaining assets to be rolled over to the spouse trust or common-law partner trust at their adjusted cost base to the deceased.

- [ ] If a spouse, common-law partner, spouse trust or common-law partner trust receives property *in specie* that is a right to receive an amount not yet due, consider filing an election under subsection 72(2) (Form T2069) to deduct from income of the terminal period a reserve in respect of that property, and to transfer the reserve to the beneficiary spouse or spouse trust for inclusion in the income of the beneficiary.

- [ ] If the terminal losses and allowable capital losses are realized in the first taxation year of the estate, file an election under subsection 164(6) to deem those losses to be losses for the taxation year in which the taxpayer died and to file an amended return for the year of death pursuant to the election.

- [ ] File a T3 trust return for each fiscal period of the estate, including stub periods which may occur at the opening and winding-up of the estate. The T3 return must be filed within 90 days of the end of the taxation year of the trust. T3 Supplementary slips must be issued to each beneficiary of the estate to whom income of the estate is paid or payable in the taxation year of the trust, and T3 Summaries must be filed with the Canada Revenue Agency.

- [ ] Allocate any capital gains, which by the terms of the will may be required to accumulate in the estate, either to the trust or to the relevant beneficiary or beneficiaries to whom the gains are payable, in order to determine liability for tax on those amounts. If the beneficiary is resident in Canada, would otherwise qualify in the year for the disability tax credit, and falls within the appropriate relationship to the testator, a preferred beneficiary election may be made in these circumstances regardless of whether amounts are actually paid or payable to such beneficiary.

- [ ] Prior to the wind-up of the estate and the distribution of its assets to the beneficiaries, obtain a clearance certificate from the Canada Revenue Agency pursuant to subsection 159(2) certifying that all taxes, interest and penalties of the deceased and the estate have been paid, or that adequate security has been given to the Canada Revenue

¶1100

Agency in respect of any unpaid tax or other amounts. If this certificate is not obtained, the personal representative will remain personally liable to the Canada Revenue Agency for any tax which remains outstanding to the extent of the value of the assets of the estate. If the estate is distributed prior to receiving the certificate, the personal representative should withhold an amount to cover any additional tax which might be owing up to the time of issuance of the certificate, and obtain appropriate indemnities from the beneficiaries.

# Appendix 4

---

## ¶1200

### Checklist of Useful Information

The following is an outline of information which should be updated on a regular basis. Such data will be useful in preparing an estimate of individual net worth and, in addition, will assist the personal representative of a deceased individual in identifying and locating the beneficiaries and assets of the estate.

☐ Family data including the date of birth, social insurance number, citizenship and residency of the individual and spouse or common-law partner; net income of spouse or common-law partner; date of birth, dependent status and net income of children; and the date of birth, relationship and net income of any other specified dependants. Note the infirmity or handicap of the individual spouse, common-law partner or any dependant.

☐ Prepaid funeral arrangements.

☐ Special non-financial objectives which the individual would like to achieve; for example, control of a family business to a specified family member, ownership of a family cottage to a specified beneficiary, special provision for a handicapped relative, income-splitting, creditor-proofing, family law protection, etc.

☐ Gifts made in prior years and identity of recipient of the gift and relationship to the donor, the type of property gifted, the year in which the gift was made and its value at that time, the year in which the property was originally acquired, its value at that time, and its value on January 1, 1972 (Valuation Day) if owned at that date. Similar information should be available in respect of any gifts received by the taxpayer and any loans outstanding, including loans to family members. Any supporting documentation should be available.

❑ The existence and location of important documents including wills and powers of attorney for the individual and spouse or common-law partner, income tax returns for recent years, domestic contract, trust deeds, annuities and other contracts, pension or deferred compensation plan documents, life insurance policies, personal balance sheet, separation agreement and divorce decree, financial statements for business ventures in which the individual has a proprietary interest, shareholder and buy-sell agreements, partnership agreements, etc. Similarly, the location and contents of safety deposit boxes should also be listed.

❑ Name and address of individual's lawyer, accountant, financial advisor, trust officer, banker, life insurance underwriter and stockbroker.

❑ Country of residence, domicile and citizenship.

❑ Value and location of cash on hand and bank accounts.

❑ Value, identity, location, ownership and beneficiaries of insurance policies.

❑ Value and location of secured receivables and loans, including mortgages.

❑ Value, cost, Valuation Day value, location and ownership of personal property including automobiles, boats, jewellery, art, coin and stamp collections, furniture and household goods, manuscripts, antiques, etc.

❑ Value, location, cost, Valuation Day value, and ownership of real estate including principal residence, recreational property, business and rental properties.

❑ Value, identity, location, cost, Valuation Day value, and ownership of portfolio investments including stocks, bonds, mutual funds and other securities.

❑ Policy number, location, survivor benefits, death benefits and beneficiary of pensions and annuities including registered retirement savings plans, deferred profit sharing plans, income-averaging annuity contracts, registered home ownership savings plan, home buyer's plan, registered retirement income funds, employee profit sharing plans, registered suplementary unemployment benefit plans, lifelong learning plan, registered education savings plan, eligible funeral arrangements, *Canada Pension Plan*, *Quebec Pension Plan*, Canada Old Age Security and U.S. or other foreign Social Security.

❐ Description, value of interest, location, cost and Valuation Day value of business interests including proprietorships, partnerships, joint ventures, syndicates, corporations, etc.

❐ Identity, value, cost, Valuation Day value and ownership of farm assets and animals, listing separately all assets having a value in excess of $1,000.

❐ Value and details of all other property interests including interests in trusts, expectancy of inheritance, powers of appointment, etc.

❐ Value, identity of creditor and security posted with respect to personal liabilities including medical, dental, legal and professional fees, utilities, income tax, credit cards, long-term debt, personal loans, instalment debt, car payments, leases, life insurance premiums, bank loans, mortgage interest, etc.

❐ Details of any continuing support or other financial obligations under matrimonial contracts including marriage or domestic contracts, separation agreements or divorce settlements.

# Appendix 5

## ¶1300

### Relevant Interpretation Bulletins

### ¶1302 Death and The Income Tax Act

## ¶1304   Trusts

# ¶1306   Other

# ¶1308

## Information Circulars
## Covering Death, Deferred Plans and Estates

|  | Information Circular |
|---|---|
| Employees pension plans | 72-13R8 |
| Registered retirement savings plans | 72-22R9 |
| Business equity valuations | 72-25R4 |
| Tax evasion | 73-10R3 |
| Payments out of pension and deferred profit sharing plans | 74-21R |
| Reassessment of a return of income | 75-7R3 |
| Transfer of property to a corporation under section 85 | 76-19R3 |
| Profit sharing plans | 77-1R4 |
| Guidelines for trust companies, etc. | 78-14R3 |
| Registered retirement income funds | 78-18R6 |
| Clearance certificates of estates and trusts | 82-6R3 |
| General anti-avoidance rule | 88-2 Supp. 1 |
| Policy statement on business equity valuations | 89-3 |
| Voluntary disclosures | 00-1 |
| Third-party civil penalties | 01-1 |

# ¶1310

## Tax Rulings

|  | Advance Rulings |
|---|---|
| Estate freeze | TR-18 |
| Non-arm's-length sale of shares | TR-29 |
| Estate freeze by way of a corporate reorganization | TR-36 |
| Sale of shares (Estate freeze) | TR-40 |
| Transfer of property to a corporation | TR-41 |
| Dissolution of a trust | TR-45 |

# ¶1312

## Advance Tax Rulings (Second Series)

# ¶1315

## Technical News

# Index

**Tax**